LAW AND HISTORY

LAW AND HISTORY

THE EVOLUTION OF THE AMERICAN LEGAL SYSTEM

Anthony Chase

THE NEW PRESS | NEW YORK

Library of Congress Cataloging-in-Publication Data
Chase, Anthony
    Law and history: the evolution of the American legal system/Anthony Chase.
    p.   cm.
    Includes bibliographical references and index.
    ISBN 1-56584-367-3 (hc)
    1. Law—United States—History. I. Title.
KF352.C46 1997
349.73—dc21   96-54048
CIP

Published in the United States by The New Press, New York
Distributed by W. W. Norton & Company, Inc., New York

The New Press was established in 1990 as a not-for-profit alternative to the large, commercial publishing houses currently dominating the book publishing industry. The New Press operates in the public interest rather than for private gain, and is committed to publishing, in innovative ways, works of educational, cultural, and community value that might not normally be commercially viable.

Book design by Luke Hayman
Production management by Kim Waymer
Printed in the United States of America

9 8 7 6 5 4 3 2 1

To Christopher

CONTENTS

ACKNOWLEDGMENTS

My primary intellectual debt is to three historians who taught at the University of Wisconsin while I was a student at Madison. Edward Gargan, Harvey Goldberg, and J. F. C. Harrison provided me with imperishable examples of real historians at work, larger than life figures who demonstrated that teaching and writing about history represent important forms of action. They will always dominate my sense of the professional horizon.

I would also like to express appreciation to students, teachers, and colleagues at three law schools (Wayne State, Harvard, and Nova Southeastern) especially those with the time and inclination to read and comment on what I have written. Student financial assistance from the first two schools and faculty summer grants and a semester sabbatical from the third, have all helped pave the way for my journey through legal culture.

I would especially like to acknowledge my continuing reliance, over many years, on friend and ally, UC-Riverside economics professor, Robert Pollin. And I would like to thank Bob's parents for their support, as well.

In one of James Garner's films, where he plays a private detective, a wiseguy is frisking him and, in the process, tears out the lining of Garner's sport coat. Garner asks the tough guy, "Does your mother know what you do for a living?" My mother not only knows what I do for a living but has provided the most enthusiastic sort of support for my work, which I have long appreciated.

Each of the individuals who took the trouble to comment on the manuscript of this book should understand how crucial their contribution has been. Last though certainly not least, I would like to thank my New Press editor, Joe Wood, and copyeditor, Rafik Nolens, for their signal work in bringing Law and History to fruition. They are the first editors ever to significantly shape my writing and I am thankful for having their help.   ANTHONY CHASE

INTRODUCTION

Some facts should be suppressed, or, at least, a just
sense of proportion should be observed in treating them.
The only point in the case which deserved mention was
the curious analytical reasoning from effects to causes,
by which I succeeded in unravelling it.
SHERLOCK HOLMES in *The Sign of the Four*

Historians, without necessarily suppressing inconvenient facts, almost invariably treat their source material selectively and with a sense of proportion, however just or unjust. This book is no exception: it is a kind of detective story, intended to help unravel the mystery of law's seemingly intricate yet important relationship to history. The method of analysis I have employed owes as much to the analytical strategies of a Sherlock Holmes as to the lawyer's reasoning of a Justice Oliver Wendell Holmes; it owes, perhaps, more to the Baker Street sleuth's "science of deduction" than to the inductive logic characteristic of lawyers trained by the case method of study so popular in American legal education.[1] My account of law's trajectory was certainly conceived under Conan Doyle's sign of four: more specifically, four wars, four key periods of development, four basic spatial or topographic metaphors that illustrate conflicts at the heart of our national politics and that constitute the dynamic element in legal history.

First, the wars: In the eighteenth century, thirteen North American colonies fought a rebellion against England, which they won, and

---

1 On the case method's origins, see William P. LaPiana, *Logic and Experience* (New York: Oxford University Press, 1994). Those seeking a more academic pedigree for the deductive approach might consult the work of French sociologist Henri Lefebvre; see, for example, *The Survival of Capitalism* trans. F. Bryant (London: Allison and Busby, 1976): "In order to pose the problem...of the reproduction of social relations—it is necessary to proceed from the total to the particular. We must search for the explanation over an extremely wide range of social phenomena" (p. 68). See also Joseph Schumpeter, *History of Economic Analysis*. "[T]he thing that comes

first is Vision. That is to say, before embarking upon analytical work of any kind we must first single out the set of phenomena we wish to investigate, and acquire 'intuitively' a preliminary notion of how they hang together or, in other words, of what appear from our standpoint to be fundamental properties. This should be obvious. If it is not, this is only owing to the fact that in practice we mostly do not start from a vision of our own but from the work of our predecessors or from ideas that float in the public mind" (pp. 561–62; quoted in Robert Heilbroner, *Behind the Veil of Economics* [New York: W. W. Norton, 1988] p. 165).

founded the United States. In the nineteenth century, northern forces defeated a rebellion by southern slave states and thereby preserved the Union. In the mid-twentieth century, the United States, along with its allies, defeated the Axis powers in World War II and, several decades later, the country was deeply divided over the nature of U.S. involvement in Vietnam. These deceptively familiar benchmarks in the American experience represent crucial events in the unfolding relationship, recounted in this book, between law and history.

The four periods that organize this rendition of legal history are familiar—certainly to constitutional historians—but the reasons I have used this particular periodization are less conventional. The first period stretches to the Civil War, the second from Appomattox and post–Civil War constitutional amendments to the New Deal, the third from World War II through Vietnam, and the fourth from Vietnam to the present.

The four "topographic"[2] or spatial models used here represent independently contradictory features of the American political landscape. They are helpful in mapping difficult legal terrain, in part because they provide a memorable framework: inside/outside, up/down, left/right, and north/south.

Inside/outside describes the different ways legal language and legal change appear from inside, as opposed to outside, the American legal profession and its culture. Up/down is shorthand for the way legal institutions (up) can mirror or resist changes in the mode of subsistence (down), the economic base, or infrastructure of society.[3] Left/right is

---

2   "A taste for topography," mystery and adventure writer John Buchan writes, "is not the same thing as a love of the natural world; it is not even the same thing as an interest in landscape" ("Literature and Topography," in *Homilies and Recreations* [London: Thomas Nelson, 1926], p. 183). To my mind, a topographic orientation reflects an appreciation for the intrinsic pedagogic utility in providing a three-dimensional visualization of the intellectual structures used in a particular analytical project. Abstraction unaccompanied by concrete images is perhaps the most striking symptom of everything that is wrong with contemporary writing in the social and human sciences. Not that writers with something difficult or conceptually elevated to say should refrain from writing; but even serious readers pray for something solid to hold on to, like a

picture or diagram, a figure in the landscape, something with real shape and dimension. There should be something concrete in theory to which one is drawn, as in music or the ocean one is drawn to the rhythm.

3   Needless to say, I am not the first to use this sort of metaphor to capture the relation between economy and society. See, for example, Lester C. Thurow, *The Future of Capitalism* (New York: Morrow, 1996): "In geology the visible earthquakes and volcanoes are caused by the invisible movements of the continental plates floating on the earth's molten inner core. Mexico's economic crisis was as unexpected and as violent as any volcanic explosion. Corporate downsizings rock human foundations (expectations about their economic futures) as profoundly as any earthquake. But no one can understand volcanoes or

about the primary social and political division within the world economy for more than a century, that between liberal (left) and authoritarian (right) forms of capitalism, and how it too has shaped legal development. North/south is a sign or symbol for the class and regional conflicts that have loomed large in the development of America's legal system.

I rely on the first two models throughout my argument, the third appears only in the second half of the book, and the fourth model only near the end. These four dichotomies—which provide, of course, only a schematic guide for the challenging field of legal history—serve to make a considerable amount of historical information much more manageable than otherwise might be the case. And, in a telling way, these concrete, "spatial" models, reflect my own preference for illustration—for history, if you will, over theory. "It is a trite but true observation," Henry Fielding remarked, "that examples work more forcibly on the mind than precepts…"[4]

Chapter One of this book, "Historical Jurisprudence," is in effect a preface to legal history: it provides a concrete application of both the inside/outside and up/down metaphors. Chapter Two, "Capital's Horizon," analyzes particular aspects of the transition from first to second periods of legal development described above—specifically, the colonial rebellion against England and the elimination of precapitalist economic formations in the United States. Chapter Three, "The Great Divide," considers further aspects of this transformation: the retooling of the common law, the assault on America's own form of mercantilism, and, eventually, civil war. This chapter ends at the point where the United States's transition from a precapitalist to a capitalist society was completed.

Thus it will be seen that America's "long revolution" begins with the establishment of national sovereignty, and it culminates only with the

---

earthquakes by looking at them. The geophysicist must probe deeper to look at the forces generated below the surface of the earth by the continental plates" (p. 6). Similarly, the legal historian must look beneath the surface, employing something like Thurow's economic plate tectonics, to understand not only the relation between surface and core, superstructure and base, but especially the process of change itself, which we might analogize to profound shifts in legal terrain taking place over the surface of time. "In continental plate tectonics," adds Thurow,

the former Dean of MIT's Sloan School of Management, "what seems static, the surface of the earth, is in reality in constant flux." Deep structural transformation in the economic substratum eventually produces corresponding alteration in the law's surface. However much the law may be in constant flux, legal institutions, as we shall see, are designed to give just the opposite impression.

4 Henry Fielding, *The History of the Adventures of Joseph Andrews and His Friend Mr. Abraham Adams* (London: John Lane The Bodley Head, 1929), p. 3.

passage of the Fourteenth Amendment. The fourth and final chapter, "Wake of the Flood," deals with the transition between the second and third periods (the presidency of Franklin Roosevelt), as well as shifts during the 1960s and after (since the Vietnam War) into yet another phase in the development of American law. It is only in the later material—especially in dealing with the Civil War and, subsequently, with the New Deal and the period after World War II—that the left/right and north/south oppositions come into focus.

Before taking up the main fault lines that have governed the course of legal transformation, it is worth commenting on the development of liberal capitalism in the United States; it has, after all, played a crucial role in the drama I am about to unfold. However, the terminology I use to describe it is critical, so it will be helpful to say something about it right at the start.

Consider two major claims about American history upon which there now appears to be general consensus. First, the eighteenth-century U.S. Constitution, though not yet based upon universal suffrage, was nevertheless liberal for its time.[5] Second, a wide spectrum of American historians now agree that "the transition to a capitalist society was accelerated during the years immediately following the American Revolution."[6] I

5   See Anthony Arblaster, *The Rise and Decline of Western Liberalism* (New York: Basil Blackwell, 1984): "We do not need to join in the debate on the precise sources of the ideas of the rebel leaders, nor speculate on whether Jefferson had read or was much influenced by Locke, to see that many of the ideas of the American founding fathers as they were embodied in the institutions of the new state do belong firmly within the developing tradition of liberal thought and practice" (p. 196).

More remarkable than the content of American liberalism, however, was the fact that it became the organizing principle of a real government; see R. R. Palmer, *The Age of the Democratic Revolution* (Princeton: Princeton University Press, 1959): "[America's] revolution was revolutionary because it showed how certain abstract doctrines, such as the rights of man and the sovereignty of the people, could be 'reduced to practice,' as Adams put it, by assemblages of fairly levelheaded gentlemen exercising constituent power in the name of the people." (vol. 1, p. 235) After surveying all those effectively denied citizenship

rights under the new constitution, Herbert Aptheker nevertheless adds that "none of this contradicts the essentially progressive nature of the Constitution of the United States *in its time...*" Aptheker, *Early Years of the Republic* (New York: International Publishers, 1976), p. 95.

On the sheer audacity of it all, see Theodore Draper, *A Struggle for Power: The American Revolution* (New York: Times Books, 1996): "In 1764, [Thomas Hutchinson] reasoned, no one would have disobeyed Parliament. A year later, a furor had gripped the populace and made it do the unthinkable. Hutchinson attributed the transformation to demagogues and opportunists acting for their own profit and advancement. For one of his intelligence and experience to think so suggests how difficult it must have been for others to digest the almost incredible transformation....The interesting debate was not between those who wanted change and those who did not. It was between those who wanted a revolutionary change and those who wanted to reform the existing system to prevent a revolution" (p. 374).

shall, to be sure, give the political designation "liberalism" real teeth, in part by restricting my definition of liberal America to a world without slaves. Market society triumphed in the United States by the beginning of the nineteenth century, but it was not until the Civil War had ended and the Fourteenth Amendment was ratified that we can accurately refer to America as a "liberal capitalist" society.[7] Having said that, one can never-

6 Gordon S. Wood, "Inventing American Capitalism," *The New York Review of Books* (June 9, 1994), p. 48.

7 Although this notion of liberal capitalism will emerge more fully as we progress, it is worthwhile providing a couple of definitional comments here. "Political liberalism," argues Francis Fukuyama, "can be defined simply as a rule of law that recognizes certain individual rights or freedoms from government control" *The End of History and the Last Man* (New York: Free Press, 1992), p. 42. When such a definition of liberalism is employed, the specific list of rights an author has in mind becomes decisive. For his list, Fukuyama relies upon the first volume of James Bryce's *Modern Democracies* (1931): Fukuyama, *End of History* 42–43, 347. A brief but stimulating contemporary discussion of liberalism is found in Ralph Dahrendorf, "Liberalism," in John Entwell and Murray Milgate, eds., *The New Palgrave: The Invisible Hand* (New York: W. W. Norton, 1989), pp. 183–87.

For a more subjective, certainly impressionistic definition drawn from a source whom we shall meet again in the next chapter, see William C. Lehmann, *John Millar of Glasgow, 1735-1801* (Cambridge: Cambridge University Press, 1960; repr. Arno Press, 1979). The author analogizes law professor John Millar's liberalism to the "fresh breezes of a humanistic, rational, historical outlook and the independence of the inquiring mind, in its implied attack upon dogmatism and the prevailing theological orthodoxy, but also a receptivity generally toward change, toward innovation..."(p. 35).

For a short but pointed definition of capitalism, W. G. Runciman's will do nicely: "By 'capitalism' I mean a mode of production in which formally free labor is recruited for regular employment by ongoing enterprises competing in the market for profit" ("The

'Triumph' of Capitalism as a Topic in the Theory of Social Selection," *New Left Review* [March–April, 1995], p. 33). See also Meghnad Desai, "Capitalism," in Tom Bottomore, ed., *A Dictionary of Marxist Thought* (Oxford: Basil Blackwell, 1983). Desai, a professor at the London School of Economics, describes capitalism as "a term denoting a mode of production in which capital in its various forms is the principal means of production. Capital can take the form of money or credit for the purchase of labour power and materials of production; of physical machinery (capital in the narrow sense); or of stocks of finished goods or work in progress. Whatever the form, it is the private ownership of capital in the hands of a class—the class of capitalists to the exclusion of the mass of the population— which is the central feature of capitalism as a mode of production" (p. 64).

New School for Social Research economist Anwar Shaikh adds that, in contrast to Desai's capitalist class, the working class is "comprised of those who have been 'freed' of this self-same burden of property in means of production, and who must therefore earn their livelihood by selling their capacity to labour (labour power) to the capitalist class" ("Capital as a Social Relation," in John Eatwell, Murray Milgate, and Peter Newman, eds., *The New Palgrave: Marxian Economics* [New York: W. W. Norton, 1990], p. 74). Capitalists thus own the means of production, as Desai points out; workers must then sell their labor to this ownership class, as Shaikh adds. And, as Adam Smith famously opened his best-known work, the nation (all social classes) live off that labor: "The annual labour of every nation is the fund which originally supplies it with all the necessaries and conveniences of life which it annually consumes, and which consist always, either in the immediate produce of that labour, or in what is purchased with that produce from

theless fairly describe the United States as a premiere example of liberal capitalism for almost the ensuing century and a half. This is important, not least because capitalist states are by no means always liberal.[8] One main task of the present work will be to demonstrate the specificity of liberal capitalism's influence in the shaping of American law.

In the second half of the nineteenth century, Germany and Japan underwent revolutions from above which, for that very reason, should not perhaps be regarded as "revolutions" at all. These two countries, which

other nations" Adam Smith, *An Inquiry into the Nature and Causes of the Wealth of Nations*, R. H. Campbell and A. S. Skinner, eds. [Oxford: Oxford University Press, 1976], p. 10).

Even setting to one side the contradiction between "liberal values" and property in human beings, the emphasis economists place upon free labor as characteristic of capitalism suggests that the existence of chattel slavery presents certain difficulties for those who might wish to apply the label "liberal capitalist" to the United States prior to the Civil War. See, for example, Karl Marx, *Pre-Capitalist Economic Formations*, Jack Cohen, trans. E. J. Hobsbawm, ed., (New York: International Publishers, 1965): "If we now talk of plantation-owners in America as capitalists, if they *are* capitalists, this is due to the fact that they exist as anomalies within a world market based upon free labour" (p. 119). The United States was neither fully liberal nor fully capitalist until after passage of what are sometimes designated "Civil War amendments." For a fuller treatment than is possible here of the debate surrounding various approaches to capitalism's definition, see Tom Bottomore, *Theories of Modern Capitalism* (London: Allen and Unwin, 1985).

8   Reminding Christian DeLacampagne, an interviewer from *Le Monde*, that liberalism and capitalism are not identical, Stanley Hoffman added that "[i]f you're speaking of political liberalism, we are fully aware that capitalism can accommodate a wide variety of political regimes. We saw it in Nazi Germany, and we see it today in China" ("Democracy and Society: An Interview with Stanley Hoffman," *World Policy Journal* [spring 1995], p. 35). See also John Dunn, Conclusion, in John Dunn, ed., *Democracy: The Unfinished*

Journey (Oxford: Oxford University Press, 1992): "The relationship between constitutional representative democracy and capitalism is both intimate and deeply untransparent. The historical services which each has rendered to the other over the last two centuries have been profound. But neither, in the end, can be wholly at ease with the other: completely confident of its ultimate fidelity" (p. 254).

Indeed, capitalism may develop more rapidly under right-wing and authoritarian regimes than under liberal regimes. Fukuyama remarks, "There is considerable empirical evidence to indicate that market-oriented authoritarian modernizers do better economically than their democratic counterparts. Historically, some of the most impressive economic growth records have been compiled by this type of state, including Imperial Germany, Meiji Japan, the Russia of Witte and Stolypin, and, more recently, Brazil after the military takeover in 1964, Chile under Pinochet, and, of course, the NIEs [newly industrialized economies] of Asia" (*End of History*, p. 123). See also Perry Anderson, "Diary," *London Review of Books* (Oct. 17, 1996): "The critical engine of [South Korean] modernisation, however, was indigenous. The military dictatorship installed by Park Chung Hi in 1961, whose underlying structure lasted for some three decades, forged the most effective developmental state of the epoch....Last but not least, the military leaders policed the most brutal work regime in the industrialised world. In the mid-Eighties, the average labour time was 53 hours a week. The levels of repression required to enforce this kind of discipline were draconian" (p. 28).

would play such a large part in shaping world events in the following century, managed to avoid civil war by preserving reactionary elements within each society's governing elite. In the same period, the United States was torn apart by a struggle to demolish the slave South which, as we shall see, was a remnant of "precapitalist" social relations. Thus, it is for good reason that Barrington Moore refers to the War Between the States as "the last revolutionary offensive on the part of what one may legitimately call urban or bourgeois capitalist democracy."[9]

As Moore elaborates in considerable detail, while Germany and Japan took a capitalist but authoritarian road to the construction of modern industrial society, the United States took the liberal capitalist route toward that end. These two ways of organizing society and politics, two different strategies of modernization, confronted each other in World War II. The titanic battle between two dramatically different approaches to governance of capitalist society resulted in a victory for liberal capitalism which, by the end of the twentieth century, had achieved genuinely global dominance. It is ironic that the outcome of the great intracapitalist war, which in a sense had preoccupied the first half of the twentieth century, was effectively decided by the Soviet Union. Both the American president and the British prime minister were in Moscow on the fiftieth anniversary of V-E Day; the symbolism was obvious. John Lukacs, after repeating a view held by most military analysts—namely, that Britain and the U.S. *together* could not have defeated the Axis forces without the Red Army—argues that those who see this century in terms of a struggle between capitalism and communism have missed the point. "The main feature of the historical landscape of the twentieth century," he writes, "is that of the two world wars."[10] Viewing this century through the lens of world war means, for our purposes, understanding modern history largely in terms of the rivalry between liberal and authoritarian capitalism. And,

9 Barrington Moore, Jr., *Social Origins of Dictatorship and Democracy* (Boston: Beacon Press, 1966), p. 112.

10 John Lukacs, *The Duel* (New York: Ticknor and Fields, 1990), pp. 9–10. See also, Eric Hobsbawm, "History and Illusion, *New Left Review* [Nov./Dec., 1996], p. 116. Gabriel Kolko has argued that Britain and France shared German "contempt for Soviet military power," and adds that Hitler's senior officers "with few exceptions enthusiastically endorsed the June 1941 attack against the USSR.

Militarily, it was vastly more precarious than anything Hitler had ever attempted, and the Soviet Union's ability to resist became the single most important factor in determining the war's military outcome" (*Century of War* [New York: New Press, 1994], pp. 29, 31). For a compelling narrative of exactly how Soviet military power managed to play this decisive role in modern history, see David M. Glantz and Jonathan House, *When Titans Clashed: How the Red Army Stopped Hitler* (Lawrence: University of Kansas Press, 1995).

again, this understanding will play an important role in the way in which I juxtapose law and history.

This book is primarily a work of synthesis. In fact, the reader may be struck by the amount of documentation I have marshalled to support my main contentions. Certainly, I have tried to provide as much direction as possible for those who wish to read the secondary literature and arrive at their own conclusions. For the sake of readability, I have relegated as much technical information and reference material as possible to the notes.

While writing this book, I spent many hours listening to books on tape, primarily readings of unabridged fiction. However, time pressures have caused me to join the apparently expanding market of consumers willing to take the shortcut provided by abridged audio tapes of current nonfiction books. James Fallows recently commented, in a radio program, that his new book on American journalism has no index because he wants to prevent people from looking through the index to find their name and only reading the paragraph or two where they are mentioned. Fallows apparently fears there are intelligent readers who simply will not take time to read an entire book.

The relationship between my text and notes reflects these kinds of pressures. Conscious of Fallows's concerns about getting a message across in a world where demands placed upon readers' time seem overwhelming, I have structured this book so that the text alone (that is, without the notes) is, in essence, an abridgement of the book as a whole, including the notes. The text itself can be read in a relatively short time. Readers who are willing at least to consult the notes can easily discover both how I have developed my ideas and how to begin to do their own research.

CHAPTER I

HISTORICAL JURISPRUDENCE

In which a wedge is driven between the letter and spirit of law and a nuts and bolts rendition of legal realism is provided. The materialist view of history is made simple; less so, dialectics, which are given a fair share in the story although not everyone will truly comprehend their significance at first reading. Further adventures are promised.

I. INSIDE/OUTSIDE

The letter is there to be filled by the Spirit—it is a counterpart to the Spirit, though it is often enough in opposition to it. In the context of salvation history it even became the written code which kills (2 Cor. 3:6), because it had hardened so much that it could no longer be moistened by the source which springs from above."
HUGO RAHNER[11]

Everyone understands the spirit of the law; lawyers are expert in the letter. When you demonstrate genuine fidelity, it is said that you have obeyed the spirit as well as the letter of the law. Thus, the law seems to have two sides or aspects from the beginning. When you have done the right thing, under the circumstances, it is said that you have at least satisfied the spirit, if not the letter, of the law. When you carefully conform your conduct to the letter of the law but ignore its spirit, you have somehow managed to escape the real import of the rule, perhaps even defeating it in the process. One of the most familiar observations made about defendants who avoid criminal sanction is that they "got off on a technicality"; in popular parlance, such evasion represents use of the letter against the spirit of the law.

The lexicon of British labor relations includes the phrase "work to rule," which means that without actually going on strike, workers follow written employment rules or production codes so closely, "to the letter," that little work can actually be accomplished. During the Vietnam War, some opponents of American policy responded rather assiduously to the requirement, printed on the Selective Service registration card itself, that they keep their draft board informed of changes in the condition of their health: these youthful dissidents kept draft board members apprised of colds, sprained ankles, even a bad day—anything to keep the draft board busy, harassed, and less effective in doing its job. After all, that's what they said they wanted, right?

11 Hugo Rahner, *Ignatius the Theologian*, trans. M. Barry (San Francisco: Ignatius Press, 1968), p. 20. While not as well known as his brother, Karl Rahner, Hugo Rahner nevertheless made an important contribution to twentieth-century Catholic thought: see Leo Donald Davis, Foreword, in Hugo Rahner, *Church and State in Early Christianity*, trans. L. D. Davis (San Francisco: Ignatius Press, 1992): "The name Rahner looms large in contemporary theology: Karl, as perhaps the most influential speculative Catholic theologian of his generation, and his older brother Hugo, equally important in the fields of Church history and patristics" (p. ix).

The point here is simple, perhaps obvious, but crucial. The law and its meaning are two separate things. Letter versus spirit, text versus meaning—there are many ways of saying it but all allude to the same duality. It is fundamental, basic to an appreciation of exactly how law is able to change over time, especially how it can sometimes change dramatically without appearing to change at all. Any law—whether in a constitution, statute, judicial decision, or administrative order—can be separated from the written text in which it is given form. Perhaps this point can be better explained by using the kind of illustration of which law professors seem so fond.

Let us say that a local veterans' organization raises money from its members and purchases a vintage World War II tank from an army surplus catalog. The group wishes to donate the tank to the city in order to have it placed in a public park across from city hall, as a memorial to local residents who gave their lives in the armed services. Although a large number of community members support such an effort to honor those who served their country, others are less thrilled. A group of environmentalists feels that a tank would spoil the otherwise natural green space which the park provides. Some parents are worried that unless the city hires a park patrol to supervise children playing near (or, God forbid, on) the tank, kids could get hurt. A handful of "beached whales" from the 1960s think that if the park is going to have a monument, it should honor those who have tried to stop wars, rather than fight them. At a special meeting of the city council, held to hear arguments on the tank issue, a lawyer representing the antitank coalition maintains that a local ordinance necessarily scuttles the tank memorial: the city's own municipal code states that "all vehicles are prohibited from entering into or being upon the grounds of any public park maintained by the city." The leader of the veterans unit says he cannot believe that law was written in order to prevent the city from honoring fallen war heroes. The attorney for the antitank coalition responds that he completely agrees: the ordinance does not stop the city from honoring soldiers, does not even prevent their being honored in a public park—but does preclude a tank (or any other vehicle) from being on park property, no matter what the reason.

The veterans leader shrugs his shoulders, says, "Well, it's a damn shame," and gives up. The council votes unanimously to abandon the tank project. The veterans leader has a daughter in law school; he had never imagined that the veterans memorial would somehow become a legal issue, so he never mentioned it to her. Later that night, his daughter yells at him on the phone: "What about ambulances? What about the dog catcher's truck? What about police cars and fire trucks...[12]

As Yale law professor Arthur A. Leff once wrote, "every natural language is to some extent ambiguous. Unlike languages of mathematical Logic, which are designed for almost no purpose but to avoid ambiguity, ordinary languages have other jobs to do..."[13] To most lawyers, the question whether this state of affairs is good or bad seems odd: it's simply what is, the way the law has always been. Ambiguity, an inevitable byproduct of the duality described above, is inherent when law is reduced to language (or at least to the normal languages that humans most regularly use to communicate with each other). It has nothing to do with "activist judges" (whether liberal or conservative) or with courts confusing themselves with legislatures: all judges make law in the process of applying abstract rules to concrete cases.[14]

12 See H. L. A. Hart, *The Concept of Law* (2d ed., Oxford: Oxford University Press, 1994): "There will indeed be plain cases constantly recurring in similar contexts to which general expressions are clearly applicable ('If anything is a vehicle a motor-car is one') but there will also be cases where it is not clear whether they apply or not. ('Does "vehicle" used here include bicycles, airplanes, roller skates?') The latter are fact-situations, continually thrown up by nature or human invention, which possess only some of the features of the plain cases but others which they lack. Canons of 'interpretation' cannot eliminate, though they can diminish, these uncertainties; for these canons are themselves general rules for the use of language, and make use of general terms which themselves require interpretation" (p. 126).

13 Arthur Allen Leff, "The Leff Dictionary of Law: A Fragment," *Yale Law Journal* 94 (1985), p. 2007.

14 Perhaps the most elegant statement of how judges actually decide cases remains Benjamin Cardozo's Storrs Lectures delivered at Yale University seventy-five years ago; see Benjamin N. Cardozo, *The Nature of the Judicial Process* (New Haven: Yale University Press, 1921), where he describes the process of judicial reasoning in considerable detail and concludes that the "law which is the

resulting product is not found, but made. The process, being legislative, demands the legislator's wisdom. There is in truth nothing revolutionary or even novel in this view of the judicial function. It is the way courts have gone about their business for centuries in the development of the common law" (pp. 115–16). Cardozo's jurisprudence "seems no less relevant now" than it did during the Progressive era, according to lawyer Lawrence Solan who, using Noam Chomsky to update Cardozo, has presented a rigorous linguistic critique of judicial discourse: see Solan, *The Language of Judges* (Chicago: University of Chicago Press, 1993), p. 27.

"[I]t would be a strange kind of interpretation," writes corporate law expert Melvin Eisenberg, "that allowed the interpreter to reformulate or radically reconstruct the text." Yet that, he says, "is just the power of a deciding court in dealing with a precedent"; he concludes that the main job of the court is "not so much to determine what the precedent was intended to stand for as to determine what it has or will come to stand for" (Eisenberg, *The Nature of the Common Law* [Cambridge, Mass.: Harvard University Press, 1988], pp. 51–52). If these many years after Cardozo, some are still surprised to find judges changing the law ("acting like legislators") presumably no one is surprised

So long as the law is written down or embodied in language, it necessarily has an elusive quality. It is precisely this feature of law which permits legal systems to survive and flourish—even long after the social conditions that brought them into being and whose values they (temporarily) gave expression have been transcended. Maintaining a superficial continuity in the face of social transformation is one of the law's premier tasks. As we shall soon see, this is what Leff had in mind with his slightly cryptic closing remarks above, about "other jobs to do": that is, whatever the value of legal certainty, lawyers have bigger fish to fry. Being clear, if that means writing rules that have only one meaning, is not the only goal of law: it is not even the most important value. In fact, it is not a goal at all—not because it is a bad idea but because it is impossible. Law cannot be anything other than what it is.

Historian of ideas H. G. Gadamer observed the ancient genealogy of this particular bit of wisdom. The "task of finding the law and coming up with a verdict," he wrote, "contains an inexorable tension that Aristotle had already thematized clearly: the tension between the universality of the valid legal framework, whether codified or uncodified, and the individuality of the concrete case." Spirit versus letter, meaning versus text, general legal framework versus decision in a specific case, and so forth. The "inexorable tension" between these oppositions, the duality of law, cannot be overcome. For better or worse a judgment must be rendered—hopefully one that disposes of concrete litigation in a way that can be accommodated within the universal values of the system as a whole. "That a concrete passing of judgment in a legal question is no theoretical statement but an instance of 'doing things with words,'" he concluded, "is almost too obvious to bear mentioning."[15] *Almost* too obvious, says Gadamer—in other words, not quite.

It is that "almost" which leads me to present this argument in the context of another tension: that between inside and outside, between what lawyers inside the legal system know and take for granted and what the commonly invoked "lay public"—those outside the profession—may not comprehend. The dichotomy between inside and outside, between those in legal culture and "out of it," between those who understand that

to find *legislators* acting like legislators. See, for example, comments by legal historian Alan Watson in his *Failures of the Legal Imagination* (Philadelphia: University of Pennsylvania Press, 1988): "It can in no way surprise us that legal change, indeed even drastic change,

can be promulgated by statute: the surprising thing, to my mind, is the extent to which change does not occur" (p. 53).

15 H. G. Gadamer, *Reason in the Age of Science* (Cambridge, Mass.: MIT Press, 1981), pp. 125–26.

law is ultimately only "a way of doing things with words" and those for whom this rather deflating little fact may come as a shock, represents a division with a long tradition and a distinguished career in American life and letters.

But maybe not for much longer. Consider, for example, the effects of Court TV, John Grisham's novels, stacks of best-sellers and reel after reel of Hollywood film, a dozen prime-time lawyer television series within a decade. In Abe Lincoln's day, it was believed that every American had something like a natural right to practice law if it truly was his calling; today, most Americans think they know enough to at least imagine themselves representing clients. Famous lawyers on the *Larry King Show*, desperately trying to remember some obscure rule from the California evidence code, shake their heads, chuckle, and reply to the viewer calling in, "Uh…actually, that's a very good question." There is a very specific kind of smile one sees frequently now on the face of lawyer-commentators across the televised spectrum: it says, "they know what we know, they're catching on." No one spending hours listening to attorneys argue to the jury, to each other, to Judge Ito and, inevitably, to television cameras in the O. J. Simpson case can help but have come to the same conclusion: law is whatever lawyers and judges say it is. This way of doing things with words may no longer be above people's heads. Perhaps the public, finally, is figuring it out.

Let us consider a couple of examples. In 1995, Norman Mailer was interviewed by PBS's Charlie Rose before a live audience at New York City's 92nd Street YMCA, which is famous for its cultural events. When Mailer's wide-ranging discussion turned to the O. J. Simpson case, he made two interesting observations (the verdict was months off). First, in his view, the trial demonstrated that law is about not truth or justice but, instead, is "a game"—no doubt Mailer's own way of describing the paradox of "doing things with words." This got a huge burst of applause, the biggest one of a night when the aging but still cantankerous Mailer's broad-brush indictments and occasionally trenchant insights were often very warmly received. What should we make of this response to Mailer's demystification of legal formality, his suggestion that the law is both a serious mechanism for adjudicating the guilt or innocence of an individual tried for first degree-murder and yet, at the very same time, a game, a contest. (Is it in fact a sport played by possibly mismatched competitors, one side nicknamed the "dream team" as if a finalist in some NCAA or NBA playoffs?)

The audience's enthusiasm for his accusation suggests that these New Yorkers were well on their way to collapsing any remaining obstacles between the inside and outside of legal culture. Having listened for months to defense attorneys and prosecutors parse evidence and tactics in the Simpson trial, how could viewers help but discern the rules of the game, the inherent ambiguity and malleability of statute, precedent, and constitutional standard? But when a questioner asked Mailer about the "sexual politics" of his novels, Mailer seemed to respond as if this was old hat—and his audience seemed to concur. It was not that the question missed its mark, merely that everyone knew the answer and had chosen either to accept Mailer's excuses or not; they had come to terms with it in their own way. How different this was from the response to his remarks on jurisprudence. If the audience was in on that secret, this knowledge was still new. As Gadamer says, it "almost" goes without saying—but not quite. Revealing law's duality was still, at least for Mailer and his audience, exciting and fun—and even a little scandalous.

Mailer's second jurisprudential comment was this: Americans are not yet prepared for the realization that law is a game. Unfortunately, he did not explain his reasons for doubting that the public is ready to see the veil of law lifted and its inner workings exposed. He *did* speak about issues of racial conflict and the Simpson case. He may have feared that, in terms of American race relations, the trial could have no good outcome. And there was of course enormous dismay, especially among white Americans, when Simpson was acquitted of the crime of murder in October 1995.[16] But the Simpson case may simply represent a near-final nail in the coffin of public confidence in legal autonomy. To paraphrase Brecht's *Mahagonny*, legal systems are neither better nor worse than the societies whose social structure and values they reflect.

Around the time of Mailer's interview, I happened to be listening to an afternoon call-in show on National Public Radio. The program asked whether teachers should present both sides in the classroom. The opening segment illustrated the theme with an anecdote about a schoolteacher telling his students that the American Revolution was no revolution at all—that it made most Americans economically worse off than they had been, and was primarily about commercial conflicts between businessmen in England and in the Colonies. The panel of guests invited that day got the ball rolling by giving different—or,

16 Jeffrey Abramson, ed., *Postmorten: The O. J. Simpson Case* (New York: Basic Books, 1996).

perhaps, not so different—views about the responsibilities of educators, the values of pluralism, the importance of academic freedom, and so on.

One guest was the then-president of the Association of American Law Schools. It was his opinion that presenting both sides of an issue was standard fare in American law school classrooms, not least because in an adversial system there are always two sides to a question—so law professors constantly force their students to argue different sides of a case. This case method has, for many years, constituted the dominant teaching mode in American legal education. The AALS president observed that, of course, there might be *some* cases that are pretty much cut and dried; but, he assured his host and listeners, law professors love to teach hard cases since that is where the action is, where the challenge of learning law and teaching legal reasoning is greatest.

Now, this commentary is too clever by half: unnecessarily, even inaccurately, it confines the focus of legal education exclusively to judicial case analysis, thereby excluding the larger issues of law's relation to society.[17] He did not even acknowledge how law schools had, during the previous decade, seen fierce debates about whether law professors should be permitted to teach precisely what the AALS president said he believed: that legal decision-making, at least in hard cases, does *not* have any definitive answer or necessary outcome. That the result of a case could turn on the ability of counsel or other factors extrinsic to legal logic— that is, it might depend on the "politics" of the legal system itself—was a very controversial proposition for some law school professors and administrators; it was certainly more controversial than this response fully revealed.[18]

Yet what seems most salient to me now is the candid acknowledgement by someone so authoritative that the essence of legal education

---

17   See, for example, Alan Hunt, *Explorations in Law and Society* (New York: Routledge, 1993).

18   See, for example, Calvin Trillin, "A Reporter At Large (Harvard Law School)," *The New Yorker* (March 26, 1984), p. 53. The battle that Trillin describes raged through legal education for a time, even though it was provoked by claims seemingly no more radical than this one: "Existing legal doctrines do not require judges or scholars to reach the results they reach because the doctrines are sufficiently ambiguous or internally contradictory to justify any result we can imagine....Saying that decisionmaking is both indeterminate and non-arbitrary simply means that we can explain judicial decisions only by reference to criteria outside the scope of the judge's formal justifications" (Joseph Singer, "The Player and the Cards: Nihilism and Legal Theory," *Yale Law Journal* [1984], pp. 19–20). The Cardozo of the Storrs Lectures, no doubt, would have found Harvard Law professor Singer's statement dry as blotting paper and would have searched for a way to make the claim sound a bit more provocative, more an active assertion of judicial independence than a passive statement of empirical sociology.

is demonstration in the classroom that hard cases can be argued either way—and, therefore, at least implicitly, law is indeterminate. The case method of law teaching—in which students argue both sides of a case—and the adversarial nature of the American legal system both mirror the dual nature of law which I have outlined, an ambiguity of law recognized by philosophers from antiquity's Aristotle to Yale's Professor Leff. And they reflect, as well, the "doing things with words" (as they say in the academy) or "law as a game" (in the language of popular culture) understanding of the legal system which seems to be dissolving the distinction between insider and outsider perspectives.

In an episode of the popular television series *Law and Order*, the gruff district attorney Adam Shiff gives a word of advice to his chief deputy prosecutor Ben Stone. Stone, striving valiantly to play it by the book, is taken aside by Shiff who bluntly instructs his junior: "Politics is part of the law, my friend. If you don't believe it, spend a day in Albany." If historic sequestration of the judicial inner sanctum is now giving way to law as an open book (and the popularity of realistic dramas such as *Law and Order* may be one sign of this), then our initial antinomy—between the inside and outside of legal culture—may be on its last legs. If the secrets of law are no longer jealously guarded by lawyers, are no longer privately held by the profession for safekeeping, but instead have become the common property of anyone who enjoys solving riddles of the realm, then a primary obstacle to understanding this book will, for most readers, have been removed in advance.

2. MATERIALISM

> *Think deep as you can, think long as you may, life depends on low reality.*
> SEAN O'CASEY[19]

Aristotle may have understood the contradiction built into any effort to apply abstract legal rules to concrete cases, but did the Greeks understand the way in which law and politics are shaped by social and economic relationships? Did they have an ancient version of what, by the nineteenth

---

19 Sean O'Casey, *Rose and Crown* (New York: Macmillan, 1952), p. 151.

century, would be described as a "materialist" approach to the study of law and society? The notion that the Greeks "had a word for it" has often been taken as a matter of faith in Western intellectual discussions, carried out in the long shadow cast by classical culture.[20] Historian of philosophy John H. Randall describes "the materialism of Democritus, Lucretius, and the eighteenth-century French materialists, like Diderot...."[21] Economist and social critic Thomas Sowell cites some of the Greek philosophers as antecedents of modern materialism, but he nevertheless distinguishes the essentially metaphysical materialism central to antiquity's debates about nature and existence from materialism as social theory.[22] A recent Oxford illustrated history of philosophy barely refers to materialism prior to Hegel and Marx, and Antony Flew's dictionary of philosophy points out the difference between a focus on matter in space and time and a focus upon the relation between historical change and social contradictions.[23]

It is also worthwhile to distinguish materialism as social theory from the popular, everyday usages of the term. Sowell observes that what economists and sociologists mean by materialism is not greed or a preoccupation with possessions—what Veblen called conspicuous consumption—however familiar the use of the term has become in conversation. G. K. Chesterton, in one of his classic rejoinders to critics of the Christian faith, treats materialism as the equivalent of obsessive rationalism or scientism, a denial of theism and a shrinking of the cosmos.[24]

Materialist approaches to the study of legal history have nothing to do with what the universe is made of, whether some people may be too preoccupied with consumerism, or with denying the authenticity of miracles. Rather, materialist jurisprudence is concerned with the social and economic forces directing the course of legal development. Richard A. Posner, chief judge of the United States Court of Appeals for the Seventh Circuit, long a professor of law at the University of Chicago, and one of

20 See, for example, Barry Hindess, "'The Greeks Had a Word for It': The Polis as Political Metaphor," *Thesis Eleven* 40 (1995): "In the extreme, the phrase represented the view that the Greeks not only had a word for politics, philosophy and other significant elements of Western civilization, but also that there is an important sense in which these things originated with the Greeks" (p. 119).

21 John Herman Randall, Jr., *The Career of Philosophy* (New York: Columbia University

Press, 1965), vol. 2, p. 378.

22 Thomas Sowell, *Marxism: Philosophy and Economics* (New York: William Morrow, 1985): "While the focus of the ancient materialists was the individual and his achievement of personal tranquility and a moral and rewarding life, the focus of the materialists who flourished in the eighteenth century was society and its reformation" (p. 40).

23 Antony Flew, *A Dictionary of Philosophy* (2d ed., New York: St. Martin's, 1984), p. 222–23.

the leading lights of the law and economics school of legal theory,[25] opens his most important book to date with an essay titled, "The Material Basis of Jurisprudence." In it, he admonishes his readers not to allow a post-communist "discrediting" of Marxism to deter them from appreciating that "a profession's characteristic modes of thought might have economic causes."[26] Posner argues, for example, that preventive medicine has generally been ignored by the medical profession because its contribution to human health does not readily translate into larger income for physicians. However, the lion's share of the essay focuses upon ways in which abstract modes of legal thought and scholarship, located in the upper reaches of our materialist model of society, have been transformed in the United States, especially during the past three decades, as a result of changes in the market for legal services and the economic organization of the American legal profession—changes, that is, in the "material basis" of social relations.

It comes as no surprise that Posner has made his way to this sort of explanation of legal thought only after mastering the inside/outside dichotomy. Like Cardozo, Posner soberly acknowledges that judicial law-making is inevitable; he candidly embraces the notion of law's inherent indeterminacy.[27] Law must simultaneously be able to adjust to social

24 G. K. Chesterton, *Orthodoxy: The Romance of Faith* (New York: Doubleday, 1990): "The Christian is quite free to believe that there is a considerable amount of settled order and inevitable development in the universe. But the materialist is not allowed to admit into his spotless machine the slightest speck of spiritualism or miracle" (p. 24). Chesterton, again, was referring to materialism as scientific worldview, not as social theory. The latter is concerned with political economy and social change, rather than with life and death or God and the human condition. Christian theologians sympathetic to ideologies of social reform, such as Hans Küng, have occasionally taken materialist theories to task for an alleged failure to deal with spiritual or existential aspects of human experience—what Küng sees as their avoidance of "questions of ultimate values, goals, meaning...." He thus notes with satisfaction a renewed appreciation of "the problem of religion" in the later work of Jürgen Habermas (Küng, *Does God Exist?* trans., E. Quinn [New York: Crossroad, 1994], p. 580).

25 See, for example, David Friedman, "Law and

Economics," John Eatwell, Murray Milgate, and Peter Newman, eds., in *The New Palgrave: The Invisible Hand* (New York: W. W. Norton, 1989), pp. 173–82.

26 Richard A. Posner, *Overcoming Law* (Cambridge, Mass.: Harvard University Press, 1995), p. 35. British High Court Judge Stephen Sedley, in a review of Posner's book, observes that at "the heart of his polemics are three pulses, legal pragmatism, Millian liberalism and legal economics, which Posner believes beat in sympathy. Powered by them, he sets out to overcome 'law' in the bad old sense—formalistic, self-referential, supposedly autonomous law of the sort his generation and mine were taught at law school and read in the judgments of a judicial generation which has now passed on" (Sedley, "Extra-Legal," *London Review of Books* [Oct. 19, 1995], p. 18).

27 "There are no tests, procedures, protocols, algorithms, experiments, computations, or observations for determining which side in the dispute is right. Some arguments can be rejected as bad, but enough good arguments remain on both sides to leave the issue

change in response to real political pressures, while at the same time give the impression of stability and fidelity to precedent.[28] Contemporary historians usually appreciate the complex, sometimes contradictory functions that law performs in society, but they also typically recognize that our law has always been result-oriented, and that Americans have rarely shied away from using law in a self-consciously purposive and instrumental fashion.[29] Somewhere between Democritus and Lucretius, the Greek metaphysicians, and our modern sociological orientation toward jurisprudence, we need to locate as precisely as possible the origin of a materialist approach to legal analysis.

suspended in indeterminacy...." (Posner, *Overcoming Law*, p. 37).

28 "As the hearings on the nomination of Robert Bork to the Supreme Court showed," Posner asserts, "the American people want two things from judges: they want particular results (such as capital punishment and the decriminalization of abortion), and they want judges who find rather than make law. These things are incompatible." However, Posner does not stop there, having bluntly described the necessary tension between "legislative" and judicial functions of courts; he goes on to observe, from a convincingly insider's perspective, how law's ambiguity permits a tentative resolution of the contradiction between spirit and letter, policy and precedent: "Judges nevertheless find it easy enough to satisfy the public's demands by giving them the results they want, clothed in the rhetoric of passive obeisance to 'the law' (including law the judges may have made up last week)" (ibid., p. 79).

At least in theory, if the division between inside and outside of legal culture completely dissolved (for example, if every American had a law degree), there would no longer be any need for judges to clothe their decisions in pious rhetoric. Posner's own examination of the fate of guild ideology and its "neutral principles" jurisprudence implies a gradual decline in the distinction between professional and public perceptions of how the legal system works. Posner appears to favor deregulation of the legal services industry, endorses authorization of paralegals to form their own law firms, and is certainly contemptuous of the "high obscurity" of legal language when it has

the function of preserving, at the level of discourse, the corporate privileges of the legal profession. One need only compare Michel Foucault's comments on why Moliere's doctors spoke in Latin to appreciate how venerable this particular allegation against the smugly learned professions happens to be (ibid., p. 80).

29 See, for example, James Willard Hurst, *The Growth of American Law* (Boston: Little, Brown, 1950): "People in the United States of all social levels and at all times mingled respect for law and for doing things in a legal way with an unashamedly practical attitude toward the law as an instrument. They would use it when it effected a purpose and otherwise dispense with it more or less openly. This paradox appeared with reference to the status of the bar" (pp. 249–50). See also Hurst's *Law and the Conditions of Freedom in the Nineteenth-Century United States* (Madison, Wis.: University of Wisconsin Press, 1956); *Law and Markets in United States History* (Madison, Wis.: University of Wisconsin Press, 1982); and *Law and Economic Growth* (Madison, Wis.: University of Wisconsin Press, 1984).

See also Robert W. Gordon, "J. Willard Hurst and the Common Law Tradition in American Legal Historiography," *Law and Society Review* 10 (1975): "Hurst's main contribution has been to expose the hitherto invisible ways in which the apparently most commonplace incidents of a legal order illuminate social values. By so doing, he managed, almost single-handed, to lower from inside the drawbridge over the moat isolating American legal from general historiography" (p. 54).

Perhaps it will be helpful to introduce this movement within material-ism (from metaphysics to social theory) with an illustration drawn from a recent motion picture, Ridley Scott's *1492: Conquest of Paradise* (1992).[30] The film's opening shot splits the wide screen in two horizontally—the upper half an evening sky illuminated by the setting sun, the lower half ocean and roaring tide—with a tiny ship far away at the center of the image. Subsequent shots reveal a man and small boy sitting on a rock by the sea, staring out across the expanse of water and sky, followed by a closeup of the man's hands, showing him carefully pealing an orange with his knife. What follows is a scene between Christopher Columbus and his young son, for whom he is about to open the secrets of mathematics and geography.

Columbus asks the lad to describe what he sees as the distant ship dis-appears over the horizon. He instructs his son to close his eyes for a moment: "Don't cheat," he says. And placing his large hand over the boy's eyes, gently strokes his cheek with one finger. "Now..." says Columbus while the boy, opening his eyes, exclaims, "It's gone!" We see a shot of the ocean, empty and perfectly still; Columbus asks, "What does that tell you?" The master mariner revolves the orange in his hand and explains, "It's round, like this. Round." His son smiles, and Columbus laughs, then affectionately tousles his son's hair. Unlike so many previous Eurocentric accounts of the Columbian expedition, Scott's film portrays the violence and barbarism that marked Europe's "discovery" of the new world.[31] At

30 See Peter Wollen, "Cinema's Conquistadors," *Sight and Sound* 7 (1992), p. 20; Carla Rahn Phillips and William D. Phillips, Jr., "Christopher Columbus: Two Films," in Mark C. Carnes, ed., *Past Imperfect: History According to the Movies* (New York: Henry Holt, 1995), p. 60.

31 In addition to Kirkpatrick Sale's *The Conquest of Paradise: Christopher Columbus and the Columbian Legacy* (New York: Knopf, 1990), on which Scott's film itself based, see David E. Stannard, *American Holocaust: Columbus and the Conquest of the New World* (New York: Oxford University Press, 1992). Remarkably, the appalling story related by Sale and by Stannard in their detailed scholarship is completely ignored by contributors to the Society of American Historians' book on historical films: see *Past Imperfect* pp. 60–65. The omission is equivalent to writing about

films on the pre–Civil War American south without mentioning slavery. Mark C. Carnes's elaborate introduction to the historians' volume nowhere indicates how or why any of its contributors were chosen. What a pity that he did not simply incorporate Peter Wollen's earlier *Sight and Sound* essay into *Past Imperfect*.

Wollen's capsule history of Columbian celebrations alone is worth the price of admission: "The second wave, which began with the expansion west and was given new impetus by Italian immigration into America, brought Columbus Day and Columbus Circle and culminated in the lavish celebrations of 1892, foremost among which was the World's Columbian Exposition in Chicago....Most significant of all was the presence of Arawaks from British Guiana in a thatched hut. Presumably these were the best available

the same time, Scott nevertheless manages to invoke the sense of curiosity and daring which have inspired modern scientific discovery—the sort of intellectual spirit that constantly shifts the extant boundaries of the knowable.[32] That is exactly what was at stake in the origin of a materialist approach to thinking about law and society.

Perhaps only Roberto Rossellini, during the period of his materialist epics like *L'eta del ferro* (1964–65) or *La Prise de pouvoir par Louis XIV* (1966), could have provided a serious historical depiction of the birth of modern jurisprudence. One wonders if this isn't precisely the kind of project to which the finest Italian filmmaker might have turned his camera had he only lived long enough.[33] Is it so difficult to visualize Rossellini's Pancinor zoom lens trailing the great Scottish professor, Adam Smith,

standins for the Arawak-speaking Taino who were encountered by Columbus on the Caribbean beach that fateful day in 1492. The Taino, who once numbered millions, had vanished from the earth within a few decades of Columbus' arrival, destroyed by forced labour, famine, slavery, slaughter and disease" ("Cinema's Conquistadores," p. 22).

32 Wollen pointedly comments on the contrast between the awe that Scott's Columbus feels when witnessing the "lush green tropical landscape" of the West Indies for the first time—an image that "will stay with him in all its vividness until his death"—and the fact that "when he saw pine trees, which could be used for shipbuilding, he immediately switched into a different register, that of practicality and exploitation" (ibid., p. 21). Much has been written on "instrumental reason" and the contradictions built into Western science. Nevertheless, the reader might usefully consult the chapter titled "Sorcerers and Apprentices—The Natural Sciences," in Eric Hobsbawm, *The Age of Extremes: A History of the World, 1914–1991* (New York: Pantheon, 1994); see also, Tad Bartimus and Scott McCartney, *Trinity's Children: Living Along America's Nuclear Highway* (New York: Harcourt Brace Jovanovich, 1991): "Why push the edge of the scientific envelope further into the unknown? Oppenheimer was asked the same question during hearings before the Atomic Energy Commission in 1954. Why, when the uranium gun bomb and the plutonium implosion bomb had been so successful against Hiroshima and Nagasaki, did the world need a hydrogen bomb—the so-called Super? 'The program in 1951,' replied Oppenheimer, 'was technically so sweet that you could not argue about that. The issues became purely the military, the political, and the human problem[s] of what you were going to do about it [the thermonuclear device] once you had it.' Technically so sweet. That, to a scientist, is romance" (p. 126).

33 Tag Gallagher suggests that, in Rossellini's hands, "the camera, one might say, becomes the eye of history…" Tag Gallagher, "Roberto Rossellini and Historical Neorealism," *Artforum* 40 (Summer, 1975). On materialist and Brechtian elements in Rossellini's historical films, see James Roy MacBean, *Film and Revolution* (Bloomington, Ind.: Indiana Univ. Press, 1975). For Rossellini's own description of how his moving or travelling lens works and how it was employed in *Louis XIV*, see Roberto Rossellini, *My Method: Writings and Interviews* 203–205 (New York, : Marsilio Publishers, Adriano Apra, ed., 1992). At the time of his death, the completed screenplay for Rossellini's biographical motion picture on Karl Marx rested on his desk, never to be filmed. It is as easy to imagine an historical epic on the life and work of the author of *The Wealth of Nations* as it is one on the author of *Capital*. See Peter Brunette, *Roberto Rossellini* 349 (New York: Oxford University Press, 1987).

founder of classical political economy,[34] as he makes his way through the brutally cold streets of Glasgow, piled high with snow, heading for class on a crystal-clear morning—Friday, December 24, 1762, to be exact, the day before Christmas. Ten years earlier, Smith had been elected to the chair of Moral Philosophy at the University of Glasgow, it was there that he began to deliver his lectures on legal history.

Smith taught the course in jurisprudence at Glasgow for a dozen years, with lectures in the morning followed by an examination, filled with Smith's illustrative commentary, ending at noon. Notes from the 1762–63 and 1763–64 terms have survived and thus it is the first class of the 1762–63 session that Rossellini might have chosen to set the stage for a cinematic reconstruction of the birth of materialist jurisprudence.[35]

34 "Marx credited the 'classical economists'—a term he coined—with delving below the surface, however inconsistently" (Sowell, *Marxism*, p. 20). Meghnad Desai observes: "A term often used synonymously with economics ....Its more specific meaning... is mainly associated with the works of Adam Smith and Ricardo, and of such authors as Malthus, James and J. S. Mill, McCulloch, Senior" ("Political Economy," in T. Bottomore, ed., *A Dictionary of Marxist Thought* [Oxford: Basil Blackwell, 1983], p. 375).

35 For a detailed account of the period in Smith's career when he developed his lectures on the economic basis of legal history, see the chapters, "Called to Glasgow University" and "Teacher," in Ian Simpson Ross, *The Life of Adam Smith* (Oxford: Oxford University Press, 1995). The notes from this course have been published as Adam Smith, *Lectures on Jurisprudence* R. L. Meek, D. D. Raphael and P. G. Stein, eds., (Oxford: Oxford University Press, 1978). See also the Introduction to Adam Smith, *Jurisprudence*, pp. 1–42; Ronald L. Meek, "New Light on Adam Smith's Glasgow Lectures on Jurisprudence," in *Smith, Marx, and After* (London: Chapman and Hall, 1977), pp. 56–91; and *Social Science and the Ignoble Savage* (Cambridge: Cambridge University Press, 1976). In his invaluable Jones Lectures at Queens University, Belfast, Cambridge University Professor of Civil Law Peter Stein, an editor of Smith's *Jurisprudence*, credits Meek, the main editor of Smith's *Jurisprudence*, with setting out in detail what evidence there

is for precursors to Smith's path-breaking legal theory. See Stein, *Legal Evolution: The Story of an Idea* 19 (Cambridge: Cambridge University Press, 1980), p. 19.

See also, Ian Ross, *Adam Smith*: "Concerning Smith's preparations for lecturing on law, we have his admission of 5 March 1769 to a Scottish judge, Lord Hailes: 'I have read law entirely with a view to form some general notion of the great outlines of the plan according to which justice has [been] administered in different ages and nations'... If the first volume of Robertson's book on Charles V (1769) is truly a guide to the scheme of the Edinburgh lectures, and thereafter to the Glasgow jurisprudence course which Callander attended as Smith's student, then they were similarly concerned with the 'Progress of Society in Europe,' tracing the changing forms of legal institutions and government responses to what Robertson was to call 'modes of subsistence' in another work, his *History of America*, 1777 (Meek, 1976: 136–145)" (pp. 106–7). Ross adds that Smith's privately taught course at Edinburgh in 1750, from which no notes survive, "must have been as extensive as that normally given in jurisprudence at Glasgow, because Smith was prepared at short notice in the autumn of 1751 to teach the subject for the Professor of Moral Philosophy there, Craigie, who was ill....A major theme was the affirmation of the value of economic liberty, and it is the evidence on this point that indicates the treatment of law and government as subject to historical change

However grim or inclement conditions outside might have been during a typical Glasgow winter, inside Adam Smith's lecture hall his listeners found him "warm and animated, and his expression easy and fluent," according to one his earliest students, John Millar, later to become the University of Glasgow's renowned Professor of Law.[36] More interesting than his account of Smith's teaching style, however, is Millar's oft-quoted formulation of Smith's legal philosophy itself. Surpassing those who preceded him, from antiquity through the luminaries of eighteenth-century French philosophy, Smith endeavored "to trace the gradual progress of jurisprudence, both public and private, from the rudest to the most refined ages, and to point out the effects of those arts which contribute to subsistence, and to the accumulation of property, in producing correspondent improvements or alterations in law and government."[37] With nearly six hundred pages of Smith's *Jurisprudence* in hand, economist Ronald

arising, in part, from economic conditions" (*Adam Smith*, p. 107).

36 John Millar is quoted in Dugald Stewart's essay, "Account of the Life and Writings of Adam Smith, LL.D.," in Stewart, *Biographical Memoir of Adam Smith* (Royal Society of Edingburgh, 1793; repr. New York: Augustus M. Kelley, 1966), p. 13. See also Nicholas Phillipson, "John Millar," in *The New Palgrave: The Invisible Hand*, pp. 211–12.

37 John Randall, as we have seen, refers to Diderot as an exemplar of eighteenth-century French materialism. Antony Flew cites La Mettrie and d'Holbach, and Thomas Sowell states that "Holbach was the central figure among the eighteenth-century materialists whom Marx regarded as his predecessors" (*Marxism*, p. 40). Ronald Meek, however, in tracking Smith's predecessors, subordinates not only the work of Diderot and d'Holbach but also that of Quesnay, Helvetius, Goguet, and Voltaire to the inspiration of Baron Charles Montesquieu's *The Spirit of Laws* (1748), which Meek calls "a horse of a different colour" (*Social Science*, p. 31).

James Bonar's catalog of Adam Smith's personal library does, in fact, include titles by most of these writers, but none save Montesquieu are represented in the list of authorities or the general index to the *Lectures on Jurisprudence*. Bonar, *A Catalog of the Library of Adam Smith* (Prepared for the Royal Economic Society, 1894, 2d ed., 1932; repr.

New York: August M. Kelley, 1966); Smith, *Jurisprudence*, pp. 591–610. Although both Meek and Peter Stein devote several pages of their respective studies of historical jurisprudence to the *content* of Montesquieu's contribution, it was as much the *spirit* of his enterprise which provided direction for Smith and the Scottish historical school. As Meek puts it, writers such as Adam Smith "were to see *The Spirit of Laws* as providing a kind of green light, an *ex cathedra* 'go-ahead', for the new social science" (*Social Science*, pp. 31–35; cf. Peter Stein, *Legal Evolution*, pp. 15–19). For an account of Smith's predecessors in developing classical political economy itself, as distinct from materialist jurisprudence, see Meek, *Precursors of Adam Smith* (London: Dent and Sons, 1973). For a concise introduction to Montesquieu's sociological jurisprudence— one more detailed than those provided by Meek and Stein—see Franz Neumann, *The Democratic and the Authoritarian State* (New York: Free Press, 1957), pp. 96–148.

John Millar is quoted in Stewart, *Biographical Memoir*, pp. 12–13. It is interesting to note in passing that it was Stewart to whom Thomas Jefferson sent his emissary when seeking British recruits for the University of Virginia faculty; see Gladys Bryson, *Man and Society: The Scottish Inquiry of the Eighteenth Century* (Princeton: Princeton University Press, 1945, repr. New York: August M. Kelley, 1968), p. 262.

Meek has tried to reduce this monumental work to its absolutely essential component parts: Smith's empirical identification of a particular society's mode of subsistence; his location of that system of production within what he regarded as the four major stages of historical development; and, finally, Smith's observation that as the mode of subsistence changes, so too does the legal superstructure because the economic base has a decisive influence over other components of the social totality.[38]

38 See Meek, *Social Science*, "The essential idea embodied in the theory is that societies undergo *development* through successive *stages* based on different modes of subsistence....The important point is that the stages should be based on different *modes of subsistence*, rather than on (for example) different modes of political organisation, or different phases of some kind of 'life cycle' based on the analogy of human life; and that these different modes of subsistence should be recognized, even if only vaguely, as in some sense *determining* elements in the total situation" (p. 6).

It might be helpful to distinguish, right away, this "modes of subsistence" theory from one of its competitors. During the ascendancy of Ronald Reagan's supply-side economics and conservative political revolution, historian Arthur Schlesinger, Jr., penned a widely read article, republished in his book titled *The Cycles of American History* (Boston: Houghton Mifflin, 1986).

When the article appeared in the book it was titled "The Cycles of American Politics," and was somewhat less ambitious than the book's title hinted. Nevertheless, Schlesinger sought to extend into the late twentieth century a view of American political life originally developed by his father, also a historian of considerable reputation. The notion was that American politics reflected a particular pattern of development that helped to explain the past and might make a rough prediction of future events possible.

The pattern or cycle revealed a "continuing shift in national involvement, between public purpose and private interest." What this meant was there are regular oscillations in U.S. political history between what Schlesinger would call liberalism and conservatism and, no matter how bleak things might have

appeared to liberal Democrats during Reagan's first term, they only had to wait a while (somewhere between twelve and sixteen and a half years), whereupon they would once again get their chance. By Schlesinger's own calculations, the liberals' turn at bat should have come around again in 1990 or 1994— though one doubts that either George Bush or Bill Clinton are what Schlesinger had in mind.

However, it is not my purpose here to dismiss Schlesinger's cyclical explanation of American politics. I only wish to indicate the difference between the sources upon which it draws and those of the economic or "modes of subsistence" theory originated by Adam Smith. Schlesinger, at one point, characterizes the deep structure of his cyclical theory this way: "The roots of this cyclical self-sufficiency doubtless lie deep in the natural life of humanity. There is a cyclical pattern in organic nature—in the tides, in the seasons, in night and day, in the systole and diastole of the human heart" (p. 27). Poetic, yes, but does it represent solid historical reasoning? Of course, Schlesinger could be right for the wrong reasons. His cyclical theory could, retrospectively, give sufficient shape and form to American politics that the subject would, at least, be rendered more teachable to undergraduates.

But the reasons Schlesinger offers for his theory, especially insofar as they reflect what Meek describes as "different phases of some kind of 'life cycle' based on the analogy of human life," seem to me questionable. Anyway, the theory of legal history I will defend, drawn as it is from Glasgow school jurisprudence, should not be confused with theories like Schlesinger's, even where both seem to identify cyclical patterns of historical development, *which ultimately they will*. It should also be noted that my own scheme

Does Millar's description of Smith's approach as a "correspondence" theory of law and society justify characterizing Scottish Enlightenment legal theory as materialist?[39] Was Smith actually arguing that "alterations" in superstructural forms of law and politics above, necessarily result from the development of productive forces and property arrangements below, at the base? Gladys Bryson, in her pathbreaking book on the Scottish historical school, carefully elucidates the role Adam Smith's jurisprudence played in an emerging science of society. Her first quote from Smith's *Lectures* is: "Till there be property there can be no government, the very end of which is to secure wealth, and to defend the rich from the poor."[40]

consists of periods that are each a good deal longer than Schlesinger's cycles.

39 See John Robertson, "Scottish Enlightenment," in *The New Palgrave: The Invisible Hand*, pp. 239–44.

40 Bryson, *Man and Society*, provides one of the first important examples of scholarship that groups together a range of eighteenth-century Scottish intellectuals (for example, Adam Smith, James Millar, David Hume, Francis Hutcheson, Thomas Reid, Adam Ferguson, Dugald Stewart, Lord Kames, and Lord Monboddo) and demonstrates their common, quite far-sighted approach to social theory. Prior to Bryson's work of 1945, Andrew Skinner cites on this topic only Roy Pascal's 1938 essay on the Scottish historical school; after Bryson, Skinner lists the work of Ronald Meek, Duncan Forbes, and W. C. Lehmann, respectively, much of which is devoted to the jurisprudential and historical views of Adam Smith and John Millar of Glasgow. See Skinner, "Adam Smith: an Economic Interpretation of History," in A. S. Skinner and T. Wilson, eds., *Essays on Adam Smith* (Oxford: Oxford University Press, 1975), p. 175.

Subsequent to the publication of Skinner's overview in the Oxford essays of 1975, and in addition to Peter Stein's *Legal Evolution*, we should add the following: John Kenneth Galbraith, *Economics in Perspective: A Critical History* (Boston: Houghton Mifflin, 1987), pp. 57–139; Robert L. Heilbroner, "Adam Smith's Capitalism," in *Behind the Veil of Economics* (New York: W. W. Norton, 1988), pp. 134–64; and David Spadafora, "The Progress of Human Culture: Scotland," in *The Idea of Progress in Eighteenth-Century*

Britain (New Haven: Yale University Press, 1990), pp. 253–320.

For the Smith quote, see Bryson, *Man and Society*, p. 161. She cites the early Cannan edition of Smith's lectures on jurisprudence as her source: see ibid., p. 268. That edition, reedited and titled "Report dated 1766" (though in all probability notes from Smith's lectures for the 1763–64 session), is gathered with the more recently discovered and considerably more extensive notes from the 1762–63 term, and together they constitute the authoritative Glasgow edition of the *Lectures on Jurisprudence*.

See also Smith, *Lectures* (from 1762–63): "[I]t is necessary that the arm of authority should be continually stretched forth, and permanent laws or regulations made which may ascertain the property of the rich from the inroads of the poor, who would otherwise continually make incroachments upon it, and settle in what the infringements of this property consists and in what cases they will be liable to punishment. Laws and government may be considered in this and indeed in every case as a combination of the rich to oppress the poor, and preserve to themselves the inequality of the goods which would otherwise be soon destroyed by the attacks of the poor, who if not hindered by the government would soon reduce the others to an equality with themselves by open violence" (p. 208).

Also consider this passage from Smith's *Lectures*, from 1763–64: "The appropriation of herds and flocks, which introduced an inequality of fortune, was that which first gave rise to regular government. Till there be property there can be no government, the

This is not exactly what we would expect from the economist to whom Thomas Sowell refers, not without reason, as the "patron saint of *laissez faire* capitalism."[41]

But should we really be surprised by Smith's seemingly modern explanation of the correspondence between law and an existing system of property relations? Across ideological boundaries, from federal judge Richard Posner and his conservative colleagues in the law and economics school to current liberal critics of the distribution of American justice— or, for that matter, from Adam Smith to his successor in the development of classical political economy, Karl Marx—we see that the more heavily a legal and political theory is based upon systematic empirical observation, the more likely it is that analysis will candidly acknowledge a simple fact "almost" too obvious to mention: law is socially produced.[42] To be sure,

very end of which is to secure wealth, and to defend the rich from the poor" (p. 404). Elaborating a bit on the same theme, Smith asserts: "Law and government, too, seem to propose no other object but this, they secure the individual who has enlarged his property, that he may peaceably enjoy the fruits of it. By law and government all the different arts flourish, and that inequality of fortune to which they give occasion is sufficiently preserved. By law and government, domestic peace is enjoyed and security from the foreign invader" (ibid., p. 489, from 1763–64).

41 Sowell, *Marxism*, p. 12.

42 All intellectual history, not just the history of law and politics, stands in the shadow of the kind of materialism initiated by Smith and his Scottish Enlightenment colleagues. See, for example, the comments of Princeton historian Felix Gilbert, included as part of a now-classic collection of essays on the writing of history: "[M]odern intellectual history arose after belief in the control of events by ideas had collapsed. It exists only in connection with, and in relation to, the surrounding political, economic, and social forces. The investigation of subjects of intellectual history leads beyond the purely intellectual world and intellectual history per se does not exist" (Gilbert, "Intellectual History: Its Aims and Methods," *Daedalus* [Winter 1971], p. 94).

In the first serious general history of American legal development, Stanford law professor Lawrence M. Friedman argues that

law should be treated "not as a kingdom unto itself, not as a set of rules and concepts, not as the province of lawyers alone, but as a mirror of society." Friedman's own approach "takes nothing as historical accident, nothing as autonomous, everything as relative and molded by economy and society." In his view, the "legal system always 'works'; it always functions....The system works like a blind, insensate machine. It does the bidding of those whose hands are on the controls. The laws of China, the United States, Nazi Germany, France, and the Union of South Africa, reflect the goals and policies of those who call the tune in those societies." (Friedman, A *History of American Law* [2d ed., New York: Simon and Schuster, 1985], pp. 12, 18).

Two centuries after Smith delivered his Glasgow lectures, his perspective has been widely adopted and is often taken for granted by historians, invoked without citations or scholarly reference. See, for example, Rosemary Horrox, "No More Feudalism," *London Review of Books* (Feb. 23, 1995): "Lawyers may have a weakness for tidying away messy realities, but they cannot generally create an intellectual model out of nothing, or force its adoption if it is too far out of step with contemporary norms" (p. 25). The social and economic forces that shape those norms are today charted, perhaps less glamorously but more soberly and realistically than before, by historians living in a world where, as Felix Gilbert puts it

Smith's analysis of what constitutes society's economic base or infrastructure and how it relates to the evolution of legal systems is more specific and more interesting than the naked proposition that law is a social artifact.[43] But whether, like Smith and Millar, we define the base as a mode of subsistence,[44] or like later economists we refer to the mode of produc-

rather bluntly, belief in the control of events by ideas has collapsed.

43 Andrew Skinner argues that according to Smith, "development will generate four distinct economic stages, each with a particular socio-political structure reflecting the mode of subsistence prevailing." Smith's colleague at Glasgow, John Millar, understood Smith's model in terms of a correspondence theory, and Skinner sees Smith's legal superstructure as a reflection of the mode of subsistence; these two views are virtually identical. Conventionally enough, Skinner adds that the "most complete and elaborate account of the whole argument" is found in Smith's *Jurisprudence* ("Economic Interpretation," p. 155).

On the other hand, American economist Robert Heilbroner, one of the most popular raconteurs of the worldly philosophy, regards Smith's *Wealth of Nations* as the most important source for the four-stage theory. In the same volume of Oxford essays that includes Skinner's article, Heilbroner claims that "Smith had already in his late twenties envisaged society as passing through four stages: 'hunting, pasturage, farming, and commerce'. In the *Lectures [on Jurisprudence]*, however, this stages-of-history sequence is introduced merely to lead to a discussion of property, whereas in *The Wealth of Nations* the scheme is reiterated with much greater historical detail and is utilized to suggest a proto-Marxian coincidence of civil institutions with the changing underpinnings of the material mode of production" (Heilbroner, "The Paradox of Progress: Decline and Decay in *The Wealth of Nations*," *Essays on Adam Smith*, p. 525).

For different editions of those works of Smith on which Heilbroner relies, see Adam Smith, *The Wealth of Nations*, E. Cannan, ed. (New York: Modern Library, 1937), pp. 653–81; E. Cannan, ed., *The Wealth of Nations* (New York: Modern Library, 1994), pp. 747–79; and

R. H. Campbell and A. S. Skinner, eds., *An Inquiry into the Nature and Causes of the Wealth of Nations*, vol. 2 (Oxford: Oxford University Press, 1976), pp. 689–72).

Heilbroner sees Smith's civil institutions (such as law) coinciding with their material underpinnings in a way that anticipates Marx's later description.

In his recent survey of the Scottish contribution, Associate Dean of the graduate school and lecturer in history at Yale, David Spadafora, adds that it "has been suggested that the Scots organized these stages along primarily economic lines, differentiating somewhat like Marx between an economic foundation and a social, political, and cultural superstructure. [William] Robertson took this view when he stated that in every examination of the 'operations of men when united together in society, the first object of attention should be their mode of subsistence. Accordingly as that varies, their laws and policy must be different.' Smith quite clearly accepted such a perspective in telling his students at Glasgow in 1762–63 that the 'four stages of society are hunting, pasturage, farming, and commerce': for him, the status of a society's development was to be identified on the basis of the central element of its economic structure. [Lord] Kames agreed and described an identical series of historical states of society…" (*Idea of Progress*, p. 271).

44 John Millar studied jurisprudence at Glasgow under Smith, with whom he shared "lasting intimacy and friendship." After concluding his studies, he spent two years in the home of Lord Kames, then was admitted to the bar in Edinburgh. "In June of 1761," adds William Lehmann, "at the almost daringly youthful age of only twenty-six, and but a year after his admission to the bar, Millar was elected to the Chair of Civil Law at Glasgow." Friends with David Hume, as well as Smith and Kames, Millar profoundly influenced both James and John Stuart Mill, generations

tion,[45] regime of accumulation,[46] social structure of accumulation,[47] or simply the international economic system,[48] this kind of up/down

of political leaders and statesmen—and, of course, the legal profession itself. See William C. Lehmann, *John Millar of Glasgow, 1735–1801* (Cambridge, Eng.: Cambridge University Press, 1960; repr. Arno Press, 1979), pp. 16–18, 151–52.

With Millar, according to Ronald Meek, "the four stages theory and the basic 'materialist' ideas and techniques associated with it become central and pervasive to a quite unprecedented degree" (Meek, *Social Science*, 160–61.) On top of everything else, John Millar was a busy attorney with both a civil and criminal practice and Lehmann provides detailed accounts by Millar's contemporaries of his trial strategies and forensic skill. At the time of his death, on the doorstep of the nineteenth century, the *Scots Magazine* reported that Millar's family had "lost a most affectionate father, his friends the life and soul of their society, the University her brightest ornament, and the country a firm and enlightened defender of her liberty." What a pity, then, that so little attention has been paid by American attorneys and law professors to this exemplary lawyer and teacher of lawyers, who "opposed every measure of public policy that, as he saw it, tended to create inequalities not of virtue and merit but of unearned privilege…" (Lehmann, *John Millar*, pp. 29, 67).

45 See, for example, Susan Himmelweit, "Mode of Production" in *A Dictionary of Marxist Thought* (Oxford: Basil Blackwell, 1983), pp. 224–27; Bob Jessop, "Mode of Production," in J. Eatwell, M. Milgate and P. Newman, eds., *The New Palgrave: Marxian Economics* (New York: W. W. Norton, 1990): "Marx used the concept of mode of production in two ways; to analyse the economic base and to describe the overall structure of societies. Thus he employed it to specify the particular combination of *forces* and *relations* of production which distinguished one form of labour process and its corresponding form of economic exploitation from another. He also employed it to characterize the overall pattern of social reproduction arising from the relations between the economic base

(comprising production, exchange, distribution and consumption) and the legal, political, social and ideological institutions of the so-called superstructure" (p. 289).

46 See, for example, Michel Aglietta, *A Theory of Capitalist Regulation: The U.S. Experience* (London: Verso, 1987); Robert Boyer, *The Regulation School: A Critical Introduction* (New York: Columbia University Press, 1990); Robert Brenner and Mark Glick, "The Regulation Approach: Theory and History," *New Left Review* (July/August, 1991), p. 45.

47 See, for example David M. Kotz, "A Comparative Analysis of the Theory of Regulation and the Social Structure of Accumulation Theory," *Science and Society* 54 (Spring, 1990), p. 5; David M. Gordon, Thomas E. Weisskopf, and Samuel Bowles, "Power, Accumulation and Crisis: The Rise and Demise of the Postwar Social Structure of Accumulation," in *The Imperiled Economy: Macroeconomics From a Left Perspective* (New York: Union for Radical Political Economics, 1987); Bruce Norton, "The Power Axis: Bowles, Gordon and Weisskopf's Theory of Postwar U.S. Accumulation," *Rethinking Marxism* (Fall 1988), p. 6; Bowles, Gordon, and Weisskopf, "Social Institutions, Interests, and the Empirical Analysis of Accumulation: A Reply to Bruce Norton," *Rethinking Marxism* (Fall 1988), p. 44.

48 See, for example Karl Polanyi, *The Great Transformation* (Boston: Beacon Press, 1957): "By the fourth quarter of the nineteenth century, world commodity prices were the central reality in the lives of millions of Continental peasants; the repercussions of the London money market were daily noted by businessmen all over the world; and governments discussed plans for the future in light of the situation on the world capital markets. Only a madman would have doubted that the international economic system was the axis of the material existence of the race.…The success of the Concert of Europe sprang from the needs of the new international organization of economy, and would inevitably end with its dissolution" (p. 18).

metaphor provides a rough and ready roadmap to guide us on our long journey across the continent of American legal history.

3. DIALECTIC

> *"For in the image of my cause I see*
> *The portraiture of his..."*
> WILLIAM SHAKESPEARE [49]

David Spadafora suggests that the Scots differentiated between base and superstructure "somewhat like Marx"; Robert Heilbroner describes Smith's stages theory as reflecting a materialist conception of history, and Thomas Sowell acknowledges that Karl Marx's labor theory of value is implicit in Smith's *Wealth of Nations*.[50] Jerry Muller nevertheless questions

---

49 William Shakespeare, *Hamlet* (v.ii.77–78).

50 Spadafora, *Idea of Progress*, p. 272; Heilbroner, "Paradox of Progress," p. 525; Sowell, *Marxism*, p. 116. With regard to David Ricardo, the third member of the "founding fathers" of classical political economy, and completing the labor theory of value trifecta, see John Kenneth Galbraith, *The Age of Uncertainty* (Houghton Mifflin, 1977): "Different products of farms or factories required different amounts of Ricardo's minimally nourished labor. The amount of labor required established the relative value of things—again the labor theory of value. Voiced in slightly different form by Marx half a century on, this proposal would shake the world" (p. 35).

See also Galbraith's *Economics In Perspective: A Critical History* (Boston: Houghton Mifflin, 1987): "The return to capital and the capitalist—interest and profits were not clearly distinguished—Smith extracted only with some difficulty from a labor theory of value. The quantity of labor and the resulting cost of sustaining it determines price. The return to capital, in consequence, must be an exaction by the capitalist from the rightful claim of the worker whose toil establishes the price and to whom the return from the sale of the product is presumably due. Or it is the appropriation of a surplus value that the worker creates over

and above what he is paid and to which, again, he has a seemingly rightful claim. And here Smith left the matter—insofar as his position is clear. This innocently subversive view would also be developed and refined in the next century by Ricardo. And it would become a major source of the revolutionary indignation and agitation of Karl Marx" (p. 67).

For more on Ricardo, see Robert L. Heilbroner, *The Worldly Philosophers* (6th ed., New York: Simon and Schuster, 1992), pp. 75–104; Ronald L. Meek, "The Decline of Ricardian Economics in England," *Economics and Ideology and Other Essays* (London: Chapman and Hall, 1967), pp. 51–74; Eric Roll, *A History of Economic Thought* (5th ed., London: Faber and Faber, 1992), pp. 155–174; Jacob H. Hollander, *David Ricardo: A Centenary Estimate* (Baltimore: Johns Hopkins Press, 1910; repr. AMS, 1982); Donald Winch, Introduction, in David Ricardo, *The Principles of Political Economy and Taxation* (London: J. M. Dent, 1973), pp. v–xviii; Piero Sraffa, Introduction, in David Ricardo, *The Works and Correspondence of David Ricardo*, vol. 1: *On the Principles of Political Economy and Taxation* (Cambridge: Cambridge University Press, 1981), pp. xiii–lxii. For further elaboration of his comments on value theory, cited above, from his book on Marxism, see Thomas

whether Ronald Meek has not represented Smith as rather "more proto-Marxist" than is justified.[51] His singling out of Meek for this criticism is ironic considering Meek's deep knowledge of *both* Marxism and the Scottish Enlightenment. As noted, Meek found in Millar a development of materialism which went further than that achieved by any other member of the Scottish historical school; yet in his assessment of Millar's jurisprudence, Meek places his finger precisely on the crucial *difference* between Smithian materialism, standing alone, and Marxism: "Of course, there is still a very deep gulf between Millar, even at his best, and Marx....In Marx's conception of history, there is a feeling for the dialectic of social change which was conspicuously lacking in Millar's."[52]

Our materialist roadmap may get us on our way but we cannot advance very far without a compass. G. W. F. Hegel, whose work comes between that of Smith and Marx, provides just that orientation and direction. Hegel's notion of contradiction is the source not simply for Marx and Engels but for every social theorist demonstrating what Meek describes as a "feeling for the dialectic of social change." But what does contradiction have to do with the relation we have tried to capture in our up/down metaphor? After all, if the superstructure is determined by the base or, in Smith's own terms, if a society's mode of subsistence decisively shapes the nature of law and government, where is there room for contradiction? If there is, in fact, contradiction between the nature of a legal system and the economic foundation upon which it has been constructed, then this

---

Sowell, *Classical Economics Reconsidered* (Princeton: Princeton University Press, 1994), pp. 97–111.

51 Jerry Z. Muller, *Adam Smith in His Time and Ours* (New York: Free Press, 1993), p. 250. Muller apparently believes that Smith was proto-Marxist but not *that* proto-Marxist. Recall that it was Robert Heilbroner, for whom Muller has considerable respect, who described Smith's notion of the relation between "material mode of production" and civil society as "proto-Marxian" ("Paradox of Progress," p. 525). See also Peter Stein, *Legal Evolution*: "Marx and his followers restored to thinking about legal change the emphasis on means of production, which Smith had introduced....[I]t is to Adam Smith that we owe the idea that the prevailing modes of production largely determine the nature of

social institutions, the form and extent of property rights and the nature of the relationships between men in society and their equality and inequality" (p. 111). Perhaps it makes as much sense to regard Meek's Marx as late Smithian as it does to regard his Smith as proto-Marxist; see Ian Ross, *Adam Smith*: "In his provocative moments, Ronald Meek used to inform his students that Marx became a Communist in the 1840s through dwelling on those passages in [*The Wealth of Nations*] which draw attention to the workers being exploited and oppressed by deceitful traders and manufacturers and indolent landlords..." (pp. 417–18).

52 Ronald L. Meek, "The Scottish Contribution to Marxist Sociology," *Economics and Ideology and Other Essays* (London: Chapman and Hall, 1967), p. 43.

disjuncture would seem to disprove materialism, at least as explanatory legal theory.

Remarkably, however, in the process of confronting this challenge to materialism, we can find the solution to one of legal history's prime riddles. The problem that has constituted such a stumbling block for the development of modern American legal and political theory—what I will later call the inability "to move beyond Beard"[53]—can be surmounted. So I pose the question again: What if law and economy, the "so-called superstructure" and infrastructure, appear to be out of joint?[54] This is a crucial query for our approach to legal history—and groundwork for a compelling and convincing answer that must be laid with care.

Not that long ago, there was heated public debate as to whether Mikhail Gorbachev was genuinely different from a rogue's gallery of commissar predecessors. All the fun, however, was taken out of trying to divine the answer when the entire Soviet system collapsed, and with it the Berlin Wall, the Cold War, the nuclear arms race, and virtually everything about the wide world which people who were middle-aged or older had taken for granted since childhood.[55] Somehow, within a decade of the fall, while everyone struggled to find the right name for what, or who, filled the vacuum, the whole thing became passé.

Only a few years earlier, such events would have been harder to imagine than a nuclear war destroying the planet, something Hollywood often visualized. By 1995, though, the most unlikely political transformation a screenwriter could have dreamt up had not only happened but had, just as quickly, been consigned to ancient history. The spy novel lost its subject matter overnight and appeared to be washed up. Was peace worth the price? Our best fiction writers, grasping fully the significance of what had happened, treated the Cold War as a vivid memory, something bittersweet, in their efforts to capture its fading aura before it was lost forever.[56] One day, perhaps, Ken Burns would make a documentary, *The Cold War*, in antique black and white. In the meantime,

53 See "Moving Beyond Beard: A Symposium," *Radical History Review* 42 (1988), pp. 7–47.

54 Jessop, "Mode of Production," p. 289.

55 See Gabriel Kolko, *Century of War* (New York: The New Press, 1994): "The unprecedented and wholly unexpected ideological and organizational collapse of the Marxist-Leninist states alone challenges our capacity to comprehend our own century…" (p. ix).

See also Eric Hobsbawm, "End of Socialism," *The Age of Extremes* (New York: Pantheon, 1994), pp. 461–99.

56 See, for example James Buchan, *The Golden Plough* (New York: Farrar, Straus, and Giroux, 1995). For an interesting work of nonfiction by Buchan's father, which renders parts of *The Golden Plough* more intelligible, see Alistair Buchan, *War in Modern Society* (London: C. A. Watts, 1966).

former Secretary of Defense Robert McNamara apologized.

Another casualty of the fall, in the view of some commentators, was Marxism. As early as 1990, John Lukacs reported a "watershed in the political and intellectual history of the world because of the evident collapse of the reputation and, consequently, of the influence of Marxism…"[57] It is not entirely clear why the fall of what was, after all, Stalin's empire should create an intellectual crisis for Marxism—not least because *western* Marxism (whether in the form of Trotskyism, the Frankfurt School of Social Research, the New Left, or the anarchists of May '68) had long since distanced itself from Soviet Marxism.[58] Yet it appears that at least some Marxists have themselves abandoned ship[59] and

57 John Lukacs, *The Duel* (New York: Ticknor and Fields, 1990), p. 243.

58 Thirty years ago, University of Wisconsin historian William Appleman Williams pointed to an inclination he believed was shared by most Americans: a mistaken tendency to confuse Karl Marx with Lenin or Stalin or the Soviet Union. See W. A. Williams, *The Great Evasion* (Chicago: Quadrangle Books, 1964), pp. 19–20.

59 I am not referring here, of course, to such inevitable apostasies as France's New Philosophers or the "second thoughts" generation in the United States whose nearly Maoist focus on self-criticism, neatly coinciding with Reagan's rise to power, makes one wonder why anyone ever listened to them in the first place. Such desperate political converts have been identified in widely differing cultures: the Japanese, for example, refer to them as *Tenkosha* (see Germaine A. Hoston, *Marxism and the Crisis of Development in Prewar Japan* [Princeton: Princeton University Press, 1986], pp. 31–32). What I *am* referring to, however, is the erosion of conviction among sincere, lifelong western Marxists such as Ronald Aronson, who writes that although the fall of communism shocked him as much as anyone else, he anticipated it would open the way for something new and liberating. "But the opposite happened," he writes, "the end of communism instead became part of a stunning defeat of those social forces, ideas, structures, projects, and even values, which for two centuries have been identified with the Left." He concludes, "Marxism is over, and we are on our own" (*After Marxism*

[New York: Guilford Press, 1995], pp. 411., 1). Some of those who understood Marxism primarily as a *practical* political philosophy believe that it declined with the disintegration of a class-conscious Western industrial working class—an event that preceded the fall of communism by many years. On the fall of the house of labor, see, for example, Hobsbawm, *Extremes*: "In most respects this conscious working-class cohesiveness reached its peak, in older developed countries, at the end of the Second World War. During the golden decades almost all elements of it were undermined. The combination of secular boom, full employment and a society of genuine mass consumption utterly transformed the lives of working-class people in the developed countries, and continued to transform it" (p. 306).

In this view, Marx was the great philosopher of proletarian revolution. The end of a (European) proletariat means, in a sense, the end of Marxism. Finally, one can still identify writers who place Marxism in a sufficiently broad historical and intellectual context that it remains possible to imagine objective forces precipitating the doctrine's rebirth, however substantially reconceptualized; see, for example, Manuel Riesco, "Honour and Eternal Glory to the Jacobins!" *New Left Review* (July/August 1995), pp. 55–67. But Riesco, too, speaks of those "who simply stop believing" (p. 56). Ironically, one of those apparently unwilling to just stop believing in the "concept of the Left" is Graham Fuller, former vice-chairman of the National Intelligence Council at the U.S.

Lukacs seemed prepared to consign Marxism to history's notorious dust-bin. Ironically, though, Marx's loss may have been Hegel's gain.[60] Long opposed by liberals because of Hegel's alleged authoritarianism (Sir Karl Popper had branded him a threat to the *open society*), and equally dis-dained by conservatives (due perhaps to guilt by association with dissi-dent schools of European Marxism), Hegelian social theory suddenly found itself in the limelight as the new, postcommunist world order spread its wings.[61] What had brought this about?

The proximate cause of mainstream political interest in Hegel was the handiwork of Francis Fukuyama, a former deputy director of the U.S. State Department's Policy Planning staff and a resident consultant at the RAND Corporation. Technically, of course, Hegel did not need reviving, for he had long since become firmly ensconced in college philosophy seminars, doctoral theses, and journals of political theory. But when was the last time that Hegelian philosophy had been debated on national affairs television programming or covered in the editorial pages of major newspapers? When had any famous dead European philosopher been

---

Central Intelligence Agency; see Graham Fuller, "The Next Ideology," *Foreign Policy* (Spring 1995): "On the spectrum of world politics today, we perceive a powerful vacuum, a gaping hole where Soviet-style Marxism-Leninism fell off the ideological map. Where is the international Left, now that its territorial bastion has collapsed? The very concept of the Left cannot disappear, regardless of the fate of its greatest champion" (p. 146). Fuller's "international Left," at least its German contingent, initially appeared disoriented by the fall; Peter Hohendahl, foreword to Jurgen Habermas's *The Past as Future* (Lincoln: University of Nebraska Press, 1994): "One of the important consequences of the German debate was the further breakup of the German left, which had begun in 1989 in the dispute over the collapse of state socialism in East Germany. While the German left had been united in its opposition to Vietnam, it could not find a common ground in the case of the Gulf War" (p. xi). But for writers who maintain that Marxism has a continuing roll to play in social and economic debate, see Howard J. Sherman, *Reinventing Marxism* (Baltimore: Johns Hopkins University Press, 1995); Saree Makdisi, Cesare Casarino, and

Rebecca E. Karl, eds., *Marxism Beyond Marxism* (New York: Routledge, 1996); Kevin Anderson, *Lenin, Hegel, and Western Marxism: A Critical Study* (Urbana: University of Illinois Press, 1995), quoted in Paul Le Blanc, "Lenin as Left-Hegelian: Reason and Revolution," *Monthly Review* (Oct. 1996): "In the light of these deep crises, most of which are connected to the persistently intractable world economic crisis, I believe it is only a matter of time before...radical intellectuals begin to return to some form of the perspectives of Hegel and Marx" (p. 44).

60 Contrast Aronson's obituary for Marx with his sense of Hegel's continuing vitality: "Still, for all its faults, Hegel's approach to history has something to tell us. It tells us first that philosophy must be, ultimately, the self-comprehension of the age, and second, that history can be looked at as the development of freedom" (*After Marxism*, p. 242).

61 See, for example, Peter Loptson, "Hegel Naturalized," *New Left Review* (May/June 1992): "Philosophical history, or speculative philosophy of history as it has also been called (usually pejoratively, by critics), is suddenly back in the mainstream, as the claimed 'end of history' is debated on every side" (p. 120).

made a party to political conversation inside the beltway or the subject of best-selling books with "blurbs" by people such as George Will, Tom Wolfe, Irving Kristol, Allan Bloom, even Edward Shevardnadze?

Perhaps with the fall of communism, Hegel was purged of any remaining Marxian taint; in any event, he was now primed for a fresh look. Some of the same sort of teleological (and Hegelian) theories of history which had once been so confidently relied upon as vindicating communism were now cast as justification for what everyone could see happening around them: the victory of liberal capitalism. In a brand-new context, thanks to Fukuyama, intellectuals and pundits, politicians and editorial writers debated "the end of history."[62] Fukuyama was both a pleasure to read and remarkably understandable (except perhaps when overexamining arguments advanced by ancient Greek moralists or the *Ecole Pratique's* Alexander Kojeve), constantly traversing his terrain from Hegel at Jena in 1806 to the victory of the VCR almost two centuries later. As those who emerged triumphant from this long struggle "sink into the soft leather of their BMW's, they will know somewhere in the back of their minds," Fukuyama concluded, that there have been "masters in the world who would feel contempt for the petty virtues required to become rich or famous in modern America."[63] Here was an authentically original thinker with the ability to reach a popular readership, a profound social theorist with a sense of irony and humor, a philosopher of history who made a living in the real world of politics.[64]

---

62 See Francis Fukuyama, "The End of History?" *The National Interest* (Summer 1989), pp. 3–18; *The End of History and the Last Man* (New York: The Free Press, 1992). See also Michael Rustin, "No Exit from Capitalism?" *New Left Review* (May/June 1992): "Fukuyama is an intellectual from the RAND Corporation, an institution where political relevance is no doubt valued very highly. This frame of concerns, and Fukuyama's sense for important issues, has given this book and its preceding *Public Interest* article (1989) a large and deserved impact..." (pp. 96–97). See also Michael J. Trebilcock, *The Limits of Freedom of Contract* (Cambridge, Mass.: Harvard University Press, 1993): "The 'End of History' has recently been proclaimed. With the transformation of Eastern Europe and the Soviet Union and the subsequent dismantling of centrally planned economies, Fukuyama

has claimed 'an unabashed victory of [classical] economic and political liberalism,' which he considers to herald the end of history in the sense that the decisive struggle between collectivist and liberal rights and market systems is now over, at least at the level of ideas or ideologies" (p. 1).

63 Fukuyama, *End of History*, p. 329.

64 According to Fukuyama, if Marx was Hegel's most important interpreter in the nineteenth century, he believes the greatest twentieth-century student of Hegel's was the French-Russian Alexander Kojeve (ibid., p. 66.) Perry Anderson regards Fukuyama himself as a "worthy successor" to Kojeve: see Anderson, "The Ends of History," in *Zones of Engagement* (London: Verso, 1992): "A fully political mind is here trained on the structure of history, seen from a philosophical standpoint. That would have been appreciated by Kojeve, in his office

With the defeat of the Nazis and emperor-system fascism, on the one hand, and the recent and dramatic fall of communism on the other, Fukuyama argued that liberal capitalism had finally mastered the globe. In so doing, it had brought the long process of human emancipation through historical development to a point of final...well, no other word for it, completion. Fukuyama deserves credit, in my view, not for his claim about human progress having today reached its zenith; rather, he deserves credit for retrieving Hegel's dialectic, the notion of movement and change as a result of contradiction. After discussing the Platonic origins of the concept of dialectic, in the form of Socratic dialogue, Fukuyama points out the crucial advance represented by Hegel's dialectical theory: "For Hegel, the dialectic takes place not only on the level of philosophical discussions, but between societies, or, as contemporary social scientists would say, between socio-economic systems"—or between antagonistic socio-economic forces *within* a single society or sovereign state. "One might describe history," he concludes, "as a dialogue between societies in which those with grave internal contradictions fail and are succeeded by others that manage to overcome those contradictions."[65]

In this view, the Roman Empire collapsed as a result of internal contradictions, only to be replaced by a medieval Christian world which developed its own set of contradictions to resolve. Likewise, American legal history traces, in outline, how a specific series of contradictions were overcome in a country which Fukuyama regards as having made a crucial contribution to the adventure of liberal democracy,[66] a nation that by any standard remains one of the three great economic powers at the beginning of the twenty-first century.[67] The expression of contradiction super-

at the Quai Branly. The functionary of the State Department [that is, Fukuyama] is a worthy successor of the *chargé de mission* at the Ministry of Finances" (p. 332). See also Fred Halliday, "An Encounter with Fukuyama," *New Left Review* (May/June 1992): "Fukuyama's theses, first enunciated in his article, 'The End of History?' in the summer of 1989, and expanded in his book, have been the centre of a notable international debate, marked by extremes of excoriation and appropriation....Fukuyama himself appears puzzled by the reception of his theses, if not ungratified by the reputation it has generated" (p. 90).

65 Fukuyama, *End of History*: "[L]et us accept," Fukuyama proposes, "the Hegelian-Marxist

thesis that history has proceeded dialectically, or through a process of contradiction..." (p. 61). Then we are positioned to analyze the way a specific "mode of subsistence" (the Scottish historical school) or—again relying upon Fukuyama's terminology—"a certain form of socio-political organization arises in some part of the world, but contains an internal contradiction which over time leads to its own undermining and replacement by a different and more successful one" (ibid., pp. 135–36.) This, in a nutshell, is the dialectical method I will apply to American legal history's four major periods of development.

66 See, for example, ibid., pp. 42–43, 64, 134, 159.

67 See, for example, Lesther Thurow, *Head to Head: The Coming Economic Battle Among*

seded by its resolution, only to be replaced by a renewed configuration of contradictions: here, in all its simplicity, is the essence of Hegel's contribution to the philosophy of history. The dynamic element in this process is *movement*—constant development, change—and the fulcrum of that process is contradiction. Superficial impressions of continuity and stability are illusory; they obscure the reality of unavoidable tension and conflict, hidden just beneath the surface. Stasis represents appearance only, contradiction is the truth. Everything, in an odd but important way, is constantly in the process of becoming its opposite.[68]

Although the point is much contested, Hegel himself apparently believed that his dialectic of historical change culminated in the Prussian military state;[69] Stalinists in their turn concluded that their system of

---

Japan, Europe, and America (New York: William Morrow, 1992).

68 Many Hegel scholars have labored long hours trying to draft coherent and accessible restatements of Hegel's dialectical method. For a few of the best, to which I will refer later, see: Peter Singer, *Hegel* (Oxford: Oxford University Press, 1983): "In the categories of our thought, in the development of consciousness, and in the progress of history, there are opposing elements which lead to the disintegration of what seemed stable, and the emergence of something new which reconciles the previously opposing elements but in turn develops its own internal tensions.... According to Hegel, the dialectic works as a method of exposition because the world works dialectically" (pp. 79–80).

Roy Bhaskar, *Dialectic: The Pulse of Freedom* (London: Verso, 1993): "In its most general sense, dialectic has come to signify any more or less intricate process of conceptual or social (and sometimes even natural) conflict, interconnection and change, in which the generation, interpenetration and clash of opposites, leading to their transcendence in a fuller or more adequate mode of thought or form of life (or being), plays a key role" (p. 3).

T. M. Knox, translator's foreword, in *Hegel's Philosophy of Right* (New York: Oxford University Press, 1967): "[T]he process is always from immediate, undifferentiated, unity (i.e., bare abstract universality), through difference and particularization, to the

concrete unity and synthesis of universal and particular, subject and object, form and content....Since the process of life is a single process, the determinations or particularizations which the concept gives to itself are an organically connected series, and they follow one another in stages of gradually increasing concreteness. The latter stages cancel the earlier ones, and yet at the same time the earlier ones are absorbed within the later as moments or elements within them" (pp. ix–x).

Randall, *Career of Philosophy*: "The dialectic movement proceeds by the development, first, of an antithesis in opposition to a thesis, and then of a further synthesis, a new and more complex relationship, in which both are taken up and their tension directed toward further advance....The antithesis is the 'negation' of the thesis, the synthesis is the 'negation' of the antithesis, a negation of a negation. If nothing new were added with the second negation, the process would obviously be back where it started. That is at bottom why Dialectic can never of itself predict the novel element to be added, but only take account of it and explain it after it has been discovered as a new fact, a further brute datum. Each step, because it adds something unpredictable, is a movement toward greater 'concreteness,' greater complexity of organization" (p. 312).

69 See, for example, Michael Forster, "Hegel's Dialectical Method," in *The Cambridge Companion to Hegel*, Frederick C. Beiser, ed., (Cambridge, Eng.: Cambridge University

bureaucratic communism completed the process Hegel defined;[70] Fukuyama candidly stated his belief in the possibility that liberal capital-

Press; 1993): "For the dialectical sequence turns out to be the same as the historical sequence—spanning the whole course of human history up to the present—in which the various shapes of consciousness and, eventually, Hegel's system have appeared. Hence Hegel is able to interpret history as a teleological process aimed at unfolding, in order, this very dialectical sequence of shapes of consciousness with the purpose of escaping earlier self-contradictions and eventually reaching the self-consistent position of his own system" (p. 136).

The outcome of this philosophical transition in Hegel from method to system, from dialectic to teleology, from critique to prophecy, is brutally described by Martin Nicolaus in his foreword to Karl Marx's *Grundrisse* (London: Penguin, 1993): "[I]t left Hegel towards the end a philosopher-pope bestowing benediction, as popes must, on the temporal emperor; here alone, in the Prussian military bureaucratic Junker autocracy, had the Absolute Mind fully revealed itself, not only to philosophy but to the senses" (p. 27). Distinguishing Hegel's teleology from his method, Nicolaus adds that the "other extreme of the contradiction that was Hegel is his work on dialectics."

"In the first place," Jean-Paul Sartre argues, in the *Critique of Dialectical Reason*, Alan Sheridan-Smith, trans., (London: Verso, 1991): "Hegel took himself to be at the beginning of the end of History, that is to say, at the moment of Truth which is death. The time had come to judge, because *in future* the philosopher and his judgment would never be required again. Historical evolution required this Last Judgment; it culminated in its philosopher. Thus the totalisation was complete: all that remained was to bring down the curtain" (vol. 1, pp. 21–22).

After identifying what he regards as important distinctions between Hegel's end of history or "ideally rational State," and the Prussian regime of Hegel's last years, Peter Singer states: "These differences are sufficient to acquit Hegel of the charge of having drawn up his philosophy entirely in order to please the Prussian monarchy. They do not, however,

make Hegel any kind of liberal in the modern sense" (*Hegel*, p. 40). Perry Anderson observes that the European liberalism of Hegel's time "was not democratic, of course, since it feared popular rule and rejected universal suffrage. Hegel was no exception in this regard. In that sense, it is naturally an anachronism to ascribe any paternity of liberal democracy to him...." ("Ends of History," p. 287). Finally, Georg Lukács adds, somewhat equivocally, that while certain criticisms of Hegel's ontology are "essentially justified," a letter that Hegel wrote in 1821 regarding Russia's future proves that "he did not envisage any fixed end to history" (*Hegel's False and His Genuine Ontology*, David Fernbach, trans. [London: Merlin Press; 1978], p. 11).

Obviously, one can debate whether Hegel's work, taken as a whole, reveals a belief in an end point or goal that is fundamental to the historical process. Further, one can argue about whether Hegel saw such an end point—if indeed he did—in the liberalism of the French Revolution and Napoleon's victory at Jena or, on the contrary, in Prussian authoritarianism. For our purposes, though, these issues are beside the point: if *any* philosopher believes that history has a predetermined direction, then that theorist (or at least that part of the theory being advanced) must be rejected. Fukuyama, sad to say, resists any distinction (Nicolaus even calls it contradiction) between Hegel's method and his system; for example, Fukuyama criticizes "Marx's collaborator, Friedrich Engels, who believed that the dialectic was a 'method' that could be appropriated from Hegel separately from the content of his system" (*End of History*, p. 61). But if Hegel's system includes a teleological view of history, it must be rejected if we are to preserve the truly dialectical quality of his method. And *that* is just what we want to do.

70 See, for example, Herbert Marcuse, *Soviet Marxism* (New York: Columbia University Press, 1958): "In line with this conception, and following Stalin's example of 1938, the 'law of the negation of the negation' disappeared from the list of the fundamental dialectical laws. Quite obviously, the Soviet Marxist conception

ism represents the goal of human history.[71] It would seem that most political thinkers drawn to such analyses find irresistible the notion that their own system or moment in time reflects an unsurpassable achievement or synthesis. Yet, as students of legal history, we are not at the moment in the business of attempting to measure regimes of government and economy by various (still much-disputed) yardsticks of human freedom; instead, we seek to use the analytical tools developed by the giants of social theory for the purpose of understanding how economic base and legal superstructure are related to each other (Smith's materialism), and how that relationship changes over time (Hegel's dialectic).[72]

But how to fuse the two visions, combine in one instrument of historical critique these two profound contributions to human knowledge? Consider the argument made by economist and essayist, Thomas Sowell of the Hoover Institution. Sowell is, perhaps, only the more recent in a long line of social theorists to span a bridge between Smith and Hegel, between materialism and dialectics,[73] but his work on Marxism demon-

---

of dialectic is most suitable to serve the ideological stabilization of the established state: it assigns to the state the historical task of solving the 'nonantagonistic contradictions' and precludes theoretically the necessity of another revolution...." (pp. 153–54). If that's not the end of history, what is?

71 Fukuyama, End of History: "It is possible that if events continue to unfold as they have done over the past few decades, that the idea of a universal and directional history leading up to liberal democracy may become more plausible to people, and that the relativist impasse of modern thought will in a sense solve itself" (p.338). The "relativist impasse" is, as Fukuyama earlier argues, a form of pessimism about the achievement of universal values, an essentially European cultural relativism which "is contradicted by the empirical flow of events in the second half of the [twentieth] century" (ibid., p. 70).

Perry Anderson, while summarizing the thrust of Fukuyama's National Interest essay and subsequent book which then deepens the argument, states that for Fukuyama's "end of history is not the cessation of all change or conflict, but the exhaustion of any viable alternatives to the civilization of the OECD [Organization for Economic Cooperation and Development]. Progress towards freedom

now has only one path. With the rout of socialism, Western liberal democracy has emerged as the final form of human government, bringing historical development to its close" ("Ends of History," p. 282). For a more recent statement of the position, see Fukuyama, Trust: The Social Virtues and the Creation of Prosperity (New York: The Free Press, 1995): "The worldwide convergence in basic institutions around liberal democracy and market economics forces us to confront the question of whether we have reached an 'end of history,' in which the broad process of human historical evolution culminates not, as in the Marxist version, in socialism but rather in the Hegelian vision of a bourgeois liberal democratic society" (p. 349).

72 For an elegant if preliminary discussion of a spectrum of issues which confronts practicing historians, see W. H. Walsh, An Introduction to Philosophy of History (London: Hutchinson's University Library, 1951).

73 Who was the first? Arguably, Hegel himself. Remarkably enough, this seems to be one of the least appreciated aspects in the development of Hegelian philosophy. In five hundred pages of The Cambridge Companion to Hegel, for example, the only reference to Smith's influence is one contributor's terse comment that Hegel

strates how widespread this particular approach to thinking about social change has become. In addition to providing his own capsule summary of the development of materialism from the ancient Greeks to nineteenth-century philosophy, Sowell locates the foundation of classical political economy (specifically, Ricardo and Marx) in Smith's work. He then turns to Hegel, arguing that dialectical, as opposed to determinist, materialism rejects the simple opposition of cause and effect in lieu of a causation that takes the form of reciprocal interaction.[74]

In making this argument, Sowell cites a letter that Friedrich Engels wrote in 1890. What, exactly, is the matter with that "determinism," as Engels puts it, "which passes from French materialism into natural science," and then manages to deny, for example, the role of accident in history? "What these gentlemen all lack is dialectic....Hegel never existed for them."[75] What Sowell, following Engels, makes possible is a clear and

---

"acquired a copy of Smith's *Wealth of Nations* (in English)..." (H. S. Harris, "Hegel's Intellectual Development to 1807," in ibid., [Cambridge, Eng.: Cambridge University Press, 1993], p. 31). A wonderful clue, however, is found in an offhand remark in the introduction: "but it has also been claimed that Hegel's philosophy is not idealism at all but a form of materialism [Lukács]" (Frederick C. Beiser, "Introduction: Hegel and the Problem of Metaphysics," in ibid., p. 21). Beiser did not need to further name his source. It was Lukacs's classic treatise on Hegel's intellectual development, written in Russia after Lukács emigrated there upon Hitler's rise to power in Germany: *The Young Hegel: Studies in the Relations Between Dialectics and Economics*, Rodney Livingstone, trans. (Cambridge, Mass.: MIT Press; 1976). Here Lukács asserts that after "the defeat of the Babeuf conspiracy and given the graveyard stillness of Germany, a radical democratic movement could not possibly have found support." Nevertheless, in the midst of this grim situation, the "contradictory strands in German idealist dialectics enabled it to dissolve the metaphysical dogmas of the old materialism and at the same time, unconsciously, and somewhat in conflict with its own idealist programme, to incorporate powerful elements of an authentic materialism" (pp. 369–70). And from whence does Hegel draw his

materialist inspiration? Lukács argues that "it is highly probable that the study of Adam Smith was a turning point in Hegel's evolution. The problem which reveals the striking parallel between Hegel's thought and the classical English economists is the problem of *work* as the central mode of human activity....[T]his problem emerges for the first time in the course of reading Adam Smith, since neither a study of the German economy which was so backward in the context of the development of capitalism, nor a reading of Steuart could really provide the necessary stimulus" (ibid., p. 172).

Quite separate from the debate over whether history has an end, or a purpose, the puzzle of why Hegel's dialectical system lacked "authentic materialism" is one of the main questions Lukács sets for himself. His short answer is that Hegel's "knowledge of the conflict between capital and labour only comes to him from reading about international economic relations, not from his own experience, from a real insight into capitalism in ordinary life. That is to say, the barrier here is an intellectual mirror of the primitive economy of Germany" (ibid., p. 176).

74 Sowell, *Marxism*, pp. 12, 28–33, 36–41.
75 Engels, "Letter to Schmidt," in Karl Marx and Friedrich Engels, *Selected Correspondence*, trans. and ed. I. Lasker (2d rev. ed., Moscow: Progress Publishers, 1965), p. 425, cited from an earlier edition in Sowell, *Marxism*, 30–31.

meaningful distinction between a determinist materialism, on the one hand, and a genuinely dialectical materialism, on the other. The difference between a relatively mechanical "cause and effect" materialist explanation and a subtle, dialectical one hinges entirely, in Engels's view, on Hegel, or more precisely, on a careful reading and appreciation of Hegel's philosophy.

Now let us return to the question posed at the beginning of this discussion, regarding the challenge presented by a potential disjuncture between law and economy. On the one hand, we should expect a certain amount of tension between economic and legal or political forces when they compete for historical center stage. But the founding proposition of materialism is that, on balance, the mode of subsistence which Smith introduced will determine the outcome of social struggles. Consequently, at some point, persistence of real contradiction between base and superstructure would seem to threaten first principles of a materialist outlook on the world. The simple truth is that such criticism would be correct—were materialism not supplemented by Hegel. It is precisely Thomas Sowell's mission to demonstrate the way materialism, by the end of the nineteenth century, had been infused with the spirit of Hegel's dialectic. He concludes that because this synthesis "is a theory of transformations, and not a theory of states of being, it is misleading to refer to the 'weight' of the economic factor, vis-à-vis other factors in the Marxian scheme. What matters is which element is more a source of change."[76]

This is a surprisingly astute reading of developments in nineteenth-century social philosophy, considering that it comes from a conservative, free market economist and, ultimately, sharp critic of Marxism—certainly as economic theory,[77] and as a foundation for Leninist politics.[78] Sowell rests his case by quoting one of Joseph Schumpeter's essays and, then, returning to Engels's aforementioned letter, he uses Engels's theory of law to portray the entire philosophy of history reflected in a synthesis of materialism with the dynamic element governing social change.[79]

---

76 Sowell, *Marxism*, p. 64.
77 Ibid., pp. 189–204.
78 Ibid., 209–17.
79 Ibid., pp. 65–66; Engels, "Letter to Schmidt," pp. 419–21, 424. Randall, in *Career of Philosophy*, remarks: "Marx himself, starting with Feuerbach's critique of Hegel, soon modified his Hegelianism by adding other elements; and in the end he managed to achieve something not far from a historical and evolutionary naturalism. But Engels remained a pretty consistent leftwing Hegelian to the end. Engels seems to have been the real formulator of dialectical materialism as a comprehensive philosophy, the St. Paul of the gospel of Marx" (p. 378). See also Gareth Stedman Jones, "Engels and the History of Marxism," *The History of Marxism*, vol. 1: E. J. Hobsbawm, ed. *Marxism in Marx's Day* (Bloomington: University of Indiana

In a modern state, Engels argues, "law must not only correspond to the general economic condition and be its expression, but must also be an *internally coherent* expression which does not, owing to inner contradictions, reduce itself to nought."[80] Never fear, suggests federal judge Richard Posner. As we have already seen, Posner acknowledges that although the demand for specific results in particular cases is incompatible with judges who merely "find" the law, they can still preserve the appearance of legal consistency, the kind of internal coherence identified by Engels, simply by clothing results in the "rhetoric of passive obeisance to 'the law' (including law the judges may have made up last week)."[81] Engels wrote in 1890, Posner a century later. In the interim, the high art of legal rhetoric was raised a notch, by Holmes and Cardozo, Roger Traynor and J. Skelly Wright, and other masters of judicial reasoning.[82] From the bench, Posner actually makes the project of "tidying away messy realities" in the structure of legal precedent, as Professor Rosemary Horrox put it, seem even easier than Engels implies.[83]

In spite of the obvious appreciation for contradiction evidenced thus far by Engels's letter, we have not yet reached its purest, most transparently Hegelian moment. "Thus to a great extent," Engels continues, "the course of the 'development of right' consists only, first, in the attempt to do away with the contradictions arising from the direct translation of economic relations into legal principles, and to establish a harmonious system of law, and then in the repeated breaches made in this system by the influence and compulsion of further economic development, which involves it in further contradictions."[84]

Hopefully, the reader will tolerate having had to wait so long to reach this point. The history of American law is the history of these "repeated breaches" and their legal consequences; just about everything in this book flows from that assumption. Still, Engels has not quite exhausted his jurisprudential interlude; the final section—virtually a blueprint for writing legal history—is well worth saving. There are three main varieties of influence exerted by state power and legal institutions on the course of economic development: first, politics "can run in the same direction, and

Press, 1982), pp. 290–326.

80 Engels, "Letter to Schmidt," p. 422.
81 Posner, *Overcoming the Law*, p. 79.
82 See, for example, Grant Gilmore, *The Ages of American Law* (New Haven: Yale University Press, 1977); G. Edward White, *Tort Law in America: An Intellectual History*

(New York: Oxford University Press, 1985); Stephen B. Presser and Jamil S. Zainaldin, eds., *Law and Jurisprudence in American History* (3d ed., St. Paul, Minn.: West Publishing, 1995).
83 Horrox, "Feudalism," p. 25.
84 Engels, "Letter to Schmidt," pp. 422–23.

then development is more rapid"; second, "it can oppose the line of development, in which case nowadays it will go to pieces in the long run"; or third, "it can prevent the economic development from proceeding along certain lines, and prescribe others."[85] In due time, I will examine specific evidence supporting each category of influence in the development of American law.

We can now answer the question that originally took us on this detour—the problem of disjunction between base and superstructure. It is the economy as a source of change (Sowell), rather than as an unmediated cause (materialism without a dialectical edge), that should draw our attention. It is the legal system's constant efforts both to remain consistent with the past and to reflect the dominant interests of the present—or perhaps even to anticipate a revolution just around the corner—which lies at the heart of legal history. Although economic forces, the mode of subsistence or mode of production, predominate, ultimately the way in which they do so is marked by uneven development and riddled with contradiction. We may even say, with the great helmsman of Waltham and La Jolla, Herbert Marcuse, that "the state belongs to the superstructure inasmuch as it is *not* simply the direct political expression of the basic relationships of production but contains elements which, as it were, 'compensate' for the class relations of production."[86] Instead of presenting the legal superstructure as a mirror that casts back upon the economy nothing but its own reflection, Marcuse believed that law is located *in* the superstructure because it is *not* identical to the system of production relations. What did he mean by this? Simply, the superstructure is where contradictions between past and present or present and future, between precedent and policy, between the letter and spirit of the law, between literal meaning and "obvious" purpose, between old and new forms of property all *are fought out.*

What remains for us to do here is point out why this sort of Hegelian intervention in the history of materialist critique not only clarifies how the base/superstructure model can be used but also answers the riddle at the heart of American thought about the relationship between law and politics. In the first third of this century, a group of American law professors, lawyers, and judges developed a view of the legal system which subsequently was labeled "Realist." Their perspective was quite similar to that of American progressive historians of the same period; as law profes-

---

85 Ibid., p. 422.   86 Marcuse, *Soviet Marxism*, p. 120.

sor Morton Horwitz correctly observes, for "many purposes, it is best to see Legal Realism as simply a continuation of the reformist agenda of early-twentieth-century Progressivism."[87]

The Realists were doing in and through the field of law something very similar to what Charles Beard was doing in the field of history. Fifty years later, in the same decade that a new generation of law teachers and students at Harvard (and elsewhere) were asking themselves how to move beyond Realism, the new American social historians were seeking to "move beyond Beard."[88] However, Beard and the Progressive historians, and Karl Llewellyn and the Realists, were themselves trying to move beyond Adam Smith. Thus, everyone was trying to employ the insights of materialist social theory to demonstrate that ideas and institutions are not independent of money and power.

What Smith could not anticipate (because he wrote prior to Hegel) and what so many American legal thinkers missed (because of their professional and political culture) was the dialectical alternative.[89] This baleful indifference to Hegel exacted a very high price from some of America's best social theorists—from those with a materialist orientation or others, perhaps, who wished only to show how large economics looms in chaneling the flow of politics.[90] Structure without movement, determi-

87 Morton J. Horwitz, *The Transformation of American Law, 1870–1960* (New York: Oxford University Press, 1992), p. 169; see also, p. 142. On the same point, see Ernst A. Breisach, *American Progressive History* (Chicago: University of Chicago Press, 1993), pp. 89–90. For more on Beard, see Richard Hofstadter, *The Progressive Historians* (New York: Knopf, 1968), pp. 167–346; William A. Williams, *History as a Way of Learning* (New York: Franklin Watts, 1973), pp. 171–99, 229–42.

88 "Moving Beyond Beard: A Symposium," *Radical History Review* 42 (1988), pp. 7–47.

89 See, for example, James Bryce, *Studies in History and Jurisprudence* (New York: Oxford University Press, 1901): "The worth of the books, abundant on the Continent of Europe but scarce in England and the United States (though a little less scarce in Scotland), which have been composed by writers of this school, will be estimated differently by those who enjoy speculation for its own sake, and by those who think it a waste of time unless it bears fruit in truths of definite practical utility. If the latter criterion of value

be accepted, the importance of these treatises cannot be placed very high....As some brilliant thinkers, at the head of whom stand Immanuel Kant and G. W. F. Hegel, have adopted this method in handling the Philosophy of Law, and have given a powerful impulse to many able disciples, it would be foolish and presumptuous to disparage their treatises. Nevertheless, the general conclusion of English lawyers has been that not much can be gathered from lucubrations of this type. They are decidedly hard reading..." (p. 611).

90 See, for example, Breisach, *Progressive History*: "With pungent hostility, Arthur Bentley would call ideas without an instrumental function in life 'soul-stuff.' Progressive historians agreed with that when they rejected Hegel's philosophy of history with its Absolute Spirit or Idea....In this sense, Progressive historians have generally and correctly been seen as history's contingent in the pragmatic revolt or the revolt against formalism" (p. 84). Breisach notes elsewhere that "Beard insisted that history constituted no Hegelian system

nation without contradiction, occasionally even materialism abandoned: this was the price paid. An important exception to this general picture is

but a development shaped by a direction, firmly set by economic forces, and specific forms, shaped by rational actions" (pp. 94–95). Looking back on the work of the Progressive historians, Beard himself wrote that "there is a class of histories which are sometimes supposed to crown all general and special histories....This type of history seeks or purports to grasp all forms and movements of human interests and ideas in all time, to bring the totality of all events in time within the unity of a single formula of interpretation. Hegel's *Philosophy of History* may be cited as an illustration. Near the opening of the twentieth century this type of history was generally and somewhat indignantly rejected by professional historians" *The Nature of the Social Sciences* (New York: Charles Scribner's Sons, 1934), p. 71.

Now, as these observations suggest, a considerable irony is at work. On the one hand, what made the progressive historians interesting was their materialism, Beard's "economic determinism," and that, of course, is what renders them coherent within the context of a liberal-reformist political movement. However, the very thing that liberated them from orthodoxy—namely, their materialist insight, *because* it came as a reaction against Hegelian idealism and "soul stuff"— contained within it an outer limit on what their scholarship might achieve. Since an anti-Hegelian bias (as well as the times) made them materialists, they were incapable of reincorporating Hegel for the purpose of transforming materialism, standing alone, into its dialectical opposite. Without Hegel, everything went haywire. One could not understand, for example, the political economy of American constitutionalism by getting at the numbered Swiss bank accounts of the Framers.

Herbert Marcuse would never make such a mistake, would never so thoroughly reduce the legal superstructure (say, the Constitution) to such an unmediated expression of the economic base. As we have seen, Engels's letter to Schmidt helped Marcuse to specify the potentially antagonistic character of the

superstructure which, again, is why the state is located where it is in Marcuse's scheme of things. Could Engels' letter be improved upon? Karl Korsch thinks so. Because Engels failed to grant aesthetics, religion, and philosophy the same degree of concreteness (relative to the economic base) that he bestows upon Law and State, Korsch specifically wishes to correct Engels's letter to Schmidt in order to "restore a genuine dialectically materialist conception of intellectual reality..." Korsch, *Marxism and Philosophy*, Fred Halliday, trans. (London: NLB, 1970), pp. 72–73. Although Korsch lived in the United States from 1936 until he died in 1961, his work hardly made a dent in American social thought prior to his death. Only with the emergence of a "New Left" in the 1960s was he "discovered" on this side of the Atlantic. See Douglas Kellner, ed., *Karl Korsch: Revolutionary Theory* (Austin: University of Texas Press, 1977).

I think that Korsch is right to chastise Engels for apparently treating art and philosophy dismissively, which Korsch believes to be the case where Engels refers to such cultural contexts as "realms of ideology which float still higher in the air" (Korsch, *Marxism*, p.72). But it remains useful to consider such realms as *relatively* remote from the economic base compared to, say, the legal system. A practical, everyday example can be found in Ross McKibbin's appreciation of a distinction between the cultural surface and real legal structure of British politics: "The recent suggestion, for example, that Labour's 'stakeholder society' could require revision of the Companies Act brought a cry of pain from nearly all the major business associations. The appropriate Labour spokesman, in the best consensual manner, hastened to say that the Act needs no tampering with: all that is required is a change of culture. Yet it has been evident for years that the Companies Act needs amendment, and if Labour really does wish to change the culture of British business—as surely it must—then it has to change the legal framework in which business operates" ("If/When Labour Gets In..." *London Review of Books* [Feb. 22, 1996], p. 3).

the late Mitchell Franklin, a professor of law first at Tulane, then Buffalo.[91] It is difficult not to marvel at Franklin's ability to capture in clear and compelling prose the complexity and feeling for movement which is the hallmark of a truly dialectical jurisprudence. "Thus, as the old legal order," Franklin wrote, "consecrating the old property relations, is threatened it becomes arbitrary and equivocal. What had seemed to be an established legal order, based on the rule of law, is threatened by the new, but real, possibilities, which require new social relations or new property relations."[92]

Here we have the mode of subsistence (Smith) giving rise to a legal superstructure which reflects and/or corresponds (Millar/Skinner) to the economic base, while new property relations, hence new social relations begin to contradict that established order (Hegel), threatening to destabilize the existing legal system (Engels). "The old rule of law," Franklin continues, "becomes the victim of such new possibilities because it reflects the course and outcome of the struggle between the old and new social forces..." What then happens to the old rule of law? It is either "destroyed and replaced by new law by revolution or it is negated and reposited by change of meaning of the old law to meet the needs of the infra-structural crisis and outcome."[93]

Here, we have what most American law school students manage to discover by the time their first-year Torts class reaches the famous cases on foreseeability, or their Contracts class takes up the Uniform Commercial Code and the Second Restatement: Law is changed either *overtly* by statute or by courts openly adopting "social policy" justifications for their decisions, or it is changed *covertly*, as when a court radically alters legal results but does so by more or less artfully reinterpreting existing precedent. Either way, law is changed when the time comes; however,

91 On Franklin, see "Special Section on Mitchell Franklin," in *Telos* (Winter 1986–87), pp. 6–57; see also, Mitchell Franklin, "Dialectical Contradictions in Law," in Erwin Marquitt, Philip Morann and Willis H. Truitt, eds., *Dialectical Contradictions* (Minneapolis: Marxist Educational Press, 1982), pp. 149–200.

92 Mitchell Franklin, "Legal Method in the Philosophies of Hegel and Savigny," *Tulane Law Review* 44 (1970), p. 770.

93 Franklin, "Hegel," 770–71. See also, Georg Lukács, *History and Class Consciousness*, Rodney Livingstone, trans. (Cambridge, Mass.: MIT Press, 1971): "This difference of structure appears even more decisively in those areas which Hegel designates those of the absolute spirit, in contrast to the forms of the objective spirit (economics, law and the state) which shape social, purely human interrelations....Even these [formations of the objective spirit] often manage to survive the demise of the social foundations to which they owe their existence. But in that event they survive as obstacles to progress which have to be swept away or by changing their functions they adapt themselves to the new economic circumstances. (The history of law is rich in instances of both possibilities)" (p. 234).

"the time," in Hegel and Franklin, is the key. This is what Sowell means when he says that the economy is a source of change, rather than a state of being: this, in a nutshell, is the difference between a static and a dialectical materialism. "As the crisis emerges, matures and is sublated during an historic epoch," Franklin concludes, "the rule of law becomes doubled or divided in societies in which the struggle is between rival systems of private property." Knocking down the final barrier that separates outside from inside legal culture (Posner), appearance from reality (Hegel), Franklin ends with a roll call of lawyering skills: "This means that legal acrobatics, legal agility, legal ambiguity, legal irony…are inevitable within the theory of the rule of law."[94] Classic examples of this process in action, provided by Franklin, come from none other than the history of American common law to which we are now, at last, prepared to turn.

---

94 Franklin, "Hegel," p. 771.

CHAPTER II

CAPITAL'S HORIZON

What happened when constitutional rhetoric was taken literally; pros and cons on whether the American Revolution really was one; a dissertation on Native-American political economy, with marginal comments on the anthropology of law. Matter prefatory to analysis of the great transformation in American law and which gives some account, at the same time, of when capitalism began. Economics and morality considered side by side.

By the time Adam Smith wrote his Wealth of Nations *the
medieval and Elizabethan institutional structures were in a
shambles. The power of the Roman Catholic Church was broken in
the sixteenth century in England, to give way to the "divine right
of kings," which, by the close of the seventeenth century had begun
to give way to the "divine right of capital." Land was well on
its way to becoming a commodity, and by the opening years of the
nineteenth century so was labor, no less and no more than any other
article of commerce, free from obligations and free of protection.*
DOUGLAS DOWD [95]

*Tom said to himself that it was not such a hollow world after all.
He had discovered a great law of human action, without knowing
it, namely, that, in order to make a man or a boy covet a thing, it
is only necessary to make the thing difficult to attain. If he had
been a great and wise philosopher, like the writer of this book, he
would now have comprehended that work consists of whatever
a body is obliged to do, and that play consists of whatever a body
is not obliged to do.*
MARK TWAIN [96]

Tracing the path of a materialist legal theory from the work of contemporary scholar and jurist Richard Posner backward to its origins in the
teaching and writing of Adam Smith and his Scottish Enlightenment
compatriots has given us a map of the historical terrain ahead.
Supplementing Smith's four-stages or modes of subsistence theory of
legal development with Hegel's dialectic, reinvigorated by Francis
Fukuyama and reincorporated into the materialist critique by Thomas
Sowell, provides the compass we also need.

   Given the materialist orientation of my critique, outlined at some
length in the previous chapter, it follows logically that I periodize legal
history in a way that stresses the mode of subsistence or mode of production in steering legal change. It does not follow, however, that economics
alone can explain the role of law in society. Smith did not think so. Even
if the primary function of law is to reconcile legal and political affairs with
the dominant mode of economic production, the law has other responsi-

---

95 Douglas Dowd, *U.S. Capitalist Development Since
1776 (Armonk, N.Y.: M. E. Sharpe, 1993), p. 67.

96 Mark Twain, *The Adventures of Tom Sawyer*
(New York: Penguin, 1986), pp. 19–20.

bilities as well. Such diverse theorists as Herbert Marcuse and the French structuralist Nicos Poulantzas appear to agree that law, beyond reflecting the infrastructure or material base of society, also helps mediate disputes within ruling elites and political parties, and helps manage conflicts between governing forces and the popular democracy.[97]

Certainly, law can also be seen as part of an elaborate effort 'designed' to convince the public that every member of the national community has an equal right to justice and must, in fact, receive equal treatment before the law. Such false promises can lead to unfounded hopes and cruel disappointment when, as Harold Laski rather charitably put it, experience teaches a bitter truth—that the margins between liberal legalism's "claims and its performance have always been wide."[98] Or as legendary Howard

---

97 Nicos Poulantzas asserts that "[a]ll too often, it is said that capitalist law just obscures real differences behind a screen of universal formalism," and adds that the "specificity of law and the juridical system is inscribed in the peculiar institutional structure of the capitalist State. Indeed, its centralizing-bureaucratic-hierarchic framework is itself possible only through being moulded in a system of general, abstract, formal and axiomatic norms that organize and regulate the impersonal echelons and apparatuses of the exercise of power" "Law," in Piers Beirne and Richard Quinney, eds., *Marxism and Law* (New York: John Wiley, 1982), pp. 192–93.

Herbert Marcuse, who comes from a quite different political tradition than Poulantzas, Marcuse nevertheless observes that the "state, being and remaining the state of the ruling class, sustains *universal* law and order and thereby guarantees at least a modicum of equality and security for the whole of society. Only by virtue of these elements can the class state fulfill the function of 'moderating' and keeping within the bounds of 'order' the class conflicts generated by the production relations" (*Soviet Marxism* [New York: Columbia University Press, 1958], p. 120. Poulantzas claims the state organizes and regulates power; Marcuse sees it as capable of moderating political conflicts. Both regard the legal system as something more than a passive mirror of economic forces and relations.

A lawyer and political theorist with a background and training quite similar to that of Marcuse, Franz Neumann argued originally in the pages of the *Columbia Law Review* that law's "moral (or ethical) function consists in the inherent elements of equality and security which it presupposes....The generality of the law is thus the precondition of judicial independence, which, in turn, makes possible the realization of that minimum of liberty and equality that inheres in the formal structure of the law" (*The Demcratic and The Authoritarian State* [New York: Free Press, 1957], p. 167). Neumann also states, however, that equality before the law "is, to be sure, 'formal,' i.e., negative. But Hegel, who clearly perceived the purely formal-negative nature of liberty, already warned of the consequences of discarding it" (ibid., p. 42).

Marcuse, too, believed that such a commitment to generality of law could be anchored in Hegel's philosophy. According to him, Hegel was convinced that the rule of law was essential to the coherence of modern society. "Conscious regulation of the social antagonisms," suggests Marcuse, "by a force standing above the clash of particular interests, and yet safeguarding each of them, could alone transform the anarchic sum-total of individuals into a rational society. The rule of law," in Hegel's social theory, "was to be the lever of that transformation" (*Reason and Revolution* [2d ed., Atlantic Highlands, N.J.] Humanities Press, 1954), p. 182. So an economic, even "dialectical materialist" history of American law cannot possibly tell the whole story.

Law School Dean Charles Hamilton Houston often observed, nobody needs to explain to African-Americans the difference between law in the books and law in action.[99] On the other hand, as British historian E. P. Thompson noted in his book on England's notorious Black Act, when people take the rulers at their word, they can, at least on occasion, contribute to the development of a principled politics as well as antisystemic social movements—in other words, an opposition which those in power may have inadvertently inspired with rhetoric that was meant to be understood only metaphorically.[100]

98 See Harold J. Laski, *The Rise of Liberalism* (New York: Harper and Brothers, 1936): "The individual whom liberalism has sought to protect is always, so to say, free to purchase his freedom in the society it made; but the number of those with the means of purchase at their disposal has always been a minority of mankind. The idea of liberalism, in short, is historically connected, in an inescapable way, with the ownership of property. The ends it serves are always the ends of men in this position. Outside that narrow circle, the individual for whose rights it has been zealous has always been an abstraction upon whom its benefits could not, in fact, be fully conferred. Because its purposes were shaped by owners of property, the margins between its claims and its performance have always been wide" (p. 9).

It is interesting to contrast these comments—particularly Laski's view of transforming real individuals into political abstractions (essential to liberal juridical method)—with the above-mentioned observations by Marcuse and Neumann. Of course, the latter were writing in an attempt to rehabilitate a liberal Hegel after the threat of fascism had been fully realized, whereas Laski's criticism of liberal legalism emerged earlier from within a context of world depression and revolutionary politics.

It is also worth noting that between Neumann's arrest and escape from Nazi Germany in 1933 and subsequent migration to the United States in 1936, he studied under none other than Harold Laski at the London School of Economics. Another student of Laski's during this period was John F. Kennedy's older brother, Joe, Jr., who would later be killed in World War II. At the time,

Joe's mother, Rose Kennedy, regarded Laski as "a little wild and a little dangerous," but Joseph Kennedy, Sr., was convinced that his sons were "going to have a little money when they get older, and they should know what the 'have-nots' are thinking and planning...." Thus he wanted both Joe, Jr., and, later, Jack Kennedy, to get a strong dose of Laski's socialist medicine. An illness prevented JFK from getting his chance to spend a year studying under Laski. Nevertheless, the future president no doubt learned something about how the other half lives from the "have-nots" themselves on a campaign trail which took him through Wisconsin and West Virginia in 1960. See Isaac Kramnick and Barry Sheerman, *Harold Laski: A Life on the Left* (New York: Allen Lane/Penguin, 1993), pp. 333–34; Nigel Hamilton, *JFK: Reckless Youth* (New York: Random House, 1992), pp. 140–43; Kenneth P. O'Donnell and David F. Powers, *"Johnny, We Hardly Knew Ye" Memories of John Fitzgerald Kennedy* (Boston: Little, Brown, 1972), pp. 147–81.

99 Mykola Kulish's (writ. and dir.) documentary film, *The Road to Brown: The Untold Story of "The Man Who Killed Jim Crow"* (50 minutes, 1989), available in VHS format from California Newsreel, 149 9th Street, San Francisco, CA 94103. See also, Genna Rae McNeil, *Groundwork: Charles Hamilton Houston and the Struggle for Civil Rights* (Philadelphia: University of Pennsylvania Press, 1983).

100 See E. P. Thompson, *Whigs and Hunters* (New York: Pantheon, 1975): "And the rulers were, in serious senses, whether willingly or unwillingly, the prisoners of their own rhetoric; they played the games of power according to rules which suited them, but

Although Supreme Court Justice Hugo Black was certainly a civil libertarian, he presumably did not intend for readers of his rather bracing decision in *Griffin v. Illinois* to take literally his assertion that the kind of trial a man gets should not depend on the amount of money he has.[101] It is difficult to imagine any factor that could be more influential. Mr. Justice Harlan was not moved to embrace *Griffin*'s high-flying rhetoric. Justice Black's egalitarian proposal could, he believed, be construed as placing an affirmative duty on government to guarantee every criminal defendant the same kind of legal representation that affluent Americans can afford; according to Harlan, this would "read into the Constitution a philosophy of leveling that would be foreign to many of our basic concepts of the proper relations between government and society." "Proper relations" may here be read as *property relations* since that is what the Levelers, as well as Justice Harlan, were really getting at.[102]

Nevertheless, before becoming too cynical about the unvarnished (perhaps naive) language of liberty, the hyperbolic discourse of radical democracy, we must consider at least one historical moment with implications that seem to cut the other way. In the first episode of the acclaimed docu-

they could not break those rules or the whole game would be thrown away" (p. 263). Here Thompson appears to echo the sentiment previously noted in the work of Marcuse and Neumann, which they drew, as we saw, from Hegel. "And, finally," Thompson concludes, "so far from the ruled shrugging off this rhetoric as hypocrisy, some part of it at least was taken over as part of the rhetoric of the plebeian crowd, of the 'free-born Englishman' with his inviolable privacy, his *habeas corpus*, his equality before the law" (ibid., p. 264).

Is it too much to identify this conception of the rule of law with Marcuse's own notion of "bourgeois idealism"? See, for example, Herbert Marcuse, *Negations: Essays in Critical Theory*, Jeremy J. Shapiro, trans. (Harmondsworth, Eng: Penguin, 1972): "But bourgeois idealism is not merely ideology, for it expresses a correct objective content. It contains not only the justification of the established form of existence, but also the pain of its establishment: not only quiescence about what is, but also remembrance of what could be. By making suffering and sorrow into eternal, universal forces, great bourgeois art has continually shattered in the hearts of

men the facile resignation of every day life. By painting in the luminous colors of this world the beauty of men and things and transmundane happiness, it has planted real longing alongside poor consolation and false consecration in the soil of bourgeois life" (pp. 98–99).

101 Mr. Justice Black, Opinion for the Court, joined by the Chief Justice, Mr. Justice Douglas, and Mr. Justice Clark, *Griffin v. Illinois*, 351 U.S. 12, 19 (1956): "There can be no equal justice where the kind of trial a man gets depends on the amount of money he has. Destitute defendants must be afforded as adequate appellate review as defendants who have money enough to buy transcripts."

102 Mr. Justice Harlan, whom Mr. Justice Stewart joined, dissenting, *Douglas v. California*, 372 U.S. 353, 361–362 (1963) "Every financial exaction which the State imposes on a uniform basis is more easily satisfied by the well-to-do than by the indigent. Yet I take it that no one would dispute the constitutional power of the State to levy a uniform sales tax, to charge tuition at a state university, to fix rates for the purchase of water from a municipal corporation, to impose a standard

mentary film series *Eyes On The Prize*, the narrator Julian Bond revisits the foundation of the civil rights movement in the South. Martin Luther King, Jr., is preaching to supporters of Rosa Parks and the Montgomery bus boycott, who crowd the aisles of the Holt Street Baptist Church, visibly moved by King's grand phrases and rolling cadences.

"And we are not wrong," King declared, that night, "we are not wrong in what we are doing. If we are wrong, then the Supreme Court of this Nation is wrong." It was 1955, just one year after the Court's historic decision in *Brown v. Board of Education*, and the year prior to Hugo Black's opinion in *Griffin*. "If we are wrong," King continued, "the Constitution of the United States is wrong. If we are wrong, God Almighty is wrong."[103] Quite a statement. Even Hugo Black's soaring rhetoric did not fly so high. Yet King's reliance upon inspirational language—drawn, in part, from the realm of law and constitution—cannot be separated from the initial success of a movement he led. Skeptics on this score may be legion but, as E. P. Thompson said of a Ghandi's anticolonial movement earlier in the century, the fact that legal rhetoric sometimes disguises the nature of ruling power and deflects opposition does not prevent it from simultaneously becoming a rallying cry for those who would dislodge that very power.[104]

fine for criminal violations, or to establish minimum bail for various categories of offenses. Nor could it be contended that the State may not classify as crimes acts which the poor are more likely to commit than are the rich....Laws such as these do not deny equal protection to the less fortunate for one essential reason: the Equal Protection Clause does not impose on the States 'an affirmative duty to lift the handicaps flowing from differences in economic circumstances.'
To so construe it would be to read into the Constitution a philosophy of leveling that would be foreign to many of our basic concepts of the proper relations between government and society. The state may have a moral obligation to eliminate the evils of poverty, but it is not required by the Equal Protection Clause to give some whatever others can afford."

Harlan places his reference to "differences in economic circumstances" in quotation marks for it is drawn directly from his dissenting opinion in *Griffin*. Describing the Levellers' disagreement with Cromwell,

British social historian J. F. C. Harrison states: "The clash between two opposing interests and ideologies could not be clearer. On the one hand were the soldiers, claiming a right to the suffrage for every freeborn Englishman, a right which they had recently asserted by fighting for freedom; on the other Ireton and Cromwell arguing that the suffrage was based on property, not natural right. Beneath the surface were other attitudes and assumptions about class divisions and the struggle of the 'Plaine Men of England against the Rich and Mightie.' These issues and arguments were not resolved, but were to be repeated continuously for the next 250 years" (*The Common People of Great Britain* [Bloomington: University of Indiana Press, 1985], p. 197).

103 "Speech by Martin Luther King, Jr., at Holt Street Baptist Church," in Clayborn Carson, David J. Garrow, et al., eds., *The Eyes on the Prize Civil Rights Reader* (New York: Penguin, 1991), p. 50.

104 E. P. Thompson, *Whigs and Hunters*, "In a context of gross class inequalities, the equity

So law has fashioned a complex career for itself throughout the history of the Republic, and it would be a disservice to those who spent their lives giving meaning to high-sounding legal phrases to suggest that the legal system is merely the static reflection of an existing distribution of wealth and power. Civil rights victories could never have been won if real people were not willing to set aside, at least for a time, a rational conviction that the system was dead set against them and that law ultimately serves he who can afford to pay the piper. Soul force, not just market forces, contribute to what O. W. Holmes called "the path of the law." Nevertheless, it is the large scale, broad-brush, material determination of law and legal transformation that I regard as historically decisive or paramount. Thus dividing legal history, as I do, into precapitalist, capitalist, state capitalist, and global capitalist periods of development should, at any rate, not take the reader by surprise.

I. REBELLION

The first of our four divisions of American legal history can, itself, be broken down into four parts (or, in a sense, projects) which, once concluded, "accomplished" the full transition from precapitalist to capitalist legal development in the United States. The initial goal was political independence—technically speaking, the establishment of national sovereignty—and this act was the primary achievement of the American colonies' rebellion against British dominion. The second enterprise was the general elimination of precapitalist economic formations in the new nation. Third was the assault on homegrown, American mercantilism, parallel to Adam Smith's attack on British mercantilism. Fourth, and finally, came the Civil War and the destruction of the slave south, the last remaining obstacle to construction of a unified national marketplace under the auspices of liberal capitalist social and economic leadership.

Although the war for independence from Britain is popularly designated the "American Revolution," considerable controversy has surrounded the issue of whether or not it really deserves to be called a

---

of law must always be in some part sham. Transplanted as it was to even more inequitable contexts, this law could become an instrument of imperialism. For this law has found its way to a good many parts of the globe. But even here the rules and the rhetoric have imposed some inhibitions upon the imperial power. If the rhetoric was a mask, it was a mask which Ghandi and Nehru were to borrow, at the head of a million masked supporters" (p. 266).

revolution at all. To my mind, the more one views revolution as a form of violent political change, the more likely one is to see the American Revolution not only as a legitimate entry within that category but, perhaps, as the most decisive and original revolution in world history. After all, it brought into being a new form of government founded on a constitution that has now been continuously in force for more than two centuries. Alternatively, if one defines revolution in social and economic terms, then America's "revolution" seems no more than an anticolonial rebellion. At least until recently, the revolution that brought the United States into being has always suffered by comparison with France's great revolution.

For example, British historian Eric Hobsbawm observed in *The Age of Revolution* that the "American revolution has remained a crucial event in American history but…it has left few major traces elsewhere. The French revolution is a landmark in all countries."[105] Assuredly, he allowed for the effects the American Revolution had on other countries immediately involved in the conflict and, in a footnote, he adds the backhanded compliment that the American Revolution *did* stimulate the one in France. But it was the French, not the American, revolution that had real international consequences: Hobsbawm parallels its impact in its time to that of the Bolshevik revolution in this century. It is well known that debates within modern French historiography over the revolution of 1789 have often been debates at least indirectly about the Bolshevik revolution and subsequent movements that it inspired. The Russian Revolution, readers do not need to be told, has slipped of late in the ranking of world-class revolutions, a predictable consequence of the disintegration of the Soviet state and its frozen empire. And the restoration of dominant commercial and business relationships in both Russia and China presages the worldwide reversal of revolutions such as those led by Lenin and Trotsky, Mao Zedong and Lin Piao.[106] Does the American (or at least capitalist) victory

105 E. J. Hobsbawm, *The Age of Revolution: Europe 1789–1848* (London: Sphere Books, 1973), pp. 75, 99. See also, Hobsbawm, *Echoes of the Marseillaise* (New Brunswick, N. J.: Rutgers University Press, 1990); Joseph Klaits and Michael H. Haltzel, eds., *The Global Ramifications of the French Revolution* (Cambridge, Eng.: Cambridge University Press, 1994).

106 The Chinese, of course, regarded the Soviet Union as capitalist thirty years ago. China scholar Maurice Meisner, describing the

political perspective of Lin Piao's 1965 manifesto "Long Live the Victory of People's War," points out that Lin believed a victorious Cultural Revolution would cause a socialist China to "become the 'revolutionary homeland,' replacing a morally bankrupt and 'capitalist' Soviet Union, whose revisionism at home and opportunism abroad were leading the forces of world revolution astray." When the Russians invaded Czechoslovakia in 1968, a crucial year for American military involvement

in the Cold War signal that it is time to reassess the relation between American and French revolutions?

The French people themselves seem to have lost some of their reverence for events that initiated their nation's modern experiment in democracy. Some French intellectuals have busied themselves with a ponderous "rereading" of their revolution. A revolution against monarchy and superstition, motivated by Kant's dictum that we should have the courage to use our intelligence, was not likely to fair well in the hands of "new philosophers" whose motto was that to think is to dominate. Such cynicism about the capacity of men and women to understand the nature of their social environment and rationally design ambitious social programs or call forth "grandiloquent world-reconstructions," as John Buchan put it,[107] tended to make the French Revolution seem like a rather hysterical episode in national history. Journalist Alexander Cockburn has described much of this French backtracking on the revolution as "part of the frenzies of French intellectual life in a time of reaction"; he also interviewed a French novelist whose description of how little history French school children are taught today, even about the great revolution, suggests that alienation from the revolutionary tradition may run much deeper than what is reflected in the rapidly shifting currents of contemporary cultural and intellectual fashion.[108]

Yet if the reputation of France's revolution is in decline, does it follow that the American Revolution's standing is on the upswing? Was it only the greater global influence of the French Revolution which caused Hobsbawm to award it pride of place? After all, the American war for independence was famously ignited by "the shot heard round the world,"

in Vietnam, Soviet transgression of an internationally recognized right of self-determination was "more harshly denounced in Peking than in any other of the world's capitals" Meisner, *Mao's China and After* (New York: Free Press, 1986), pp. 398–99). See also, Maurice Meisner, *The Deng Xiaoping Era* (New York: Hill and Wang, 1996). U.S. criticism was muted; however brutal the Russian invasion of Czechoslovakia, it did not compare with American actions in Vietnam.

After quoting Marx and Engels's famous prediction that capitalism would, in time, compel all nations "on pain of extinction, to adopt the bourgeois mode of production," Harvard University professor of international trade Jeffrey D. Sachs adds that Marx and Engels's "proposition was put to the test from the 1840s onward, and has been nearly vindicated, but only after 150 years of wrenching confrontations between capitalism and traditional societies." Echoing Fukuyama, Sachs concludes that the "puzzle is not that capitalism triumphed, but that it took so long. China was the first to feel the onslaught," but, in many respects, the last to submit. ("Consolidating Capitalism," *Foreign Policy* [Spring 1995] p. 55).

107   John Buchan, *Pilgrim's Way* (Cambridge, Mass.: The Riverside Press, 1940) pp.77–78.

108   Alexander Cockburn, "Tête à Tête," *Interview* (March 1989), pp. 83–85.

and the American Constitution which revolution brought into being is again today, as it was at the end of the World War II, much imitated by drafters of charter documents in emerging democracies. Barrington Moore questions the radical credentials of the American Revolution on the ground that although it may have involved some "elevated issues," nevertheless at "bottom it was a fight between commercial interests in England and America." Since this skirmish did not result in any basic transformation of social or class relations in the colonies, Moore wonders whether it has really earned the right to be designated a "revolution."[109]

There is no denying that class relations and social structure remained largely unaltered by the American Revolution.[110] If we confine our focus

109 Barrington Moore, Jr. *Social Origins of Dictatorship and Democracy* (Boston: Beacon, 1966), p. 112. See also Michael Mann, *The Sources of Social Power* (Cambridge, Eng.: Cambridge University Press, 1993): "Whether the War of Independence was 'revolutionary' has always, rightly, been controversial. A revolution can be defined sociologically as a violent transformation of dominant power relations; but real-world revolutions are a matter of degree. American events were decidedly ambiguous" (vol. 2, p. 149).

See also John Agnew, "The United States in the World Economy," in Bertell Ollman and Jonathan Birnbaum, eds., *The United States Constitution* (New York: New York University Press, 1990): "The settlement along the Atlantic coast of North America that became the territorial-economic core of the United States was a product of European commercial-political expansion in the seventeenth and eighteenth centuries.

American independence from Britain was the result of the breakdown of routinized trans-Atlantic relations brought on by the British revenue legislation of 1764..." (p. 29). Citing the Stamp Act, the Townshend Acts, and the Currency Act of 1764, Columbia University professor of economic history Stuart Bruchey suggests that such "British legislation thus affected not only the interests of merchants and traders but also those of settlers and land speculators. It is difficult not to believe that the cumulative grievances provoked by these laws led the colonists down

the path to revolution" (*Enterprise: The Dynamic Economy of a Free People* [Cambridge, Mass.: Harvard University Press, 1990], p. 108).

Similarly, Immanuel Wallerstein argues that there were sharp divergences of interest between the British and their colonists in North America and that, eventually, they led to war. These contradictory interests were brought to a head when the "British moved to make the settlers begin to pay for the costs of empire and to enforce vigorously the mercantilist commercial regulations" (*The Modern World System* [San Diego, Cal.: Academic Press, 1989], vol. 3, p. 203). Wallerstein emphasizes the deepening economic crisis, adding that the "opposition to the Stamp Act in 1765 and the Townshend duties in 1767 had first of all to do with their immediate financial impact, both directly as taxes and indirectly in terms of their effects on the balance of trade; and both colonists and their friends in Great Britain feared it as 'a killing of the goose that was laying the golden eggs.' And, as in most economic crises, the negatives cumulated" (p. 206).

Finally, see Robert Heilbroner and Aaron Singer, *The Economic Transformation of America* (3d ed., Fort Worth, Tex.: Harcourt Brace, 1994): "It is often *increases* in taxes, rather than the level of taxes, that bring discontent; and certainly the rise in English imposts, whether or not tax levels were low by comparison with England's, brought discontent to the colonies. To make matters worse, after 1763 the British

to the question of whether or not the American war of independence, standing alone, constituted a revolution, we might well answer that it did not. However, if we pose a larger question—whether the colonies' declaration of independence and establishment of national sovereignty figured as part of something—then America's rebellion *can* be seen as the beginning of a genuinely revolutionary social movement. Even as skeptical an observer of American history as Moore describes the Civil War as a revolution.[111]

Taken together, then, colonial insurrection and civil war, along with the transformation that took place in between, should be seen as part and parcel of the real revolution gripping the modern world: the market's *prise de pouvoir*, the rise to power of capitalism.

2. PRECAPITALIST ECONOMIC FORMATIONS: NATIVE-AMERICAN POLITICAL ECONOMY

The grey stones have grown weary imploring their gods to destroy the hated race of conquerors and now they show no more than the fatigue of inanimate objects, fit only for the admiring cries of some tourist or other. What use was the patient labour of the indians who built the palace of Inca Roca, subtly shaping the edges of stone, when confronted with the violent energy of the white conquistador and his knowledge of bricks, vaulting and rounded arches?
ERNESTO CHE GUEVARA [112]

Gordon S. Wood's overview of early American historiography, on which I based some of my introductory remarks, divides historical opinion on the

government, hardpressed for revenues, began to enforce the Navigation Acts strictly rather than carelessly and loosely as it had done before" (p. 75).

110 In addition to Moore, see John Agnew, "The United States and the World Economy": "Despite its seemingly revolutionary character, however, the American revolt is noteworthy because it created no serious interruption to the 'flow' of American development....Although there was some land confiscation and a large variety of political reforms, the American Revolution was remarkably conservative compared, say, to the later French and Russian Revolutions. Most importantly, social institutions were left untouched: the class structure, the ideas of people concerning government, the distribution of wealth, the capitalistic economy" (pp. 31–32).

111 Moore, *Social Origins*, p. 112.

112 Ernesto Che Guevara, *The Motorcycle Diaries*, Ann Wright, trans. (London: Verso, 1995), p. 91. See also Laurence Whitehead, "Furibundo de la Serna," *London Review of Books* (Nov. 2, 1995), p. 20.

advent of American capitalism between those to whom Wood (following Allan Kulikoff) refers as "market historians" and those whom he calls "moral historians." The latter, so called in part because of their attraction to E. P. Thompson's notion of "moral economy," have argued that the transition to capitalism in the United States came relatively late, due to significant resistance among New England farmers to the penetration of an entrepreneurial mentality. The market historians, conversely, argue for an earlier date; most of them suggest that a profit motive was built into American society from the beginning.

Before we can address this question, though, we must take up a more basic one: Who counts as an American? Wood points out that, according to the market historians, "nearly every white American" embraced an entrepreneurial self-concept, from the seventeenth century forward.[113] But why choose the 1600s as a starting point? Who were the *nonwhite* Americans, implicitly referred to in Wood's remark, and what sort of political economy did they embrace? Unless Native-Americans, for example, are demoted from status as first-Americans to the category of non-Americans, on what theory can it be asserted that America has always been capitalist? Like the social historians Wood chides for engaging in essentially moral critique (which Wood suggests may be good for the soul but does not necessarily lead to good history), perhaps enthusiasm for entrepreneurial societies and the profit motive led some market historians astray, even to the point of forgetting the obstacle that Native-American society posed to the development of a continent-spanning capitalist civilization.

To be sure, Adam Smith is regarded as one of the most vigorous proponents of free market capitalism in the annals of economic philosophy. But that did not lead him to ignore Native-American political economy. On the contrary, he built it into the basic structure of his jurisprudence, making it the foundation for one of his four stages of social and political development.[114] And Smith was not alone in regarding Native-American political economy as precapitalist.

---

113   Gordon S. Wood, "Inventing American Capitalism" *New York Review of Books* (June 9, 1994): "America did not have to become capitalistic, said Louis Hartz in his *Liberal Tradition in America*, the book that best summed up postwar thinking about America's past; it had been so from the beginning. From the seventeenth century on, it seemed, nearly

every white American 'had the mentality of an independent entrepreneur'—eager to make money and get land and get ahead" (p. 44).

114   See Ronald L. Meek, *Social Science and the Ignoble Savage* (Cambridge, Eng.: Cambridge University Press, 1976): "Many different influences no doubt contributed to the making of the four stages theory. In this book,

Echoing a point made in the eighteenth century by the Scottish historical school and constantly reiterated by modern social science, anthropologist Peter Farb begins by observing that the institution of private property is not general but, rather, is specific to particular periods and peoples.[115] Farb then describes the social organization of the Northern

however, I shall be directly concerned with only one of these—that of the contemporary literature about savage societies, and in particular about the American Indians.... The contemporary literature about the American Indians, I shall claim, played an important part in determining some of the leading emphases of the four stages theory, and the form of a number of its chief propositions" (pp. 2–3).

See also Robert L. Heilbroner, "The Paradox of Progress," in Andrew S. Skinner and Thomas Wilson, eds., *Essays on Adam Smith* (Oxford: Oxford University Press, 1975): "Hence in *The Wealth of Nations* we meet a sequence of four different organizational modes through which society will tend naturally to pass, provided that it does not meet insuperable obstacles of nature or human misunderstanding. The sequence begins with 'the lowest and rudest state of society, such as we find it among the native tribes of North America,' and terminates in the fourth stage, of which *The Wealth of Nations* virtually in its entirety must be the reference, characterized by a commercialization of agriculture, an encouragement to manufactures, and above all, by the pervasive presence and influence of the division of labour with its associated benefits of increased productivity" (p. 525). The language from Smith quoted by Heilbroner is found in the Glasgow Edition of Smith's work: see Adam Smith, *An Inquiry into the Nature and Causes of the Wealth of Nations*, R. H. Campbell and A. S. Skinner, eds. (Oxford: Oxford University Press, 1976), pp. 689–90.

Finally, of course, we have Smith's lectures on jurisprudence: see, for example, Adam Smith, *Lectures on Jurisprudence*, R. L. Meek, D. D. Raphael, and P. Stein, eds., (Oxford: Oxford University Press, 1978): "In Tartary, where as we said the support of the inhabitants consist[s] in herds and flocks, *theft*

is punished with immediate death; in North America, again, where the age of hunters subsists, theft is not much regarded. As there is almost no property amongst them, the only injury that can be done is the depriving them of their game. Few laws or regulations will [be] requisite in such an age of society, and these will not extend to any great length, or be very rigorous in the punishments annexed to any infringements of property" (p. 16). In contrast to Gordon Wood's "market historians," Adam Smith regarded the earliest American mode of subsistence as still three historical stages away from capitalism.

115   Peter Farb, *Man's Rise to Civilization: The Cultural Ascent of The Indians of North America* (2d ed., New York: Penguin, 1978): "Private property, division of labor, the presence or absence of priests, and many other characteristics of societies do not exist at random but only at particular stages" (p. 14). Alan Ryan points out that, in the nineteenth century, "Mill and Marx accused their contemporaries of discussing economics as if all the world had the legal institutions of the North Atlantic seaboard" (Alan Ryan, "Property," in John Eatwell, Murray Milgate, and Peter Newman, eds., *The New Palgrave: The Invisible Hand* [New York: W. W. Norton, 1989], p. 227). Andras Hegedus adds that a valuable feature of Marx and Engels's critique of property was that "it challenged the assumption commonly made in the West at that time that bourgeois forms of property must everywhere be the norm, and thus stimulated much historical research...as well as anthropological research which has shown the absence of private property, at least in land, among many tribal peoples" (Andras Hegedus, "Property," in Tom Bottomore, ed., *A Dictionary of Marxist Thought* [Oxford: Basil Blackwell, 1983], p. 399). Ryan, incidentally, observes that Mill and Marx "willingly exempted" Adam Smith from their criticism; p.227.

Algonkians with their economic relations based upon cooperative hunting, the sharing of game, and production for use rather than profit. He candidly acknowledges the Algonkians' lack of experience with a capitalist marketplace economy prior to the arrival of European traders.[116] University of California anthropologist Robert H. Lowie makes a point about the Cree which is similar to Farb's.[117] In describing Oglala and Blackfoot attitudes toward property, he emphasizes the significance of generosity toward the poor and identifies public opinion as an important restriction upon the setting of prices.[118] Prices and property were seen as social conventions, controlled by community standards.

Wilcomb E. Washburn, remarking on the high status of women among the Iroquois, suggests that their authority may have arisen not from ownership, but, rather, from access to economic resources; Iroquois land was communally owned. There was no regular market among the Seneca; production with them, too, was for use rather than profit. While describing the Huron system of pooling resources among longhouse members, Washburn even feels compelled to place the word "property" in

116 "Before the arrival of Whites, a typical Algonkian band hunted cooperatively and shared its game. Because the outcome of the hunt was uncertain, a custom grew up whereby several families looked out for one another; such an arrangement represented a simple form of insurance, guaranteeing a supply of food when hunting was poor. But a shift in economic patterns took place when the Algonkians started to produce for trade rather than for use. The most important economic ties were no longer within the band; they now extended outside the band to include the White trader. Rather than being in a cooperative relationship with the rest of the band, the band members were now in a competitive one. Neighboring families no longer were insurance against hardship; instead, they became hindrances to the limitless acquisition of furs" (Farb, *Civilization*, p. 62).

117 Robert H. Lowie, *Indians of the Plains* (Lincoln: University of Nebraska Press, 1982): "Quite generally, the Indians were for the first time tempted by fur traders to kill game for gain" (p. 117).

118 On generosity to the poor, see Lowie, *Indians of the Plains*: "A most important difference

between the Plains Indians and Tahitians concerns material property. Whereas in Tahiti a monarch could appropriate the possessions of a lesser man, on the Plains any comparable act was unthinkable. On the contrary, a great man could maintain his status best by lavish generosity to the poor. Such liberality, next to a fine war record, was the basis for high standing" (pp. 112–13). Elsewhere, Lowie remarks: "Although reciprocal obligations were recognized, altruistic behavior was imposed in certain situations. A Blackfoot or Crow stumbling on a fellow tribesman butchering was sure to receive an ample portion of meat. Any self-respecting man gave presents to the poor, and no one could hope to rise to the position of a headman who failed to live up to his people's idea of generosity" (p. 115).

On public opinion, see ibid.: "To illustrate by Blackfoot data, the ownership of a bundle was supposed to ensure long life, success, happiness; in consequence, it also brought social prestige. To buy a bundle was a safe investment, for it was readily negotiable and the new buyer was under pressure of public opinion to offer at least the price exacted at one time from the seller" (p. 116).

quotes.[119] In addition to these tribes from the Northeast and the Plains, anthropologists and historians have found similar patterns among Native-American cultures of the Southwest. Elizabeth A. H. John, for example, in surveying the lives of Native-Americans resident from the Red River to the Rocky Mountains, from the Arkansas River to the Rio Grande, has identified communal economic practices among the Caddo people.[120] John is also effective in her portrayal of the cooperative social relations upon which the adobe dwellings of the Pueblo were ultimately founded.[121] Tragically, the failure of Spanish settlers in the "new world" to appreciate and respect the personality of Native-Americans for whom the Southwest was an old world, and the homeland of ancient traditions, led to violence and destruction.[122]

119 Wilcomb E. Washburn, *The Indian in America* (New York: Harper and Row, 1975): "The agricultural lands adjoining Iroquois village sites were worked and controlled by the women, who were occasionally spoken of as 'owning' the land, though most authorities assert that the land was communally and not individually owned" (p. 31). Among the Seneca, surplus production had little individual value, particularly if there was a hard winter and corn reserves had to be shared out. Washburn adds: "Hoarding brought recriminations. The Iroquois system was geared to cooperation in behalf of larger social units, not to individual competition" (p. 31).
See Howard Zinn, *A People's History of the United States* (New York: Harper Perennial, 1990): "In the villages of the Iroquois, land was owned in common and worked in common. Hunting was done together, and the catch was divided among the members of the village. Houses were considered common property and were shared by several families. The concept of private ownership of land and homes was foreign to the Iroquois" (p. 20). "The communal emphasis of such a system," Washburn continues, "was reinforced by the storage facilities in the longhouse shared by several Huron families where large casks to store corn were located in the porch or in some corner rather than in the divisions belonging to individual families. The traditions of reciprocity and sharing among the members of the longhouse encouraged the *de facto* pooling of all individual resources"

(Washburn, *Indian in America*, p. 33).

120 Elizabeth A. H. John, *Storms Brewed in Other Men's Worlds* (Lincoln: University of Nebraska Press, 1975): "The productive Caddo economy also commanded respect. Their agriculture was a communal enterprise, producing two varieties of corn, half a dozen kinds of beans, squash, sunflower seeds, and tobacco. Only the *Grand Xinesi* was exempt from labor.... In poor years, the discipline and cohesiveness of their society were manifest in the unstinting generosity with which they shared all that they had and in their diligent protection of the precious seed corn for another year" (pp. 167–68).

121 John, *Storms Brewed*: "The compact village structure lent itself not only to defense but to the cooperative way of life fundamental to Pueblo agriculture. The people of each village shared the labor of the fields and the religious observances they believed essential to their common enterprise....Those sober, egalitarian societies, built upon the principles of harmony among themselves and with the spirits of their universe, vested principle leadership in village headmen, whose duties were primarily religious" (p. 4).

122 John, *Storms Brewed*: "Misleading appearances cost the Pueblos heavily. Tales of their similarities to the Indians of Meso-America, in houses, textiles, and crops, led Spaniards to guess that 'another Mexico' lay northward. In reality, the Pueblo Indians differed sharply from those of the Valley of Mexico in their egalitarianism, their

It is one thing, of course, to provide evidence of precapitalist economic formations among Native-Americans prior to the arrival of European settlers; yet it is something else again to argue that the precapitalist character of Native-American political economy contributed to the near destruction of these historic peoples at the hands of invading Europeans. Historian Charles Sellers at the University of California, not only suggests that Native-American economic "allocations were based on need, and the idea of private property hardly existed," but, further, concludes that by "1815 Indians and their cultures were nearing extinction in the eastern United States....Native Americans were destroyed by lack of immunity to both the microbes and the market brought by whites."[123]

The commodification of hunting and the sale of animal pelts, according to Sellers, eroded the ethic of tribal sharing and production for use. Wilcomb Washburn makes the same point, relying on a Native-American source.[124] Sellers's argument finds further illustration in an event noted by Ronald Takaki, also a professor at Berkeley, who cites a petition from the Connecticut Mohegans which seems to reflect their awareness of the transformation the market was imposing upon their tribe.[125] While subordination to the market caused the disintegration of Native-American culture from within, violence and military force wielded by Europeans threatened Native-American survival from without.

---

minimization of war, and the disciplined austerity of their lives. Theirs was not a society or a land that could heap wealth upon conquerors, but misunderstandings persisted even when Spaniards came to stay in New Mexico" (p. 7).

123   Charles Sellers, *The Market Revolution* (New York: Oxford University Press, 1991), p. 7.

124   "As Indians stepped up their harvest of animal pelts to exchange, taboos broke down, and overkilling disrupted the Indian ecology. As they accumulated pelts for their commodity value, the ethic of sharing came under strain....If these forces of cultural demoralization were not enough, the market was happy to supply all the firewater Indians could pay for" (Sellers, *Market Revolution*, p. 7). See also, Mahican chief Hendrick Aupaumut, *History of the Muhheakunnuk Indians*, quoted in *First Annual Report of the*

American Society for Promoting the Civilization and General Improvement of the Indian Tribes in the United States (New Haven, Conn., 1824), p. 42, quoted by Wilcomb Washburn, *Indians in America*: "It was a law among them not to kill any more game than was necessary for their own use—none even to barter, which might have produced a temptation to waste their animals. By this regulation their game was preserved undiminished, the consumption being no greater than the natural increase. The law continued in force, until the *Chuckkathuk*, or *white* people, came to his island" (p. 56).

125   Ronald Takaki, *A Different Mirror* (Boston: Little, Brown, 1993), p. 46. See also, Charles Sellers, *Market Revolution*: "Confrontation between white and Native American cultures presented in the starkest terms a contrast, and for some a choice, between the cultures of land and market" (p. 8).

At one level, of course, the significance of the market was simply that it helped furnish European invaders with an incentive for removing Native-Americans from the land. An expanding marketplace went hand in hand with imperialism and military conquest. Westward, the course of empire took its way.[126] At another level, however, the mentality of the market, its ideological perspective on the world, also provided a ready-made justification, even legal rationale, for the dispossesion of the Native-Americans.

The disparity between Native-American and European political economy, between precapitalist and market approaches to economic organization, permitted settler ideologues to characterize the Native-American economy as no economy at all, to assert that Native-Americans had no regard for proper notions of land ownership, and finally, to claim they did not have a right to the land.[127] Native-Americans, justly described as the first ecologists, had, in fact, cultivated and improved the land for centuries.[128] But because their whole approach to the land was antithetical to the orientation of market capitalism, they and their civilization were to be forcibly evicted.[129]

126 "Behind the English invasion of North America, behind their massacre of Indians, their deception, their brutality, was that special powerful drive born in civilizations based on private property. It was a morally ambiguous drive; the need for space, for land, was a real human need. But in conditions of scarcity, in a barbarous epoch of history ruled by competition, this human need was transformed into the murder of whole peoples" (Zinn, *People's History*, p. 16). Sellers assesses the cumulative impact, the threat from within and without: "Native American cultures were already decimated and demoralized, therefore, when they encountered the decisive phase of the genocidal process, the inexorable advance of white settlement over Indian lands" (*Market Revolution*, p. 7). "But the most 'decisive' impetus of the Market Revolution," concludes Takaki, "was cotton....The income derived from the export of cotton helped to finance enterprises throughout the American economy. The development of the cotton export sector depended on the appropriation of Indian lands and the expansion of slavery. The major cotton-producing states—

Alabama, Mississippi, and Louisiana—were carved out of Indian territory. Tribe after tribe in the South was forced to cede their lands to the federal government and move west of the Mississippi River" (*Different Mirror*, p. 82).

127 David E. Stannard, *American Holocaust* (New York: Oxford University Press, 1992): "An obvious conclusion derivable from such an ideology was that those without a Western sense of private property were, by definition, not putting their land to 'good or profitable use,' as [Thomas] More phrased it, and that therefore they deserved to be dispossessed of it....In practice this became known as the principle of *vacuum domiicilium*, and the British colonists in New England appealed to it enthusiastically as they seized the shared common lands of the Indians" (pp. 234–35).

128 "There exist sufficient examples of Indian concern for killing only so much as he needed and only in the proper manner to support the assertion that the Indian was the first ecologist" (Washburn, *Indians in America*, p. 56).

129 "In point of fact, the Indians had thoroughly 'improved' the land—that is, cultivated it—

If Adam Smith took stock of such precapitalist modes of subsistence, modern economic historians have frequently treated Native-American concepts of communal property and production for use as if they were invisible or incomprehensible to the modern mind. For example, the authors of a popular American economic history text—which typifies an entire genre of contemporary textbook writing—include a dense, two-page discussion of "American Indians" which simply fails to acknowledge the precapitalist nature of Native-American economic organization.[130] They acknowledge that "too often" unscrupulous settlers employed deception, even violence to deprive Native-Americans of legitimate land titles; and they admit that "Indians came to be regarded as an obstacle to be removed so that their land could be taken." While the "interest of English traders," they conclude, "lay in preserving the general shape of the American Indian economic system, trade tended to disrupt the tradi-tional native economic life-style."[131] The economic historians quoted here not only fail to explain why they believe traders had a stake in preserving the "general shape" of a precapitalist economy but, further, refer to one of Adam Smith's basic modes of subsistence as merely an "economic life-style."[132]

Contemporary Harvard economist and proponent of "shock therapy" for postcommunist countries Jeffrey Sachs describes the capitalist under-mining of traditional societies as a process which he acknowledges, quot-ing Marx, "compels all nations, on pain of extinction, to adopt the bourgeois mode of production."[133] The textbook writers cited above

for centuries. They also possessed carefully structured and elaborated concepts of land use and of the limits of political dominion, and they were, as Roger Williams observed in 1643, 'very exact and punctuall in the bounds of their Land, belonging to this or that Prince or People.' This was, however, not private 'ownership' as the English defined the term, and it is true that probably no native people anywhere in the Western Hemisphere would have countenanced a land use system that, to return to Tawney's language, allowed a private individual to 'exploit [the land] with a single eye to his pecuniary advantage, unrestrained by any obligation to postpone his own profit to the well-being of his neighbors.' And thus, in the view of the English, were the Indian nations 'savage'" (Stannard,

American Holocaust, p. 236).

130   Sidney Ratner, James H. Soltow, and Richard Sylla, *The Evolution of The American Economy* (2d. ed., New York: Macmillan, 1993), pp. 38–39.

131   Ibid., 39. The authors correctly indicate that "the native culture lacked some of the basic elements of European culture..." (p.38). Foremost among these elements, however, were capitalist social relations and a market conception of private property, inexplicably omitted from the textbook's list (writing, the wheel, the plow, livestock, iron implements, and firearms).

132   Ibid. Later, the authors refer to Native-American economy as a "tribal way of life" (p. 262).

133   Sachs, "Consolidating Capitalism," *Foreign Policy* Spring 1995, 55.

describe the same process, as it unfolded in North America, as a "life-style" change, without a word about Native-American attitudes toward property or profit.

The economics historians' theoretical failure is reminiscent of western jurisprudential incomprehension when confronted with anthropological notions of "primitive" or customary law. Only with the development of legal sociology (during the rise of what I call here the state capitalist period of American legal history) did social scientists begin to elaborate complex descriptions of precapitalist legal institutions. Lawyer and anthropologist Sally Falk Moore, for example, describes the dramatic impact which Bronislaw Malinowski's research on the Trobriand islanders had upon contemporary legal thinking.[134] After reading *Crime and Custom in Savage Society*, law professor Karl Llewellyn teamed up with anthropologist E. Adamson Hoebel, and together they produced a landmark in modern legal thought, *The Cheyenne Way*. Both Sally Falk Moore and William Twining point to the ultimate failure of modern jurisprudence to come to grips with either Malinowski's insights on what followed—the work of Llewellyn and Hoebel and those whom they inspired.[135] Instead of trying to understand the law of precapitalist society

134   Sally Falk Moore, *Law as Process* (London: Routledge and Kegan Paul, 1978): "*Crime and Custom* excited enormous interest outside the field of anthropology—particularly among academically minded lawyers, whose outlook was broadened considerably....This attention to law as a phenomenon existing outside the traditional sphere of European-style legislatures, codes, courts, and police was something new and important" (p. 219).

135   In spite of initial attention paid to the discoveries of legal anthropology, a significant antidote to the ethnocentrism of Western social science, Moore is compelled to observe that "many recent works on jurisprudence...treat the law of technologically simple societies as the historical or typological precursor of modern law—as an early stage subsequently replaced by that supposed apogee of excellence, the Western European tradition, or perhaps still better, the Anglo-American tradition.... Malinowski's work, then, persuaded people outside the anthropological field that there was such a thing as law in nonindustrial

societies....But this knowledge was received only to be placed in a very narrow niche reserved essentially for exotica and historical background, rather than being understood as something that might have theoretical relevance to the present, either because of similarities or because of contrasts in systems" (ibid., pp. 219–20).

William Twining, *Karl Llewellyn and the Realist Movement* (Norman: University of Oklahoma Press, 1985): "When *The Cheyenne Way* was published it was immediately recognized to be a work of major significance....It is indicative of the breadth of the authors' frame of reference that different reviewers considered it from the point of view of its significance for anthropological method, sociological jurisprudence, legal practice in the United States, juristic method, the economics of primitive societies, comparative law, and interdisciplinary cooperation...

[D]isappointing, however, was the fact that the book made a much greater impression upon anthropologists than upon jurists. By and large this has continued to be the

on its own terms, legal scholars tend to pass over it, treating it merely as "a phenomenon that has been superseded, rendered obsolete by later improvements."[136]

Thus, from Adam Smith's anchoring of jurisprudence in a "modes of subsistence" theory of social determination through Richard Posner's identification of legal culture's "material basis" in society, the tradition of materialist theory of law[137] has demonstrated over and over that a clear understanding of the economic organization of a society permits one to extrapolate its system of law and governance. Conversely, if one fails to grasp the economic infrastructure (which is surely true of much modern writing about Native-American society) then the corresponding legal

case, as can clearly be seen by a brief survey of the subsequent literature of 'primitive law'" (p. 166).

136   Moore, *Law as Process*, pp. 219–20.

137   Perhaps the most famous "materialist" theory of Native-American law and society was that advanced in the nineteenth century by Lewis Henry Morgan. With Adam Smith and more recent writers as well, Morgan shared the view that historical development was unilinear— that is, civilization developed through specific sequential stages toward an end point or goal. However, unlike the Western social scientists whom Moore criticizes for seeing all "stages" of civilization as stepping stones leading to a rough replication of Anglo-American triumph, Morgan's sequence had a rather alarming finale, viewed from the perspective of late-nineteenth-century corporate capitalism.

Discussing Morgan's classic work *Ancient Society* (1877), historian Brian W. Dippee points out that Morgan believed "the desire for property had become an 'unmanageable power' among civilized men," and, Dippie continues, "in words that made his book a bible for Marxist thinkers, [Morgan] concluded that it carried within it 'the elements of self-destruction.' The idea was intriguing, suggesting a stage beyond civilization when everyone would share in a spirit of mutual dependence that transcended the selfishly personal and completed the process of social evolution....Tribal values were, in embryonic form, the values of the future. The implications of Morgan's remarks and the tribal ethic could make no impression

upon the America of Jay Gould, John D. Rockefeller, Andrew Carnegie, and J. P. Morgan" (*The Vanishing American: White Attitudes and U.S. Indian Policy* [Lawrence: University Press of Kansas, 1982], p. 110). Nor, I think, would Francis Fukuyama be likely to extend his "end of history" over the horizon envisioned by Morgan.

"One need not accept Morgan's simplistic notions of stages of barbarism," argues Wilcomb Washburn, "in which he placed the various Indian nations according to the practices he discovered among them, or his overexuberant attribution of communism to aboriginal societies in order to appreciate the significance of his description of a system dominated by communal rather than individual goals" (*America*, p. 33). While rejecting Morgan's evolutionism, we can still profit from his empirical observation of precapitalist societies and, perhaps, draw some methodological lessons from his work, as well. Sally Moore suggests that Morgan's underlying postulate was "that ideology was more durable than organization, hence that cultural expression would lag behind social reality. According to this view, new forms of social organization would arise first, and these would produce their corresponding systems of classification. Incongruities could be explained as the result of a period of overlap between old ideology and new organization" (Moore, *Process*, p. 35). This admirable description of Morgan's method, his underlying postulate, comes perilously close to restating the dialectical principle itself.

superstructure will also remain invisible. So long as economists and historians suppress the precapitalist profile of traditional Native-American society, lawyers and legal philosophers will inevitably be mystified by that society's elaborate system of legal rules and process.

3. PRECAPITALIST ECONOMIC FORMATIONS: EUROPEAN SETTLER POLITICAL ECONOMY

In short, if there is to be any such thing as dialectical materialism, it must be a historical materialism, that is to say, a materialism from within.…It is at the heart of a society which is organised and stratified—and which is also rent by strife—that the appearance of a new machine will bring profound changes which will reverberate from the infrastructures to the superstructures; it is within a society which possesses tools and institutions that the material facts…which condition it and in relation to which it is itself defined, will be discovered.

JEAN-PAUL SARTRE[138]

There are three serious, scholarly overviews of American legal history; five, if you include casebooks; seven if you aggregate publications of legal historians whose research has had a unique impact on scholars working within the field since 1950.[139] All of these writers present a picture of American legal development compatible with the one I have provided

138 Jean-Paul Sartre, *Critique of Dialectical Reason*, Alan Sheridan-Smith, trans., (London: Verso, 1991), p. 33.

139 Overviews: see Lawrence M. Friedman, *A History of American Law* (2d ed., New York: Simon and Schuster, 1985); Grant Gilmore, *The Ages of American Law* (New Haven: Yale University Press, 1977); Kermit L. Hall, *The Magic Mirror: Law in American History* (New York: Oxford University Press, 1989). Casebooks: Stephen B. Presser and Jamil S. Zainaldin, eds., *Law and Jurisprudence in American History* (3d ed., St. Paul, Minn.: West Publishing, 1995); Kermit L. Hall, William M. Wiecek, and Paul Finkelman, eds., *American Legal History* (New York: Oxford University Press; 1991). Aggregate publications: James Willard Hurst, *The Growth of American Law* (Boston: Little, Brown, 1950); James Willard Hurst, *Law and the Conditions of Freedom* (Madison: University of Wisconsin Press, 1956); *Law and Economic Growth* (Madison: University of Wisconsin Press, 1984); *Law and Markets in United States History* (Madison: University of Wisconsin Press, 1982); Morton J. Horwitz, *The Transformation of American Law 1780-1860* (Cambridge, Mass.: Harvard University Press, 1977); Morton J. Horwitz, *The Transformation of American Law 1870-1960* (New York: Oxford University Press, 1992).

thus far; in fact, the historical periodization they share now seems virtually unassailable. Yet only one of them emphasizes periodization over detail and focuses primarily on the outlines of legal history. It is for these reasons that the work of Grant Gilmore stands out, especially *The Ages of American Law*, a brief but inspired book that is based upon the Storrs Lectures delivered at Yale in 1974.[140]

"The law of the primitive agricultural settlements which were painfully hacked from the wilderness in the seventeenth century...had no more relevance to the law of our own industrialized society than the law of the Sioux or Cheyennes," Gilmore writes. It "is true," he adds, "that, as the colonies prospered and their populations multiplied, courts were instituted and a professional class of lawyers and judges emerged. Even so, it is pointless to speak of an 'American law' before the 1800s."[141]

140   When Glmore gave his Storrs Lectures, U.S. military forces were still in Saigon, Richard Nixon had only just gone "whining into exile in the luxurious home he had created for himself (partly with taxpayers' money) in California," and the emerging fourth, or global capitalist, period in American legal history had not yet been defined with sufficient clarity to deserve a classification of its own (Hugh Brogan, *The Penguin History of the United States of America* [London: Penguin, 1985], p. 688). Thus Gilmore—like Karl Llewellyn earlier—still divided American legal history into three parts: "I have adopted a tripartite division of our legal past which was, so far as I know, first put forward by the late Karl Llewellyn, whose last book, *The Common Law Tradition*, published in 1960, was principally devoted to what he called his 'periodization' of American law. Llewellyn's three 'periods' run from, roughly, 1800 until the Civil War; from the Civil War until World War I; from World War I until the present (or, at all events, the recent past)" (Gilmore, *Ages* p. 11). It is hard to imagine what Gilmore meant by his concluding parenthetical remark unless he wished to imply that perhaps a fourth period was already underway. Also, whereas his (and Llewellyn's) first period concludes with the Civil War, as does mine, his second period stretches from the Civil War to World War I, rather than World War II, as in my periodization. To be sure, one can look at these two world

conflagrations as one long war. The "end of the First World War," according to Immanuel Wallerstein, "represented far more a truce in a 'thirty years' war' than a definitive victory for the Allies. Germany had lost a battle in its struggle with the US to be the successor hegemonic power to Great Britain; it had not yet lost the war. It set out, under Weimar, to reconstruct its position in preparation for a second round" ("The USA in the World Today," in *The Politics of the World Economy* [Cambridge, Eng.: Cambridge University Press, 1984], pp. 69–70).

In fact, however, by "World War II," I mean 1932, and by "World War I" Gilmore actually means the 1920s: "After World War I the formalistic approach which had been dominant in American legal thought for fifty years, went into a protracted period of breakdown and dissolution. There appears to be a general agreement that a principal feature of the new approach, *which became manifest during the 1920s*, was a root-and-branch rejection of the formalism or (in a term which came to have a wide vogue) the conceptualism of the preceding period" (ibid., p. 12). Thus, our periodizations diverge at most by a decade.

Finally, among those whom Gilmore cites as sharing this tripartite periodization are three individuals who would become increasingly influential in American legal thought in the years following Gilmore's lectures: Morton Horwitz, Lawrence

Now, at one level, this comment is obviously wrong. Native-American law (certainly including that of "the Sioux or Cheyennes") not only deserves to be regarded as American law but, as Sally Falk Moore and many others have pointed out, could have considerable relevance for contemporary legal theory and history—again, for starters, because of the utility in assessing similarities or contrasts in systems.[142] At another level, though, what Gilmore is trying to get at is the *disparity* between American legal culture (crucially, that of European settlers in the colonies as well as that of Native-Americans) before and after 1800.

It is at this point that we must return to Gordon Wood's analysis of contemporary scholarly argument about when America became a capitalist society. After detailing the debate between "market" and "moral" (or social) historians, he comes down on the side of one leading authority, Winifred Barr Rothenberg. Rothenberg's empirical research has convinced Wood that a market economy emerged in New England during the 1780s, only *after* the end of the American Revolution. Contrary to market historians, Wood confidently concludes that it was only in the 1780s that market society finally came to predominate in America.[143]

If Native-Americans resisted the violent expropriation of their land to the point of near extinction as a people, many European settler communi-

---

Friedman, and Duncan Kennedy.

   For Kennedy's periodization, see his "Toward an Historical Understanding of Legal Consciousness: The Case of Classical Legal Thought in America, 1850–1940," in James Boyle, ed., *Critical Legal Studies* (New York: New York University Press; 1992), pp. 193–214. Karl Llewellyn was not a historian; but his commentary on common law reasoning, from which Gilmore draws a model periodization, should not be missed: see *The Common Law Tradition: Deciding Appeals* (Boston: Little, Brown, 1960).

141 Grant Gilmore, *Ages of Ameican Law*, p. 8.

142 Moore, *Law as Process* p. 220; Karl Polanyi, *The Great Transformation* (Boston: Beacon Press, 1957): "Max Weber was the first among modern economic historians to protest against the brushing aside of primitive economics as irrelevant to the question of the motives and mechanisms of civilized societies. The subsequent work of social

anthropology proved him emphatically right" (pp. 45–46).

143 Wood argues that "Rothenberg is able to date the emergence of a market economy in New England in the decade following the American Revolution....Although [she] spends a good deal of time criticizing the moral economy historians, whom she affectionately calls her 'dear enemies,' her book actually works to reconcile the differences between the market and social historians" (Wood, "Inventing Capitalism," pp. 47–48). After surveying additional evidence for Rothenberg's specific dating scheme, Wood adds: "It is not surprising therefore that Rothenberg should have located the emergence of a New England market economy in the 1780s....In the 1780s, we can actually sense the shift from a premodern traditional society to a modern one in which the business interests and consumer tastes of normal people were coming to dominance" (p. 49).

ties in the "new world" also resisted the rise of the market. Ascertaining exactly when that resistance was eclipsed by a triumphant market is at the heart of the debate between moral and market historians, as elaborated by Wood.

Rothenberg herself argues that "with respect to all these indicators there is a break point between 1785 and 1800"; she concludes, this break point "makes the case...both as strongly and as strongly empirical as I think it can be made, that Massachusetts agriculture, the preindustrial economy that rested upon it, and the farm family it rested upon were all transformed by and under the subtle dominion of regional and inter-regional markets for labor, farm commodities, and capital that emerged soon after the Revolution."[144] Thus, Wood, the moral economy historians, Rothenberg, legal historian Grant Gilmore, and Charles Sellers *all* believe that something crucial—what historian Karl Polanyi in his most famous work even calls the *great* transformation[145] was being realized in the United States around 1800. As Wood notes, contemporary historians (regardless of school) seem ill prepared to challenge this time frame.

In a recent edition of a key work from the "new economic history," for example, Vanderbilt economist Jeremy Atack and *New York Times* journalist Peter Passell appear to accept 1800 as a turning point in the growth of per capita income in the United States; for practitioners of this school of economic history, per capita income represents an important category of economic development. Relying upon the empirical research of Robert Gallman, the authors argue that colonial per capita income for the white

144 Winifred Barr Rothenberg, *From Market-Places to a Market Economy: The Transformation of Rural Massachusetts, 1750–1850* (Chicago: University of Chicago Press, 1992), p. 243. Rothenberg suggests in a footnote on the same page that "what we have called a *proto-market* process had emerged by 1750 and that, on the other hand, the onset of price-responsive behavior in the supply of pork appeared, in the regression analysis, to come between 1810 and 1820." So it is fair to argue that Rothenberg's line falls where Wood suggests, right after the American Revolution, and, a little more generally, between 1785 and 1800, with a somewhat wider concentric circle broad enough to encompass the period between 1750 and 1820, if econometric standards are relaxed. Yet she remains remarkably confident about her concrete

designation of the last fifteen years of the eighteenth century, at least with respect to what she characterizes as the hegemony of a market economy in Massachusetts.

145 "For a century the dynamics of modern society was governed by a double movement: the market expanded continuously but this movement was met by a countermovement checking the expansion in definite directions. Vital though such a countermovement was for the protection of society, in the last analysis it was incompatible with the self-regulation of the market, and thus with the market itself" (Polanyi, *Great Transformation*, p. 130). It is the incompatibility of traditional common law doctrine with the "self-regulation of the market," that provided the dynamic element in nineteenth-century American legal transformation.

population in 1710 was somewhere between $28 and $45 per annum. When European settlement began a century earlier, they assert, per capita income could not have been much lower. Describing the same category of data during the century after 1710, Atack and Passell suggest that "on the eve of the Revolution, per capita income was perhaps one-third higher— a very modest increase, certainly, compared with what came later. After 1839, for example, per capita income in real terms grew at an average annual rate of about 1.6 percent for more than a century," reaching $109 in 1839, and $205 in 1880. Thus, the growth rate between 1710 and 1775, the authors contend, was only about one-half of one percent per year, and the per capita income figures rise from about $30 (the earliest period of settlement), to $30–45 (1710), to about $60 (century's end). Dramatic improvement finally comes in the nineteenth century.[146] Thus, per capita income figures for whites also reflect the same overall patterns shown by Rothenberg's data for the economy as a whole.

Nevertheless, after summarizing the arguments of the moral economy historians, Atack and Passell note skeptically: "If farmers in the seventeenth and eighteenth centuries had such [anti-commercial] attitudes and behaved in these ways, then they were very different from their nineteenth century successors and heirs." This, of course, is exactly Wood's point: they *were* different. Sellers, for his part, suggests that the difference between Native-American economy and a market economy was about as stark as one can imagine. The transition from precapitalist to capitalist society does not happen overnight—but it *does* happen.

Atack and Passell bolster their rejection of the moral historians' emphasis on 1800 by citing, of all people, Winifred Rothenberg. "Data drawn by Winifred Rothenberg from farm account books," they claim, "show farmers who purposefully and consistently produced more than their families could consume....Indeed, the very fact that they kept account books is testimony to their commercial attitudes."[147] Such conduct, the new economic historians contend, simply reflects commercial traditions that settlers brought with them from Europe.

No one disputes that "commercial traditions" existed in the seven-

---

146 Jeremy Atack and Peter Passell, *A New Economic View of American History* (2d ed., New York: W. W. Norton, 1994), pp. 3–6.

147 Ibid., pp. 32–33. Contrast Rothenberg's remark that "Using the behavior of farmers' own prices to diagnose the emergence of a market economy does not mean that I have to impute modern economic motivations to individual farmers whose account books I used" (*From Market-Places*, p. 52).

teenth and eighteenth centuries, both in Europe and North America. Commercial attitudes among some farmers, however, *do not* a capitalist society make, as Rothenberg explicitly demonstrates in her contribution to the debate and, indeed, as Maurice Dobb observed half a century ago.[148] Atack and Passell cite Rothenberg's 1992 book, though not the above-mentioned conclusion to her research;[149] readers may assume her book compliments their distinctions, rather than proving just the opposite: that there *is* a turning point, and that it comes at the end of the eighteenth century. Yet such a dividing line corresponds perfectly with Atack and Passell's own empirical data on rapid increases in per capita income.

Francis Fukuyama sees capitalism (liberal capitalism, to be sure) as the *end* of history, the market economists envision it stretching back to the *beginning* of history, or at least as far as the historian's eye can see. How does one criticize capitalism, or even place it in perspective, if there has never been anything else? This is simply "the end of ideology," a second time around.[150] Another group of writers, outside this new "end of ideol-

---

148 Rothenberg distinguishes between commercial or marketplace attitudes, on the one hand, and societies built upon market economies, on the other: "If in the hegemony of the market economy lies the genesis of the modern world, then we shall need first to distinguish it from its look-alike, marketplace economies the existence of which can be traced back so far in human history that 'the tendency to truck and barter' was long thought to be 'innate'" (*From Market-Places*, p. 5).

See also, Maurice Dobb, *Studies in the Development of Capitalism* (New York: International Publishers, 1947): "Both Sombart's conception of the capitalist spirit and a conception of Capitalism as primarily a *commercial* system share the defect, in common with conceptions which focus attention on the fact of acquisitive investment of money, that they are insufficiently restrictive to confine the term to any one epoch of history, and that they seem to lead inexorably to the conclusion that nearly all periods of history have been capitalist, at least in some degree. As our knowledge of earlier economic societies has increased, the tendency

on the part of those who give such meanings to the term has been to extend the boundaries of Capitalism further back in time" (p. 8). This is the process Wood describes as taking place within the canons of new economic history. Yet unlike Dobb he does not venture a sociological or historical explanation of why this should happen now.

149 Atack and Passell, *New Economic View* p. 33 n5.

150 See, for example, Jackson Lears, "A Matter of Taste: Corporate Cultural Hegemony in a Mass Consumption Society," in Lary May, ed., *Recasting America: Culture and Politics in the Age of Cold War* (Chicago: University of Chicago Press; 1989), for the argument that, in the United States, "the emphasis on national uniqueness and homogeneity...pervaded postwar social thought. The tendency to see American culture as a monolithic and autonomous entity required a systematic inattention to power relations" (p. 42). See also Eric Hobsbawm, *The Age of Extremes* (New York: Pantheon, 1994): "The major texts of Golden Age reformism Crosland's *The Future of Socialism*; J. K. Galbraith's *The Affluent Society*; Gunnar Myrdal's *Beyond the*

ogy" circle, have arrived at a quite different conclusion. Winifred Rothenberg and Gordon Wood;[151] an older generation of scholars who

Welfare State; and Daniel Bell's *The End of Ideology*, all written between 1956 and 1960, rested on the presumption of the growing internal harmony of a society that was now basically satisfactory, if improvable, that is to say, on confidence in the economy of organized social consensus. That consensus did not survive the 1960s" (p. 286).

Rothenberg observes that as "Central and Eastern Europe and the former Soviet Union struggle to reinvent a market economy, their struggle against daunting odds bids fair, finally, to remove from the word capitalism the embarrassment, 'the whiff of brimstone' that attaches to it" (*From Market-Places*, p. 242). That the social systems she identifies face an uphill climb with regard to establishing *liberal* capitalist societies is beyond dispute; but why their chances of creating full-fledged capitalist economies should be regarded as slim is hard to understand. On the contrary, it is unlikely that they would be permitted by the United States to construct *any other kind* of economy. Though it is, perhaps, outside Rothenberg's main field of historical research, she surely realizes that such prevention has been a main theme of American foreign policy in this century: see, for example, William Appleman Williams, *Americans in a Changing World* (New York: Harper and Row, 1978).

It is not so much a question of whether the word "capitalism" will lose its problematic character but, rather, whether (at last) it will simply disappear from economic and political discourse altogether, as the society to which it refers is rendered invisible by historians and social scientists. What is remarkable, wrote Maurice Dobb with reference to the term "capitalism" itself, "is that in economic theory, as this has been expounded by the traditional schools, the term should have appeared so rarely, if at all." Dobb, a Cambridge University economist who also wrote books for the lay reader, of course knew why: "If Capitalism does not exist as an historical entity," he concluded, "critics of the present economic order who call for a change of system are tilting at windmills..." (*Capitalism*, pp. 1–2).

151 "We are just now finding out about the nature and extent of these social and cultural changes in late-eighteenth century Anglo-America—changes that quickly spread through the relatively egalitarian society of New England....It is not surprising therefore that Rothenberg should have located the emergence of a rural New England market economy in the 1780s....The few years following the end of the War of Independence clearly revealed for the first time all the latent commercial and enterprising power of America's emerging democratic society. In the 1780s we can actually sense the shift from a premodern traditional society to a modern one in which the business interests and consumer tastes of ordinary people were coming to dominate" (Wood, *Inventing Capitalism*, p. 49).

A good many "ordinary people" during the nineteenth century, perhaps half the U.S. population, might question whether *their* interests and *business* interests were really identical: see, for example, Keith Ian Polakoff, Norman Rosenberg, Grania Bolton, Ronald Story, and Jordan Schwarz, *Generations of Americans* (New York: St. Martin's, 1976): "an American upper class did exist in the middle of the nineteenth century, as it had during the eighteenth. As compared to earlier times, in fact, the upper class of 1850 was probably more firmly established economically and more dominant socially and perhaps politically. For all the sense of movement and progress from 1815 to 1850, the wealthy as a rule made policy for the nation and shaped its culture while reaping the major benefits of its economic growth."

Turning to the "ordinary people" of American society, the authors observe that at "the other end of the scale, 50 percent or so of the population—the 'laboring classes'—lived at or near the subsistence level. Within this broad group were approximately 3.5 million slaves, perhaps an equal number of rural whites, and some 4 million nonagricultural workers of varied origins....Luckless laborers made up the bulk of the nation's paupers—the roughly 200,000 urban poor with no means

established the classical interpretation of Puritan New England's economy[152] as well as a younger generation of social historians;[153] a number of
economists and historians who do not fit comfortably within any
school;[154] practitioners of the dismal science adept at popularizing

of support except crime or beggary. Industrial
workers also fared poorly" (pp. 273–74).

152   See, for example, Samuel Eliot Morison,
Builders of the Bay Colony (Boston:
Northeastern University Press, 1981): "The
idea of *laissez faire*, that each person should be
free to buy cheap and sell dear, to follow what
calling he pleased and choose between work
and idleness, was utterly strange to the early
New England puritan. He brought with him
from England the contrary ideal of regulation,
of social and economic life carefully ordered
in the interest of the common good. The
founders of Massachusetts Bay brought no
gospel of economic freedom; on the contrary,
they attempted to preserve in New England
both the class distinctions and economic
restrictions of Old England" (p. 162). Richard
Tawney remarks: "Of English-speaking
communities, that in which the social-
discipline of the Calvinist Church-State
was carried to the furthest extreme was the
Puritan theocracy of New England....
Naturally the authorities regulated prices,
limited the rate of interest, fixed a maximum
wage, and whipped incorrigible idlers; for
these things had been done even in the house
of bondage from which they fled. What was
more distinctive of the children of light was
their attempt to apply the same wholesome
discipline to the elusive category of business
profits." (*Religion and the Rise of Capitalism*
[Gloucester, Mass.: Peter Smith, 1962], pp.
127–28). Tawney uses the phrases "children of
light" and "wholesome discipline" ironically.

See also Bernard Bailyn, *The New England
Merchants in the Seventeenth Century*
(Cambridge, Mass.: Harvard University Press,
1955): "The divergence between the merchants
and most of the rest of the Puritan population
manifested itself more explicitly in public
condemnations for malpractice in trade,
particularly overcharging, usury, taking
advantage of a neighbor's need....To be both a
pious Puritan and a successful merchant
meant to live under what would seem to have

been insupportable pressures" (p. 44). Carl
Bridenbaugh notes: "Village authorities
sought to dominate the economic life of the
townsmen. At almost every point inhabitants
found themselves limited in their actions and
inspected in their dealings, for prevailing
theory held that the individual owed more to
the group than did society to him....Save at
Charles Town colonial authorities everywhere
exercised great care to insure fairness in all
dealings, and their records teem with accounts
of 'Corders of Wood,' 'Cullors of Staves,'
'Packers of flesh and fish,' 'Searchers of
leather,' 'Measurers of Salt,' and so on. To
describe the activities of all these officers
would result only in wearisome detail.
Their duties were all much the same: the
examination of products for quality and the
supervision of gauging and measuring to
insure fair treatment to both inhabitants and
strangers" (*Cities in the Wilderness* [New
York, N.Y.: Knopf, 1955], pp. 49, 51).

153   See, for example, Allan Kulikoff, *The
Agrarian Origins of American Capitalism*
(Charlottesville: University Press of Virginia,
1992): "Early American class relations, then,
grew from agrarian capitalism in England and
from reactions against it. Settlers and their
descendants could hardly survive outside
the North Atlantic system, with its trade
and credit networks, but many refused to
fully accept the commodification of land,
goods, trade, and labor that capitalism
inspired. Instead they created—through the
development of staple agriculture or the
search for marketable goods, through the
formation of labor systems that would permit
both economic independence and commerce,
through complex class struggles over the
use of land—dynamic and modern social
formations tied to the world market but not
fully of it. Southern planters devised a
noncapitalist and increasingly anticapitalist
slave regime in the colonial and antebellum
eras; northern farmers relied on petty
commodity production and local exchange to

keep capitalist class relations at bay" (p. 27).

Describing the politics of stagnation in Boston at the beginning of the eighteenth century, UCLA historian Gary Nash argues that the "idea of a regulated market, where the retailing of farm produce would be closely supervised and controlled, was an ancient one that went to the heart of the concept of what has been called a 'moral economy.' At issue was whether the supply of food at reasonable prices to the urban laboring classes was so transcendently important that it should never been compromised by either country producers' or city vendors' considerations or private profit." Nash concludes that "some controls were placed on the retailing of the necessities of life. Boston was unique among the northern capitals in allowing the private retailing of produce by itinerant traders rather than centralizing sales in a public market place. Even in Boston, however, the magistrates set the price of bread according to the current price of wheat" (*The Urban Crucible* [Cambridge Mass.: Harvard University Press, 1986], p. 80).

Looking specifically at the second half of the eighteenth century, University of Maryland historian James A. Henretta argues that "the newfound centrality of the 'market' in American ideology and society foreshadowed the eventual triumph of the monied interest. For the market, along with private property, wage labor, and sophisticated financial instruments, constituted the institutional core of early modern 'capitalism.' In the short space of the fifty years between 1750 and 1800, these ingredients of a capitalist order had risen in prominence as the traditional limitations on economic development in America—the shortage of labor, of extensive markets, of entrepreneurs, and of political purpose had been overcome" ("The Transition to Capitalism in America," in Henretta, Michael Kammen, and Stanley Katz, eds., *The Transformation of Early American History* [New York: Knopf, 1991], p. 238).

"Even had market orientation been greater than it was in the late eighteenth century," adds British historian Christopher Clark, "rural New England would not necessarily have been capitalist in character. As scholars of slavery have shown, it is possible to participate in long-distance trade without altering the fundamentally noncapitalist character of a social structure. Only over time, and under circumstances that need to be explored, did market involvement help bring about the creation of capitalist social relations in the New England countryside....In short, the evolution of rural capitalism was defined, not by the adoption of any one particular set of practices, but by the accretion of a series of distinctive forms and organizations that together came to form a new economic system." Crucially, Clark sees that process of evolution taking place during two distinct phases of transformation, 1780–1820s and from then until the Civil War (Clark, *The Roots of Rural Capitalism* [Ithaca: Cornell University Press, 1990], p. 15).

154   William R. Brock, for example, who is certainly not a "materialist," nevertheless acknowledges that "quantitative evidence bears massive testimony" to the economic transformation that occurred in the United States in the century following the American Revolution. "Without accepting or rejecting dogmatic assertions of economic determinism one can readily agree that every aspect of life—social, intellectual, and psychological—will be profoundly influenced by economic changes of this magnitude." And those aspects of life we refer to as "legal" were no exception: Brock, *The United States, 1789–1890* (Ithaca: Cornell University Press, 1975), p. 68.

Yale economics professor William N. Parker, looking at the same transformation that so impressed Brock, explains that between "1790 and 1840, along its rivers, its streams, and its coastline from Salem to Bridgeport, southern New England experienced a notable Industrial Revolution, lagging behind England's by only a few years. By the standards that economic historians— bourgeois or Marxist—apply, New England's Industrial Revolution was a success. To a Marxist it appears to have broken the mold of a precapitalist form: that of the patriarchal family economy, or some would hold, that of an equally ancient form, the communal village. A new class, merchants and petty capitalists, exhibiting its ingenuity in workshop and marketplace, replaced priests and a king—the latter by a violent revolution

economic ideas;[155] even a notoriously difficult European philosopher;[156] all seem to agree on this: the transition from precapitalist to capitalist

that proved to be the forward shadow of its great counterpart in France. In Yankee counting houses and mills, American business civilization was born…" (Parker, "New England's Early Industrialization: A Sketch," in Parker, *Quantity and Quiddity: Essays in U.S. Economic History* [Middletown, Conn.: Wesleyan University Press, 1987], p. 39).

155   See, for example, John Kenneth Galbraith, *A Journey Through Economic Time* (Boston: Houghton Mifflin, 1994): "The industrial capitalism that developed in England and southern Scotland in the eighteenth century had the locational dynamism that survives to this day. From Britain the new system went, over the course of the next hundred years, to the German states, to France, in a more limited fashion to Scandinavia and Italy and across the Atlantic to the United States" (p. 2).

Remarking on the "ability of Christian doctrine to adjust to economic need"—in my terms, superstructural accommodation of economic change—Galbraith argues that "by the time of the Renaissance Popes, the Church itself would have become reconciled to the accumulation of wealth by its priests. Indulgences would be marketed in an orderly manner; churchly offices would have their going price; the rich, once held to have a difficult access to heaven, would now enter in an expeditious way as their solvent survivors purchased a prompt passage for them through purgatory—a design that must have caused a serious congestion of the righteous poor in that inhospitable station." Galbraith concludes his amusing peroration by observing that "Christian doubts as to the righteousness of moneylending have never been wholly expunged. As noted in the last chapter, the loan shark is, to this day, outside the boundaries of conventional respectability, and only in relatively recent times have bankers been safely within" (*Economics in Perspective* [Boston: Houghton Mifflin, 1987], pp. 21–23).

"[W]hen we examine the general culture of capitalist life," suggests Robert Heilbroner, "we are most forcibly struck by an aspect that precedes and underlies this rationalization,

namely the presence of an ideological framework that contrasts sharply with that of precapitalist formations." Heilbroner distinguishes the "all-embracing world view, usually religious in nature," characteristic of precapitalist societies, from the ideology of capitalism which precipitates "changes in the attitude toward acquisitiveness itself, above all the disappearance of the ancient concern with good and evil as the most immediate and inescapable consequence of wealth-gathering….The problem of good and evil was thus removed from the concerns of political economy and relegated to those of morality…" (*Behind the Veil of Economics* [New York: W. W. Norton, 1988], pp. 47–49).

156   British cultural theorist Raymond Williams went to considerable lengths to persuade Anglo-American intellectuals that the work of European philosopher Lucien Goldmann, for example, not only has strong affinities with that of Goldmann's English-language counterparts but, furthermore, is well worth whatever effort might be required to decipher his structuralist categories of thought. *See,* for example, Raymond Williams *Marxism and Literature* [New York: Oxford, 1977). In a long essay on the Enlightenment, Goldman asserts that by the end of the eighteenth century "the citizen no longer regarded his social position as the outcome of divine grace or punishment, but as the result of his own conduct; whether his actions were appropriate and successful or misdirected and profitless, they were, at least in economic terms, morally neutral and incapable of being judged by standards of good and evil. In the Middle Ages it was possible to talk in terms of 'just' or 'unjust' prices; in the eighteenth century there were only correctly or mistakenly calculated prices. The right price was the one that fixed the difference between cost and selling price in such a way as to maximize profit; the wrong one was any that failed to secure the maximum gain." (Lucien Goldmann, *The Philosophy of the Enlightenment*, trans. by Henry Maas, [Cambridge: MIT Press, 1973], p. 54). The unfolding of American common law between the Revolution and the Civil

economy, from premarket communities to societies organized on the basis of the market, transformed both Europe and North America by the early nineteenth century. The social and cultural consequences of that revolution were overwhelming; they reconstituted the whole of life right down to the ground. Broadly understood, it is a revolution which continues today.[157] That such a profound shift in economic and social structure might leave legal arrangements somehow unscathed is inconceivable.[158]

War perfectly mirrors the transformation that Goldmann describes.

157 See, for example, Manuel Riesco, "Honour and Eternal Glory to the Jacobins!" *New Left Review* (July/August 1995): "The transition to capitalist modernity is not yet complete— far from it. With regard to the economic structure, the key to the transition to capitalism in general appears to be so-called primitive accumulation—that is, expulsion of peasants from the land and their subsequent conversion into potential workers. In 1994, however, according to UN figures, more than 70 percent of the world's population still lived and worked on the land...It seems clear, then, that much is still lacking for the process to be completed" (p. 58).

158 Rothenberg, describing "the process of modernization itself," whereby "markets embedded within and *constrained by values antithetical to them within the culture*" were replaced by a market economy, suggests that the "immense transformation that ushered in the modern world appears to have been an omnivorous process, ultimately (although not simultaneously) reshaping all institutions in its path"—including, she adds, "property rights [and] legal institutions" as well as "the tenets of religious belief..." (From *Market-Places* pp.2–3; emphasis added). Although the concrete reshaping of property rights and legal institutions is the aspect of this "immense transformation" upon which I will focus, it is worth considering another aspect cited here by Rothenberg—the reshaping of religious belief.

In his description of early New England society, Samuel Eliot Morison points out that "Max Weber, a German economist of the last century, propounded the interesting theory that Calvinism released the business man from the clutches of the priest, and sprinkled

holy water on economic success. According to him, John Calvin defended the taking of interest on loans, which the mediaeval church had condemned under the name of usury....Whatever may be thought of this theory in relation to what Calvin actually thought and wrote, it will not hold water here" (*Builders of the Bay Colony* p. 160; Max Weber, *The Protestant Ethic and the Spirit of Capitalism* [New York: Routledge, 1992]). Morison then precedes to contrast his view of the anticommercial character of Massachusetts Bay's Puritan faith with Weber's famous theory about Protestantism and the rise of capitalism.

Contrasting Weber's theory with Bailyn's argument that New England "merchants resented the communal norms of the Puritan ministry, preferring in their place the greater freedom of the marketplace," Boston University historian David Hall laments the general failure of historians of colonial America to utilize Weber's "rich framework of interpretation" and he argues that the "alternative to a static conception of Calvinism is to recognize that Calvinism remained ambivalent in important ways" ("Religion and Society: Problems and Reconsiderations," in Jack P. Greene and J. R. Pole, eds., *Colonial British America: Essays in the New History of the Early Modern Era* [Baltimore: Johns Hopkins University Press, 1984], pp. 325, 335–336). Hall rejects the traditional and "oversimple contrast between 'community' and 'individualism.'"

While he is right about this, the basic question—whether religion was an obstacle to capitalism's development in New England *or* it facilitated that growth—is not so cut and dry. First, we must establish *when* religion's relation to society is being assessed. All institutions change over time. Puritanism

So what was the content of that alteration in legal doctrine and institutions precipitated by the rise of capitalist social relations? No one has more succinctly presented it than Harvard historian David S. Landes who, having surveyed the abolition of antiusury laws in Britain and Europe—as well as recognition of foreign corporations and the rise of new commercial instruments like checks—suggests that in the nineteenth century, "the gains of the middle decades were simply a continuation of trends that went back to the eighteenth century and beyond. The history of commercial and civil law in the West, is in large measure the story of the progressive adaptation of the usages of an agrarian, community-centred, tradition-bound society to the requirements of an industrial, individualistic, and rational—hence mobile—capitalism."[159] Landes regrets the extent to which economists have ignored the legal aspect of this story (or worse, left it to "legists"); fortunately, though, American legal historians—especially those who have pursued a comprehensive overview of American law—have been less guilty of ignoring economic influence in legal development. Certainly the lawyers and judges who were there, who led the way in transforming nineteenth-century American law itself, were extremely conscious of the relation between law and commerce.

At the end of World War II, long before the moral and market historians began their debate over the origins of American capitalism, Columbia University's Joseph Dorfman published a detailed analysis of the historical development of economic ideas in the United States. In his chapter on Puritan political economy, Dorfman observes that New England's leaders "believed in the just price as presented by Ames," and he illustrates application of just price doctrine in the "celebrated case" of Robert Keayne in 1639.[160] On the one hand, merchant Keayne was tried and convicted of

---

may have helped to consolidate an anticommercial regime up to a point, but as it changed with the times, it may have hastened the process of precapitalist society's disintegration. Or perhaps a precapitalist economic infrastructure made room for both precapitalist legal and theological institutions in early New England, but as this economic infrastructure changed (between the first third of the seventeenth and nineteenth centuries), the juridical and religious superstructures built upon it also changed in quite fundamental ways.

159 David S. Landes, *The Unbound Prometheus* (New York: Cambridge University Press, 1969), pp. 198–99.

160 Joseph Dorfman, *The Economic Mind in American Civilization 1606–1865* (New York: Viking, 1946), vol. 1, p. 46. On Ames's theory of the just price, referred to by Dorfman, see R. H. Tawney, *Religion and the Rise of Capitalism*: "The most influential work on social ethics written in the first half of the seventeenth century from the Puritan standpoint was Ames's *De Conscientia*, a manual of Christian conduct which was

overpricing (nails, gold buttons, a bridle, and so forth) by the General Court and, then, severely admonished by the church for his misconduct. Historians Samuel E. Morison, R. H. Tawney, Bernard Bailyn, and Carl Bridenbaugh, described above as authors of the classical interpretation of Puritan New England's economy, make predictably good use of the Keayne litigation in bolstering their arguments.[161] Nevertheless, Keayne's

intended to supply the brethren with the practical guidance which had been offered in the middle ages by such works as *Dives et Pauper*. It became a standard authority, quoted again and again by subsequent writers....
His teaching with regard to prices is not less conservative. 'To wish to buy cheap and to sell dear is common (as Augustine observes), but it is a common vice.' Men must not sell above the maximum fixed by public authority, though they may sell below it, since it is fixed to protect the buyer; when there is no legal maximum, they must follow the market price and 'the judgment of prudent and good men.' They must not take advantage of the necessities of individual buyers, must not overpraise their wares, must not sell them dearer merely because they have cost them much to get....Nor was such teaching merely the pious pedantry of the pulpit. It found some echo in contrite spirits; it left some imprint on the conduct of congregations" (pp. 216–17).

161 See, for example, Morison, *Builders of the Bay Colony*: "If any of the deputies present [at Keayne's trial] had come over in the *Arbella*, they might have replied out of Governor Winthrop's shipboard sermon, in which he expressly condemned usury, oppression, and extortion. Keayne got off with the lower fine, and a censure from the Boston church, which made him 'with tears acknowledge and bewail his covetous and corrupt heart.' Master Cotton took the occasion to deliver a sermon on business ethics and to announce the following principles which the godly should follow in trade....A man may not sell above the current price, i.e., such a price as is usual in the time and place, and as another (who knows the worth of the commodity) would give for it, if he had occasion to use it....If Massachusetts ever came to an attitude of fawning on the wealthy and successful, it

would not be the fault of her parsons" (pp. 161–62). R. H. Tawney remarks: "The scandal was terrible. Profiteers were unpopular—'the cry of the country was great against oppression'—and the grave elders reflected that a reputation for greed would injure the infant community, lying as it did 'under the curious observation of all Churches and civil States in the world.' In spite of all, the magistrates were disposed to be lenient....Here, if he had been wise, Mr. Keayne would have let the matter drop. But, like some others in a similar position, he damned himself irretrievably by his excuses" (*Religion and the Rise of Capitalism*, p. 129).

Bailyn observes: "Finding evidence in the social teachings of Calvinism for the rectitude of his life, [Keayne] could impute only sinfulness to those who attempted to blacken his name. But his enemies also drew upon religious ideas for the justification of their attack. To them it seemed clear that by all the relevant Calvinist standards of justice in business, Keayne had sinned. In his scramble for profit he had trampled underfoot the notion of a just price. He had dealt with his debtors usuriously. He had put the increase of his own wealth above the common good. No amount of public benefaction could make up for such evil practices" (*The New England Merchants*, p. 43). Elsewhere, he writes: "What was the effect of Puritanism on the business lives of merchants like Robert Keayne? It was not a simple, singular influence....Calvinism in its New England Puritan form accounts not for a new 'spirit of capitalism' but rather for a delicate balance of tensions in the life of the pious merchant—a balance as heavily weighted with medieval business ethics as with Protestant worldly asceticism. The growth of capitalistic society involved not the perpetuation but the destruction of this Puritan balance" (Introduction to the *Apologia*

trials and tribulations, for Dorfman, have another side: Dorfman believes that this celebrated Massachusetts case "illustrated the difficulties" involved in regulation of commerce, in placing sharp limits upon merchant ambition, even at this early date. In reducing Keayne's two-hundred-pound fine by half, the magistrates indicated that Keayne was not alone in offending against the community's commercial code of behavior limiting profit taking and, indeed, "that a 'certain rule' could not be found for an equal rate between buyer and seller."[162]

On the one hand, the classical interpretation—reinforced by more rigorous research carried out over the past few decades—reveals a precapitalist America in which many of New England's European settlers resisted the market revolution and all that it portended. On the other hand, both Dorfman (early on) and some of the market historians (later), have correctly pointed out that the theocratic society's antimarket sanctions were sometimes ambiguous and, ultimately, temporary. This means not that America "has always been capitalist," but, rather, that commercial attitudes were a thorn in the side of even early New England's "children of light" (Tawney's phrase) and reflected something more important still—a premonition of what was to come.

Materialist jurisprudence obviously helps us to explain the outcome of Robert Keayne's prosecution in relation to the underlying precapitalist political economy that he sought to escape or transcend. The mode of production, Adam Smith's "mode of subsistence" (in this case, literally, a subsistence economy)[163] was decisive in creating a legal culture that located Robert Keayne not within but *beyond* the pale (recall Galbraith's

of Robert Keayne [Gloucester, Mass.: Peter Smith, 1970], p. xi).

    See, finally, Bridenbaugh, *Cities in the Wilderness*: "The magistrates found Keayne the worst of all offenders, because of his wealth and the fact that he sold 'dearer' than most tradesmen. His dealings so outraged community sentiment that some members of the Boston church demanded his excommunication. Aware of his duty as upholder of the social discipline, the Reverend John Cotton took the case as subject for his weekly lecture, and expounded from the pulpit the medieval doctrine of the just price" (p. 50).

162 Dorfman, *Economic Mind*, p. 47.
163 "[P]eople who settled at any distance from navigable water mainly produced use values for subsistence rather than the market's commodity values for sale. Profound cultural differences arose from these contrasting modes of production. The market fostered individualism and competitive pursuit of wealth by open-ended production of commodity values that could be accumulated as money. But rural production of use values stopped once bodies were sheltered and clothed and bellies provided for. Surplus produce had no abstract or money value, and wealth could not be accumulated. Therefore the subsistence culture fostered family obligation, communal cooperation, and reproduction over generations of a modest comfort" (Sellers, *Market Revolution*, p. 5).

distinction between the banker and loan shark). However, adding a dialectical dimension to this critique enables us to understand exactly why Dorfman felt Keayne's debacle revealed some of the "difficulties" implicit in any attempt to fathom the "economic mind" of early New England, and why the Massachusetts court itself had a problem identifying a "certain rule" applicable to Keayne's situation.

Thus we return, briefly, to the exemplars of dialectical reasoning previously invoked: Hegel, please recall, was reintroduced into the conversation about contemporary societies by Fukuyama.[164] Engels described the challenge faced by any legal system compelled to maintain an appearance of inner coherence while, at the same time, necessarily keeping pace with

164   "If Marx was Hegel's greatest nineteenth-century interpreter, then Kojeve was surely his greatest interpreter in the twentieth century" (Francis Fukuyama, *The End of History and the Last Man* [New York: The Free Press, 1992], p. 66). Hans-Georg Gadamer, after describing Kojeve's *Introduction to the Reading of Hegel* as "epoch making," suggests that Kojeve found his "own way to Hegel, which is determined by the bloodletting of the Russian October Revolution and by the ensuing wish to acquire a better understanding of Marx..." (Gadamer, *Hegel's Dialectic*, P. Christopher Smith, trans., [New Haven: Yale University Press, 1976], p. 66). See Alexandre Kojeve, *Introduction to the Reading of Hegel*, James H. Nichols, Jr., trans. (Ithaca, N.Y.: Cornell University Press, 1980): "History is what judges men, their actions and their opinions, and lastly their philosophical opinions as well. To be sure, History is, if you please, a long 'discussion' between men. But this *real* historical 'discussion' is something quite different from a philosophic dialogue or discussion. The 'discussion' is carried out not with verbal arguments, but with clubs and swords or cannon on the one hand, and with sickles and hammers or machines on the other. If one wants to speak of a 'dialectical method' used by History, one must make clear that one is talking about methods of war and of work. This real, or better, active, historical dialectic is what is reflected in the history of philosophy. And if Hegelian Science is dialectical or synthetical, it is only because it describes that *real* dialectic in its totality..." (p. 185).

See also Theodor W. Adorno, *Hegel: Three Studies*, Shierry Weber Nicholsen, trans., (Cambridge, Mass.: MIT Press, 1994): "If, however, one were to make precise inquiries into its own verification, then it is precisely Hegel's conception of the dialectic, which the ignorant tend to dismiss as a conceptual straitjacket, that the most recent phase of history has verified....[I]n terms of his own ideology, and as the henchman of more powerful interests, Hitler attempted to eradicate bolshevism, whereas it was his war that brought the giant shadow of the Slavic world down on Europe—that same Slavic world of which Hegel had already made the ominous statement that it had not yet entered history" (p. 10). Thus, in Adorno's view, Hitler made war on communism not without hope that the Americans would recognize their true interests and enter the conflict on the antibolshevik side, (in other words, that of authoritarian capitalism or fascism); as a result, Soviet domination fell on the heads of the East Germans (and, conversely, made West Germany a satellite nation, at least temporarily, of the United States). New England's Puritan parsons, whom Morison said would be the last ones to transform Massachusetts along commercial lines, ended up helping to provide capitalism with a crucially needed set of legitimating ideas— the Protestant ethic of hard work and honest acquisitiveness. Work by Europeans in the new world and the wars they made upon its inhabitants, as Kojeve acutely observes, provided America with its *real* historical dialectic.

changes in the underlying economic structure. With the rise of commercial—including "sharp"—practice within the Bay Colony, evidenced by
confrontations like that between Robert Keayne and an early (and antimarket) version of the "Protestant Establishment,"[165] came increased
pressure upon Church and State to find ways of reconciling economic
change with existing codes of conduct. What Engels referred to as
"repeated breaches made in this system by the influence and compulsion
of further economic development" eventually did in the precapitalist
structure of community values and anticommercial doctrines, which
Keayne held in such obvious contempt. But this "dialectical overcoming"
(*Aufheben*) of the precapitalist legal order took another 150 years.[166]

Another way to illustrate this approach to historical change is simply
to provide several concrete, if diverse, examples drawn from Austrian
social democracy, Japanese communism, British cultural studies, and
French economics. Viennese legal theorist Karl Renner's main contribution to legal history was his elaborate explanation of how law is generally
able to fulfill the challenge of maintaining an appearance of internal
coherence during dramatic infrastructural shifts. Using "norm" and "substratum" rather than "superstructure" and "base," Renner writes that "in
spite of the norm, the substratum changes, yet this change of the substratum takes place within the forms of the law; the legal institutions automatically change their functions *which turn into their very opposite*, yet this
change is scarcely noticed and is not understood."[167] Skeptics need only

---

165   See E. Digby Baltzell, *The Protestant
Establishment: Aristocracy and Caste in America*
(New York: Random House, 1964).

166   "But one can say that the Hegelian Dialectic
is entirely summed up by a single fundamental
category, which is that of *dialectical
Overcoming (Aufheben)*. For what is to be
'overcome' is precisely the Immediate, and
the 'overcoming' itself is Mediation through
negating action which creates the
Mediated..." (Kojeve, *Introduction to the
Reading of Hegel*, p. 208). See also John
Herman Randall, Jr., *The Career of Philosophy*
(New York: Columbia University Press, 1965):
"On the one hand, 'to sublimate' means 'to
make an end of, to annul'; on the other, 'to
preserve, to maintain'; what is sublimated
(*das Aufgehobene*) is 'something also preserved,
that has lost only its immediacy, but is
not therefore annihilated.' And thirdly,

sublimation means 'raising to a higher form,"
(vol. 2, p. 312). We have already provided
T. M. Knox's description of how later stages
in an historical process manage to cancel out
earlier ones while, nevertheless, absorbing
elements from the earlier stages. And this
might be a good point for the reader to review
the various nutshell versions of Hegel's
dialectic, including Knox's, provided in the
previous chapter.

167   Karl Renner, "The Development of Law," in
Austro-Marxism, Tom Bottomore and Patrick
Goode, ed. and trans. (Oxford, Eng.: Oxford
University Press, 1978), p. 269; emphasis
added. See also Renner, "The Development of
Capitalist Property and the Legal Institutions
Complementary to the Property Norm,"
in Vilhelm Aubert, ed., *Sociology of Law*
(New York: Penguin Books, 1969): "Upon
the enclosed estate there stands the manor

recall Richard Posner's comment along these same lines—that it is relatively easy for experienced lawyers and judges to disguise change when it is "clothed in the rhetoric of passive obeisance to 'the law' (including law the judges may have made up last week)."

Consider another illustration. In 1927, the Japanese Communist Party (JCP) split into two factions that continued to engage each other in theoretical debate down to the beginning of World War II, at which time the party's surviving militants constituted the backbone of Japanese resistance

---

house of the old noble family, and the peasant's farm is surrounded by his own land. Property is distinctly fenced off, noticeboards announce that it is 'private' and that 'trespassers will be prosecuted'. In contrast, let us consider the most striking example of modern development, a privately owned railway. We enter the station hall, but though this is registered property like the manor and the farm, it does not even come into our minds that we have entered somebody else's property. No one inquires who is the owner, his identity has become a matter of indifference....We get our ticket which the other party is obliged to give us, there is no trace of bargaining, of freedom of contract, of conditions and terms; published by-laws fix everything in advance. We board the train and do not think for a split second that we have hired Mr. X's private vehicle, though lawyers may still construe it in this way" (p. 41). Renner is describing how legal institutions are modified over time in relation to large-scale transitions in the form and ownership of property and how the everyday experience of life is changed, too, almost unconsciously. The transition in property relations from an era of manor houses and noble families to that of the great railway barons and corporate public utilities brings into being new legal norms. "But these new norms," Renner concludes, "could not accomplish more than to give a precise legal form to what had existed in the world of facts long before they intervened. The specific features of a public utility were established in the substratum before the norm got hold of them" ("The Development of Capitalist Property," p. 42). The time it takes the legal norm "to get hold of" new features within

the system of infrastructural or economic relationships—the tendency of cultural and legal expression to lag behind changes in social reality—is what Morgan meant by the durability of ideology. Thus, American common law during the first half of the nineteenth century was catching up with changes that had been taking place for some time. Remnants of a precapitalist legal order inevitably came into sharp conflict with new economic arrangements precipitated by the market revolution.

On Renner's contribution, see Tom Bottomore, "Karl Renner," in Tom Bottomore, ed., *A Dictionary of Marxist Thought* (Oxford: Basil Blackwell, 1983), p. 416; Richard Kinsey, "Karl Renner on Socialist Legality," in David Sugarman, ed., *Legality, Ideology, and the State* (New York: Academic Press, 1983), pp. 11–42. Paul Hoffman notes: "Renner would make a political comeback after World War II as chancellor and eventually as president of a resurrected Austria. A biographer suggested after his death that Renner's pro-*Anschluss* statement in 1938, 'which was also in keeping with his German-national conviction,' was to some extent prompted by the circumstance that his son-in-law was Jewish. The Gestapo had arrested Hans Deutsch, a former director of the city-controlled Hammer bakery who was the husband of Renner's daughter Leopoldine; Deutsch was later released and allowed to emigrate to England. Renner's 1938 declaration may thus have been 'a personal arrangement with the people in power at the time.' In any case, it convinced many Social Democrats that it was useless to resist the Nazis" (*The Viennese* [New York: Anchor Doubleday, 1989], p. 238).

to fascism. One of the factions, the *Koza*, or "so-called feudal school," according to Johns Hopkins University professor Germaine A. Hoston, "argued that the existence of semi-feudal *remnants* in Japan's political superstructure—e.g., the emperor system, the Privy Council, and the dominant *kokutai* ideology—constituted proof that Japan's bourgeois-democratic revolution was not yet complete and would have to be finished before the JCP could embark on a socialist revolution."[168] The *Koza* faction of the JCP was able to penetrate the sophisticated legal and political forms that dominated Japanese society between the wars, interpret those forms as predominantly "remnants" of a previous (authoritarian) period, and on that basis question the liberal credentials of prewar Japanese constitutionalism.[169] This demonstrates that the concept of "remnant"—which can be understood to encompass the meaning that Professor Randall and others assign to sublimated elements (*das Aufgehobene*) in Hegel's system—might be useful to legal historians identifying elements of a superseded legal regime that survive within its successor.

Turning to British literary theory of the 1970s, specifically the work of Raymond Williams, we discover a reformulation of remnant as residual. By *residual*, Williams means superstructural elements "effectively formed in the past, but...still active in the cultural process." He adds two more concepts. First, there is the *dominant*, representing the hegemonic, the primary organizational structure at a given moment in time. Second, is the *emergent*, which refers to "new meanings and values, new practices, new relationships and kinds of relationship [which] are continually being created."[170] If we consider the capitalist period of American legal history (from the Civil War to World War II), we can identify not only a dominant legality but, also, both remnants or residual elements of the precapitalist legal order and emergent elements (precursors or forerunners) of the state capitalist period. Drawing upon French economic theory, University of Wisconsin social historian Harvey Goldberg distinguishes between *l'économie dominant* and *l'économie subordonné*, which jointly structure a

168 Germaine A. Hoston, *Marxism and the Crisis of Development in Prewar Japan* (Princeton: Princeton University Press, 1986), pp. xi–xii, emphasis added; see also, George M. Beckmann and Okubo Genji, *The Japanese Communist Party, 1922–1945* (Stanford: Stanford University Press, 1969).

169 See, for example, John W. Dower, ed., *Origins*

of the Modern Japanese State: Selected Writings of E. H. Norman (New York; Pantheon, 1975); Dower, *Empire and Aftermath: Yoshida Shigeru and the Japanese Experience, 1878–1954* (Cambridge, Mass.: Harvard University Press, 1979).

170 Raymond Williams, *Marxism and Literature*, pp. 121–27.

given society.[171] In this model, the commanding system of production subordinates residual elements, at least for the time being.

Renner would emphasize how a profound shift in economic organization separating the seventeenth-century Bay Colony from Rothenberg's market society in Massachusetts after 1780 was papered over by the relative continuity of legal forms. Different aspects of the same rule can be emphasized from one period to the next, depending upon the current of economic change, thereby accommodating shifts in the substratum without doing violence to legal norms. In the language of JCP economists or cultural theorists such as Raymond Williams, we can describe the economic perspective reflected in Keayne's challenge to the system as a precursor or "forerunner" of capitalist hegemony; eventually, within the context of a dominant market system, religious and legal opposition to commercial exploitation can be seen as residual, a remnant of past practice.

"In 1640," according to Dorfman, "the General Court of Massachusetts declared that because of the scarcity of money many debtors could not meet their obligations though their goods be sold for half their worth." We need to look rather closely at this statement and what it implies. When Dorfman, documenting the views of the General Court, refers to goods being sold "for half their worth," he is referring to two contrary methods of evaluation. One way to value goods sold is by relying on the price at which they are sold; this is one meaning that can be given to the phrase "market price." In certain circumstances, someone may be forced to sell goods "for half their worth"; in contrast to the market value, then, is the *real* value which, in this illustration, is twice the market value. The point is not that this value is "real" in any epistemological sense but, rather, that it refers to a system of valuation independent of the immediate market. Saying that something sold "for less than it is worth" implies a system for valuing things which is distinct from the transaction that determined the selling price.

Dorfman continues: "But on an 'equal valuation' [many debtors] could

<hr/>

171   According to Professor Goldberg, the subordinated economy "means those economic systems of precapitalist societies whose practices after all, in some manner, however imperfectly, reflected the moral code and the customary usages of the community"; by contrast, the dominant economy refers to "the economic system of the emergent capitalist societies in which the purposes of profit and of production at any cost ran roughshod and transcended any other moral, cultural and psychological consideration" (Goldberg, "The Ideology of Private Property," Goldberg Center History Lecture Audiotapes [Madison: University of Wisconsin, Jan. 24, 1977]).

not only pay their debts but live comfortably on the remainder. Therefore the assets of debtors are to be valued by three 'indifferent men.'"[172] The clear implication is that a panel of "indifferent men" is more likely to value the goods at their actual worth than is the market. Or, perhaps, the figure arrived at through an indifferent evaluation itself constitutes the actual value or worth of the goods in question. We can certainly compare this commentary with that provided by John Cotton, in the sermon he delivered on business ethics in the wake of the Keayne debacle: "A man may not sell above the current price, i.e., such a price as is usual in the time and place, and as another (who knows the worth of the commodity) would give for it, if he had occasion to use it...."[173]

This admonition is quoted in most accounts of Keayne's confrontation with the New England authorities; the most recent assessment, by University of Virginia historian Stephen Innes, is no exception. Yet instead of relying upon it to demonstrate that Cotton rejected the "idea of *laissez faire*, that each person should be free to buy cheap and sell dear," Innes argues just the opposite. He suggests that "Cotton's just price was the going market price of a product." He concludes that "the current market price was the true price," and adds that what "was not acceptable was fraud, collusion, or the failure to perform one's contractual obligations."[174]

One could argue that Innes has read back into the early seventeenth century a free market ideology more characteristic of a later period of legal development. Certainly, the notion that an article's true value is whatever you can get for it, absent fraud or misrepresentation, reflects a doctrine that legal historians have associated with the classical theory of contract, which triumphed only after the market revolution—that is, *not* in the seventeenth century. For the moment, though, it is worth asking how Innes gets his market theory from Cotton.

Innes and Morison quote the same passage from Cotton's sermon, but Innes stresses the first part of the rule (prohibiting prices above what is usual for the time and place) without emphasizing the second part ("and as another (who knows the worth of the commodity) would give for it...")[175] Innes softpedals the second half of the injunction, wherein

172   Joseph Dorfman, *Economic Mind*, p. 48, quoting *Massachusetts Colonial Records*, vol. I, p. 307.

173   John Cotton's sermon is found in *Winthrop's Journal*, 1:317–18, quoted in Morison, *Builders of the Bay Colony*, p. 161.

174   Stephen Innes, *Creating the Commonwealth* (New York: W. W. Norton, 1995). pp. 170–71.

175   "A man may not sell above the current price, i.e., *such a price as is usual in the time and place*, and as another (who knows the worth of the commodity) would give for it, if he had occasion to use it..." (ibid., p. 170; emphasis added by Innes).

Cotton says "and": ethical business practice must satisfy *both* parts of the standard. You should not charge more than the current price of goods, *and* you should not charge more than the goods' *real* value. There is an entire view of the world contained within this language and we do not want to miss it.

Just as in Dorfman's example of prohibitions on goods being sold at only half their worth, or the requirement of an independent valuation by individuals without a stake in the transaction, Cotton's economic theory reflects a potential split between market value and real value, between the current price and what would be paid by "another," someone outside the deal, who *knows* the worth of the commodity. There is, then, a knowledge that is not market knowledge: it constitutes the regulatory yardstick in Massachusetts Bay, suggesting a regime of social regulation of prices. Under market capitalism, on the other hand what is there to know other than the market price? It is not that what one otherwise knows no longer counts. It is that there is nothing else to know at all. Economically speaking, other than by and through the market, there is no longer any mechanism for valuing things. The market price becomes the real value and what had been the real value no longer exists. Marx put it well in the *Communist Manifesto*: "All that is solid melts into air." So Innes starts with Morison's (and everybody else's) Cotton, emphasizes going prices in lieu of real values, limits market rule exceptions to fraud and misrepresentation, and ends by asserting that in New England the "final basis of the price was the blind, supply/demand-driven unconscionable force of the market." Would that it were so, Keayne must have prayed.[176]

---

176 Contradicting what seems to me the main thrust of his whole book, Innes endorses Rothenberg's judgment that the market revolution in America did not succeed until the end of the eighteenth century: "Much appears to support a 'pre-capitalist' portrayal of early New England. The primitive state of accounting procedures, the continuation of medieval restrictions on the free use of property, and the absence of banks, a reliable currency, and general incorporation laws, meant that Bay Colonists could not have been full-blown Weberian 'rational-calculators' even if they had so desired. Perhaps *the* most important 'diagnostic of market penetration—synchronicity and convergence in the behavior of prices'—did not emerge until late in the eighteenth century in

Massachusetts" (ibid., p. 42).

How does Innes square his history of price controls with the one that is so central to Rothenberg's whole argument? She contends, in the same text to which Innes refers, that in 1635, "after a brief experiment in legislating prices and wages at the provincial level, that responsibility devolved by statute on the towns. It is likely that these less remote, more informal—and, in a 'shame culture,' more effective—pressures from the community acted to fix customary prices for some time. The question is, for how long a time? According to the argument to be presented [in her book], the *increased scattering* of farm prices and of farm wages after 1750 constitutes evidence that the regime of socially controlled prices was beginning to break down *by the*

More than a century after Robert Keayne was punished for profiteering, in November of 1758, in Braintree, Massachusetts, John Adams was admitted to the Suffolk bar and began to practice law in the Inferior Court of Common Pleas. The following summer, reflecting on the everyday problems that lawyers encounter, the novitiate attorney (and future president) made the following entry in his diary:

> It is a natural, immutable Law that the Buyer ought not to take advantage of the sellers Necessity, to purchase at too low a Price. Suppose Money was very scarce, and a Man was under a Necessity of procuring a £100 within 2 Hours to satisfy an Execution, or else go to Gaol. He has a quantity of goods worth £500 that he would sell. He finds a Buyer who would give him £100 for them all, and no more. The poor Man is constrained to sell £500s worth for £100. Here the seller is wronged, tho he sell [them?] voluntarily in one sense. Yet, the Injustice, that may be done by some Mens availing them selves of their Neighbours Necessities, is not so Great as the Inconvenience to Trade would be if all Contracts were to be void which

mid-eighteenth century" (Rothenberg, *From Market-Places*, pp. 44–45; latter emphasis added). Innes asserts, however, that peacetime "wage and price controls in fact were in effect for a *total* of forty-three months during the period from 1630 to 1684....From 1634 through the onset of the depression of 1640, the General Court's confidence in the efficacy of wage and price controls eroded steadily" (*Creating the Commonwealth*, pp. 177–78).

It could be argued that Innes and Rothenberg are talking about apples and oranges—formal regulation (Innes) and informal regulation (Rothenberg). But Innes does not stop there: "By the end of the first decade [i.e., the 1630's], all New Englanders—those from agricultural Dedham as well as those from commercially oriented Springfield—recognized that in order to import what they needed, they had to sell their products in markets that they could create but not control. Through the series of government decrees on this issue can be discerned the triumph in early Massachusetts of the doctrine of economic freedom" (ibid., p. 78). For Innes, uncontrolled markets reigned by the middle of the seventeenth century; the Puritans opted for economic freedom—not, as

Rothenberg has it, for statuory devolution of what remained, for at leastanother century, a regime of socially controlled prices. It is far from clear how he can buy into Rothenberg's dating of price convergence while rejecting everything else. The two historians appear to locate the breakdown of socially controlled prices more than a century apart.

Rothenberg's seventeenth- and eighteenth-century system of price regulation, whose disintegration is itself a significant symptom of the ascendency of market society, seems to me to represent clear evidence of a society still shaped by precapitalist economic conditions. Rodney Hilton observes: "It is unwise to speak of a capitalist system when the political and legal superstructure of society is still one shaped by pre-capitalist economic conditions. Political power, even in the hands of a ruling class whose economic basis is decaying can still retard the development of new economic and social forms. The history of England under the Tudors and Stuarts and of central and eastern Europe in the 19th century illustrates this point" ("Capitalism—What's in a Name?" in *Class Conflict and the Crisis of Feudalism* [London: Verso, 1990], pp. 201–2).

were made upon insufficient Considerations. But Q. [Query] What Damage to Trade, what Inconvenience, if all Contracts made upon insufficient Considerations were void.[177]

It is instructive to compare this eighteenth-century view of legal and commercial relations with Innes's analysis. On the one hand, we have Innes's claim in *Creating the Commonwealth* that under both Roman law and medieval practice, "the just price in ordinary circumstances was established primarily through the forces of supply and demand....Goods were 'worth as much as they can be sold for, commonly."[178] This rule,

---

177   L. H. Butterfield, ed., *Diary and Autobiography of John Adams*, vol. 1: *Diary, 1755–1770* (Cambridge, Mass.: Harvard University Press; 1962), p. 112. Morton Horwitz notes: "In Massachusetts, the eighteenth century rule was that a defendant in an ordinary contract case could offer evidence of inadequacy of consideration in order to reduce his damages. At three separate points in his student notes, written around 1759, John Adams indicated that 'sufficient Consideration' was necessary to sustain a contract action. 'No consideration, or an insufficient Consideration, a good Cause of Motion in Arrest of Judgment,' Adams noted in one of these entries" (*The Transformation of American Law, 1780–1860*, p. 165).

178   Innes, *Creating the Commonwealth*, p. 167. "The just price," Innes adds, "was an expression of the community's estimation, as arrived at by the market....Ethical principles typically entered over consumer information, not the price mechanism" (ibid., 167–68). Such stark generalizations about "Roman Law and medieval practice" are rather one-dimensional; two of the historians upon whom Innnes relies (Rothenberg and Jacques Le Goff) paint a more complex picture.

In her own treatment of medieval practice, Rothenberg briefly surveys the history of just price doctrine and medieval usury laws, concluding that "despite church doctrine, the charging of interest was in fact tolerated in Catholic Europe throughout much of the medieval period." She adds that, eventually, "canon law itself came to justify the charging of interest 'to make the creditor whole.' Until the change in canon law, however, the

prohibition of interest, whether vigorously enforced or not, constituted one of the most important constraints placed by church and state on economic activity" (From *Marketplaces*, pp. 8–9). Rothenberg emphasizes both social limitations placed upon the emergence of capitalism and the way such legal and religious constraints were gradually eroded, eventually not only coming to terms with economic change but, in fact, sanctifying it.

"Granted," Jacques Le Goff writes, "the economy of the thirteenth-century West is not the economy of the Trobriand Islands during the early twentieth century; but, though it is more complex, the notion of *reciprocity* nonetheless dominates the theory of economic exchanges in a society founded upon 'a network of relations' that are Christian and feudal" (*Your Money or Your Life: Economy and Religion in the Middle Ages* [New York: Zone Books, 1988], p. 19). "Just" prices and prohibitions on usury make sense within a society dominated by relations of reciprocity. With the growth of a money economy, however, "and when the wheel of fortune turned faster for knights and for noblemen," he concludes, "as well as for the burghers of the cities buzzing with work and business throwing off their old fetters, then Lady Usury became an important personage. The Church grew alarmed. Nascent canon law and, shortly afterwards, scholasticism—which tried to conceive of and to prescribe the relationship between the new society and God—sought to stem this growing usury. If I recite the litany of the principal measures taken by church councils and the most important texts, it is simply to show the

according to Innes, was applied in Puritan New England, where notions of just price were subordinate to market exigencies and were "fully responsive to the fluctuations of supply and demand." Exceptions to this rule were confined to cases of fraud, misrepresentation, or "imperfect price information." Once again, Innes's New England economy was shaped by "the blind, supply/demand-driven unconscionable force of the market" and, in Innes's version, even Gov. John Winthrop endorses buying cheap, selling dear, and admits that "even among the saints, sharp bargaining practices had been normal from the beginning." Capitalism, it would seem, really was there "from the beginning."[179] Historian Joyce Appleby, in her blurb on the jacket of *Creating the Commonwealth*, states that the book "retrieves the concept of capitalism from polemics and abstractions by embedding its practices and values in the cultural milieu of seventeenth-century New England." If by this she means that there were commercial attitudes embedded in the culture of early European settlements in North America, then she is on solid ground; however, it seems more likely that she believes that Innes's research proves what he says it does—that New England's Puritan society was, indeed, capitalist from the beginning. Here, I think, is just the point where we can most dramatically contrast Innes's (and perhaps Appleby's) view with John

---

spread and the strength of the phenomenon, and the stubbornness with which the Church fought it" (pp. 23–24).

Le Goff too acknowledges the way the language of prohibition and just price was hollowed out and lost its meaning; also like Rothenberg, he emphasizes the element of disruption which necessarily surrounds the emergence of a new social and economic order and how extensive a change actually had to take place in order to destroy precapitalist European society. Medieval ethical principles concerned all aspects of economic life, no t just "consumer information," and provided a considerable barrier to economic transformation, for a time. See also, Le Goff, *Medieval Civilization*, Julia Barrow, trans., (Oxford: Basil Blackwell, 1988): "When there was economic growth in the medieval west— as happened, as we have seen, in the eleventh and twelfth centuries—this growth was only the result of a growth in population....It was normal that this indifference and even

this hostility to economic growth should be reflected in the monetary economy sector and should put up strong resistance to the development within this sector of a spirit of profit....In fact, all medieval social categories were subjected to strong economic and psychological pressures, the effect if not the aim of which was to oppose all accumulation appropriate to bring about economic progress" (pp. 224–25).

179 Stephen Innes, *Creating the Commonwealth*, 170–172. With regard to the basic nature of New England's Puritan political economy, he concludes that even "taking into account the issue of historical anachronism, the weight of evidence—particularly in light of the English background of the early migrants—stands squarely on the capitalist rather than precapitalist side of the ledger....There is ample evidence that in their productive capacities, exchange ethics, and political economy, the Bay colonists were discernibly and irrevocably capitalists" (ibid., pp. 44–45).

Adams's perspective on early development of American political economy and the law of contract.[180]

We can apply Innes's assessment of Bay Colony capitalism to the specific hypothetical that Adams raises in his diary entry. In any economy governed by supply and demand, where legal regulation of contractual relationships is subordinated to market forces, it is incoherent to suggest, as Adams does, that there could be a "natural, immutable Law that the Buyer ought not to take advantage of the sellers Necessity, to purchase at too low a Price." Innes argues that, according to Cotton, scarcity of a commodity in no way renders unethical raising the price for that commodity. And the rule cuts both ways: a merchant who has paid "too dear" when prices are elevated must absorb the loss when commodity prices decline.[181]

No fraud is evident in the case described by Adams; neither are misrepresentation or ignorance of prices. Arguably, there is no coercion present, a fine distinction Adams conveys with his ironic comment that the debtor sells his possessions voluntarily, "in one sense."[182] Innes argues that the commercial law of Massachusetts Bay provided the unlucky or improvident neither escape nor protection from the vicissitudes of the market. Thus, if Puritan New England was indeed, and "irrevocably," a capitalist society (as the United States would indeed become by the middle of the nineteenth century), it is hard to imagine a natural immutable law in 1750 protecting individuals who enter a risky contract with unhappy results.

---

180 "In their behavior in the marketplace, *in their public policies regarding property, law, contract, and (especially) land tenure*, as well as in their Weberian virtues of industry, enterprise, and prudence, the New Englanders, I will argue, had clearly crossed the threshold that separates a pre-capitalist from a capitalist society" (ibid., p. 45; emphasis added).

181 Ibid., pp. 170–71.

182 *Diary and Autobiography of John Adams*, p. 112. See also, Edward Andrew, *Shylock's Rights: A Grammar of Lockian Claims* (Toronto: University of Toronto Press, 1988): "Adam Smith observed that 'when commerce is introduced into any country probity and punctuality always accompany it.' Smith noted: 'Of all the nations in Europe, the Dutch, the most commercial, are the most faithful to their word. The English are more so than the Scotch...' However, the honest Dutchman, Mandeville, averred that 'where Trade is considerable Fraud will intrude.' The apparent contradiction is that what the Dutchman called vice the Scots called virtue. However, closer analysis reveals that Mandeville was not criticizing the principle of contractual fidelity; he merely pointed out that merchants and manufacturers employ the arts of salesmanship and other business skills which appear to pre-commercial peoples as vice or fraudulence" (pp. 75–76). John Adams's evenhanded self-questioning and his sense of irony reflect a thoughtful attorney caught between the values of precapitalist social life and those of a market society.

Innes effectively provides a rough version of classical American contract law, the commercial doctrine that arose in the period immediately after the market society described by Rothenberg had become firmly established. But one cannot make sense of Adams's ambivalence on the question if the matter had been settled a century earlier, as Innes claims, in a capitalist or even *protomarket* New England. It is not just that the example Adams provides is virtually identical to the one that Dorfman draws from the Massachusetts Colonial Records for 1640; if Adams could no longer envision real value as distinct from market value, then how could he describe the goods sold by the poor man for one hundred pounds as actually being "worth" five times that much? Their worth, following Innes, should have been neither more nor less than what they sold for on the market. It is hard to understand how Adams could speak these words, or record them in his diary, if it had been uniformly accepted for a century that "Goods were 'worth as much as they can be sold for.'"[183]

Lester Thurow, describing just the sort of superstructural adjustment I have described here as taking place within American law once the market had triumphed, suggests that the emergence of capitalism necessitated a corresponding ensemble of ideological adjustments. "In the Middle Ages," he asserts, "avarice was the worst of all sins and the merchant could never be pleasing to God"—or pleasing to the courts, we might add, and the popular values such courts reflected in Massachusetts in the seventeenth century, as shown in the trial of Robert Keayne. "Capitalism," continues Thurow, "needed a world where avarice was a virtue and the merchant could be most pleasing to God. The individual needed to believe that he or she had not just the right, but the duty, to make as much money as possible." And this, of course, precipitated precisely that transformation in Protestant religious values and doctrinal interpretation which Tawney and, earlier, Max Weber described with such clarity and insight. What idea or social philosophy was crucial to this capitalist refashioning of religion and law, culture and commitment? Thurow concludes: "The idea that maximizing personal consumption is central to individual welfare is less than two hundred years old. Without this belief the incentive structure of capitalism has no meaning and economic growth has no purpose."[184] In other words, the very idea that Thurow sees as forming the ideological backbone of acquisitive society and the raison d'etre of capitalist civilization is less than two hundred years old. America

183 Innes, *Creating the Commonwealth*, p. 167.
184 Lesther C. Thurow, *The Future of*   *Capitalism* (New York: William Morrow, 1996), p. 11.

could not have been capitalist in the 1640s—dominated by Innes's unconscionable market forces — if Thurow is right and the idea animating capitalism came into being only within the last two hundred years. But Thurow is not alone, as we have seen, in recognizing that it was only during the last two decades before 1800 that the market finally triumphed.

Adams's diary entry presents a straightforward juxtaposition of a quite sophisticated market view of the legal system with a serious and realistic alternative. On the one hand, he proposes that the injustice of a single case can hardly counterbalance the larger economic disservice that would be done by subjecting all market transactions to a rule permitting contractual rescission simply on the basis of "insufficient Considerations." On the other hand, even setting aside the question of injustice, Adams bluntly asks what concrete damage would be done to trade if the law required adequate (not equal) consideration in all cases. If the answer is that commercial inconvenience would be considerable, indeed intolerable, you have an argument for pretty much doing away with contractual notions voiding agreements where consideration is inadequate (as in the properly capitalist period). If, however, the answer is that commercial disruption would not reach an unacceptable level so long as the number of contracts thus rescinded was sharply limited and confined to egregious cases, then you have an argument for a limited inadequacy of consideration rule (characteristic of the state capitalist period).

Of course, one can always answer Adams's query by asserting that because Justice trumps Inconvenience, fairness ranks higher than profits, and the law should not enforce contracts unless it is clear that there is an approximate equality of consideration being exchanged. It was just such a doctrine against which Robert Keayne so vigorously rebelled.

What is admirable in Adams's presentation, however, is that he invites a systematic, cost/benefit comparison of how two divergent legal rules, two different social policies, would turn out if actually adopted. This is an approach contemporary historians and economists might do well to follow, rather than seeking to insulate contemporary economic decision-making from criticism or trying to "retrieve capitalism" (and the history of commercial law) from polemical debate. Regardless of the precise point in time where we draw a line indicating that America became "fully capitalist," we should not draw that line, in my view, prior to Adams's meditation on the nature of a developing American contract law in the 1750s.[185]

---

185 New York University legal historian William E. Nelson, describing the Massachusetts legal system in the prerevolutionary period, argues that to the "extent that the legal system

was capable of affecting social reality, it insured that the distribution of wealth did not change substantially or rapidly over time and that men had well-defined places in their community and well-defined relationships with the community's other men. Incentives for individuals to compete with each other for control of economic resources were eliminated, and one cause of social instability was thereby reduced." Perhaps needless to say, Robert Keayne was that extraordinary individual who felt it was sometimes necessary to swim against the current, and thus sought to compete for available economic resources as well as impose new definitions on his relationships with other members of the community.

Reversing our up/down metaphor (and Renner's norm/substratum distinction) while still echoing the Bailyn/"moral economy" school synthesis, Nelson concludes that the "total picture of the law of exchange that emerges, then, is one of a substratum of doctrine insuring that exchanges of goods and services would normally occur at the rates that were customary or otherwise reasonable at the time of the exchange....In short, it did not allow people to increase their wealth by making speculative or otherwise one-sided exchange bargains. It sought rather to promote stability by insuring that a person who gave up wealth in one form would receive equivalent wealth in return" (*Americanization of the Common Law: The Impact of Legal Change on Massachusetts Society, 1760–1830* [Athens: University of Georgia Press, 1994], pp. 46, 61). After briefly quoting from the work of Bailyn and James Henretta, Stephen Innes states in a footnote that "[s]upporting this perspective from the vantage point of law and jurisprudence, William E. Nelson asserts that customary standards of reasonableness governed wage and price levels in early New England" (*Creating the Commonwealth*, pp. 360). He then provides a brief quote

from Nelson, which says exactly what he just finished saying and ends his treatment of Nelson's research right there.

Harvard University Professor of Government Shannon C. Stimson finds Nelson's research a good deal more useful and more compelling. Specifically relying upon Nelson's interpretation of *how* "customary standards of reasonableness" were imposed through law, she concludes that "the scope of colonial jury determination reached beyond determinations of fact to substantive questions of law. William Nelson has argued that the power of the colonial jury to 'find law' was almost unlimited. He attributes this power to various rules and practices regulating the division of function between judges and juries. For example, Nelson notes that the frequent use of the general issue, which left to juries the ultimate determination of the legal consequences of the facts of the case as well as 'the practice of giving juries conflicting instructions on the law emanating both from counsel and from the several judges of the court', encouraged juries to 'select the rules for determining the legal consequences of the facts'" (*The American Revolution in the Law* [Princeton: Princeton University Press, 1990], p. 49).

See also Horwitz, *Transformation of American Law*: "Modern contract law is fundamentally a creature of the nineteenth century. It arose in both England and America as a reaction to and criticism of the medieval tradition of substantive justice that, surprisingly, had remained a vital part of eighteenth century legal thought, especially in America. Only in the nineteenth century did judges and jurists finally reject the longstanding belief that the justification of contractual obligation is derived from the inherent justice or fairness of an exchange" (p. 160). Rothenberg, though not always agreeing with him, nevertheless, makes good use of Horwitz's research; inexplicably, Innes does not.

CHAPTER III

THE GREAT DIVIDE

*A disputation on the common law of contract and how it
was rent by a new system of social relations; the sad plight of
various litigants related; Aristotle and Corwin admitted in
evidence on the rule of law itself. The latter is placed in doubt
while reconciliation of constitutional decisions on matters
pertaining to the Contracts Clause and monopoly grants is
made into an intellectual adventure, of sorts. A digression
concerning Justice Scalia is followed by further adventures
of mercantilism before the courts; a discourse on three legal
theorists, not always recognized as such, introduces
application of their ideas to law and economic change in the
United States. The riddle of apparent doctrinal contradiction
is resolved. Charles River Bridge portrayed as mercantilism's
Gettysburg, and then the War itself is explained in terms
of liberal versus authoritarian capitalist approaches to
nineteenth century social transformation. A bridge is crossed.*

At that moment, the holy Mael clasped his hands and sighed deeply.

"Do you see, my son," he exclaimed, "that madman who with his teeth is biting the nose of the adversary he has overthrown and that other one who is pounding a woman's head with a huge stone?"

"I see them," said Bulloch. "They are creating law; they are founding property; they are establishing the principles of civilization, the basis of society, and the foundations of the State."

"How is that?" asked old Mael?

"By setting bounds to their fields. That is the origin of all government. Your penguins, O Master, are performing the most august of functions. Throughout the ages their work will be consecrated by lawyers, and magistrates will confirm it."

ANATOLE FRANCE[186]

Anatole France's aphorism about the bridges of Paris (revealing that the neutrality of legislation and equality before the law still mask an underlying inequity) may no longer reflect a particularly radical point of view. An African-American member of the Los Angeles Police Department, interviewed on ABC's *Nightline* the day after O. J. Simpson was acquitted said that the message the jury sent by their verdict was that if you have enough money, you can buy your way out of jail. France's point, that economic status indeed affects the availability of legal rights—has become conventional wisdom, notwithstanding the clichéd imagery of "blind justice" to the contrary.

The point that France wished to make in the above quoted excerpt from *Penguin Island*, however, remains a good deal more difficult to grasp. We are so accustomed to thinking in Hobbesian terms of law *and* order,[187] the rule of law versus anarchy and violence, lawfulness contrasted with civil disobedience, working within the system versus tearing it down, and

186 Anatole France, *Penguin Island*, A. W. Evans, trans. (New York: Dodd, Mead, 1909), p. 52.

187 Consider the following description of the Hobbesian perspective by University of Chicago political scientist Russell Hardin: "If Hobbes' vision of anarchy, including the anarchy of revolutionary times when government fails, is compelling, then his account fits the problem of maintenance of an extant government against revolutionary threats better than it fits the problem of choosing an initial government. We can all more readily coordinate on the unique extant government than on any of the many possible forms of government we might create out of our anarchy. Mutual advantage is essentially the central moral claim for Hobbesian order. We obey a particular government because failure of the government through revolution will be worse for virtually all of us, at least for all of us in the present generation" ("My University's Yacht: Morality and the Rule of Law," in *The Rule of Law* [New York: New York University Press, 1994], pp. 209–10).

so on, that it is easy to forget a cardinal fact of modern social life: law and violence often go hand in hand. I do not mean to point out that the forces of law and order are sometimes compelled to rely upon the use of violence. That is true; the state constantly seeks reinforcement of its monopoly on the "legitimate" use of force. Rather, what I want to point our here is how law and violence, legal change and violent change, are part of a single, continuous process. Viewed in this light, law and violence are identically symptomatic of a deeper shift in the substratum or infrastructure of society. The rise and consolidation of capitalism in the United States in the decades following the Revolution had a dramatic impact on the development of the common law. What state judiciaries could not accomplish, constitutional lawyers and judges sought to achieve. And what remained undone, after both common and fundamental law had been transformed, was accomplished through civil war. Thus, legal change and the deployment of massive military force served the same revolutionary goals.

It is especially ironic that some of the most violent moments in nineteenth century American history (for example, Shiloh, Antietam, Gettysburg), seem in retrospect to have been absolutely crucial events, essential in their own right to the development of a liberal rather than authoritarian form of capitalism in the United States.[188] Anatole France's association of legality with violence, property with conquest, strikes home—certainly on any dispassionate reading of modern history. But in the United States in the middle of the nineteenth century, what alternative was there?

I. THE COMMON LAW

We begin by looking closely at the development of the common law of contract during the first half of the nineteenth century. An 1822 New York case, *Seymour v. Delancey*,[189] decided by a nationally renowned jurist, Chancellor James Kent, involved an owner of two farms who agreed to

---

188 "For five years civil war raged. In terms of casualties and destruction it was by far the greatest war in which any "developed" country was involved in our period, though relatively it pales beside the more or less contemporary Paraguayan War in South America, and

absolutely beside the Taiping Wars in China" E. J. Hobsbawm, *The Age of Capital 1848–1875* [London: Weidenfeld and Nicolson, 1975], p. 142).

189 *Seymour v. Delancey*, 6 Johns Ch. 222 (1822); for case excerpts, see Stephen B.

exchange them for a one-third interest in urban property situated in Newburgh, New York. The exchange did not, in fact, take place at the time of the agreement and, subsequently, the farm owner's heirs were sued by the owner of village lots (i.e., the urban property just mentioned) who sought performance of the original contract. Kent refused to enforce the contract because "at the date of the agreement, the village lots were not worth half the value of the country farms." Relying upon "a very great weight of authority" for the proposition that a contract should not be enforced "where the consideration is so inadequate as to render it a hard bargain, and an unequal and unreasonable bargain," Kent went so far as to suggest that "inadequacy of price may, of itself, and without fraud or other ingredient, be sufficient to stay the application of the power of this Court..." Kent believed that, in *Seymour*, the value of the interest in village lots was inadequate to the point of giving the character of "hardship, unreasonableness and inequality to the contract..."

"What was not acceptable," asserts Stephen Innes, describing what he regards as the state of market exchange in New England by 1641, "was fraud, collusion, or the failure to perform one's contractual obligations."[190] Two centuries later, Chancellor Kent's understanding of what is unacceptable is clearly broader: *also* unacceptable, according to Kent's "very great weight of authority," is any exchange in which inadequacy of consideration is so great as to make the bargain hard or unreasonable. Fraud and misrepresentation need not be shown. In point of fact, from Dorfman's discussion of Puritan restrictions on the sale of goods at half their worth, to John Adams's diary entry a century later, to Kent's ruling in *Seymour*, there is consistent evidence of a common distinction between market values and real values.

"After observing that under the civil law contracts for sale of land were rescinded by judicial authority if the price was below half the value of the land," note Stephen Presser and Jamil Zainaldin, "and that even under the Code Napoleon rescission could be granted if the price was $7/12$ths below the 'real value', Kent refused specific performance."[191] So long as the law distinguishes between market values and *real* values, it is impossible to argue that the market alone dictates prices and knowledge about them. So

Presser and Jamil S. Zainaldin, *Law and Jurisprudence in American History* (3d ed., St. Paul: West Publishing, 1995), pp.279–281; Kermit L. Hall, William W. Wiecek, and Paul Finkelman, eds., *American Legal History* (New York: Oxford University Press 1991), p. 175.

190 Stephen Innes, *Creating the Commonwealth* (New York: W. W. Norton and Co., 1995), p. 175.

191 Presser and Zainaldin, *Law and Jurisprudence*, p. 280.

long as contracts go unenforced because of inadequacy of consideration—a degree of inequality in the values exchanged that seems harsh and unfair—then exchange ethics cannot be collapsed into "the blind, supply/demand-driven unconscionable force of the market." The history of contract law, outlined in this chapter, provides as strong a challenge to Innes' account as did the history of commercial relations surveyed in the last chapter.

"Another indication of the equitable nature of damage judgments in the eighteenth century," argues Harvard legal historian Morton Horwitz, "was the almost universal failure of American courts either to instruct juries in strict damage rules or else to reverse damage judgements with which they disagreed." After assessing a juridical practice which ran directly contrary to the market-driven contract theory, Horwitz concludes that "the community's sense of fairness was often the dominant standard in contract cases."[192] If the community's sense of fairness was often the measuring stick for the legitimacy of economic exchange in the eighteenth century, it would be surprising indeed to discover that market forces had exhausted that measurement in the previous century.

Horwitz points out that the "prevailing legal theory of consideration was expressed by Chancellor Kent as late as 1822, on the very eve of the demise of the doctrine that equity would not enforce unfair bargains. In contract actions at law, he wrote, where a jury determined damages for breach of contract, 'relief can be afforded in damages, with a moderation agreeable to equity and good conscience...' Eighteenth century American reports amply support Kent's statement."[193]

In both law and equity, then, judges and juries constructed rules that, on balance, continued the regime of social control of prices, at least until the beginning of the nineteenth century. That is just the point in time, however, when an emergent capitalist organization of exchange relations finally provoked superstructural adjustment. If eighteenth-century contract doctrine remained "essentially antagonistic to the interests of commercial classes," as Horwitz asserts, all that would soon change.[194] What subsequently happened to Kent's decision in *Seymour*, on appeal, provides a clear signal of what was coming.

The owner of the village lots, dissatisfied with Kent's imposition of a non-market ethic of exchange, was unwilling to abandon his claim on the

---

192 Morton Horowitz, *The Transformation of American Law, 1780–1860* (Cambridge, Mass.: Harvard University Press, 1977), p. 166.
193 Ibid., p. 165.
194 Ibid., p. 167.

country farms and, thus, appealed the decision in *Seymour*.[195] One way to look at the result on appeal is to focus on facts that were omitted from Kent's analysis. Consider, for example, that "the owner of the two farms against whom the action was brought had previously purchased the two-thirds interest in the city lots, and that he might have suspected that the city lots would dramatically rise in value if a proposed Navy Yard were built in town."[196] Seen in this light, the agreement into which the parties originally entered appears to have been a "risking" one where the value of the city lots was, in fact, speculative.

Why should courts remake contracts where the element of uncertainty of value may well have been bargained for by the parties themselves? In *Seymour*, it can be argued, the owner of country farms offered them in exchange because he would receive, in return, the missing piece of the puzzle—the outstanding portion of the city lots he already owned—which might become more valuable if a naval yard project, was approved. Seen from this perspective, this was not a case of inadequacy of consideration at all. And there is a point, in Senator Sudam's appellate opinion, where he admits that a contract is enforceable only when the agreement is "*fair, just* and *reasonable*; that the contract must be founded on *adequate consideration*; and that it must be free from *fraud*, *misrepresentation*, *deceit* or *surprise*" (emphasis added). One could wager then, that Sudam and Kent agreed as to the law but simply disagreed on the relevant facts.

However, the better view of the second *Seymour* decision is that it hinged more on legal than factual disagreements between the two tribunals. In the view of the appellate court, the doctrine endorsed by Kent no longer corresponded to the exigencies of a growing capitalist economy. While paying lip service to the doctrine of inadequacy of consideration, Sudam appears to reject that traditional mechanism for protecting those who are incautious in their commercial dealings. "I cannot assent to the doctrine," he wrote, "that inadequacy of price may, of itself and without fraud or other ingredient" be sufficient to preclude the court from enforcing contracts since it is well known that "purchases are constantly made upon speculation; that the value of real estate is fluctuating; and that there, most generally, exists an honest difference of opinion in regard to any bargain, as to its being a beneficial one, or not." What most haunted Sudam was the specter of an entrepreneurial economy frustrated by med-

---

195 *Seymour v. Delancey*, 3 Cow. 445 (1828); for case excerpts, see Presser and Zainaldin, *Law and Jurisprudence*, pp. 280–281; Hall et al., *Legal*

History, pp. 175–177.

196 Presser and Zainaldin, *Law and Jurisprudence*, p. 280.

dling judges, "interfering with the contracts of individuals," as he put it, "and sporting with their vested rights."[197]

In the *Seymour* decisions, then, and throughout early-nineteenth-century case law, we see the courts beginning to move away from traditional equitable doctrines of contract; in so doing, they demonstrate an increased willingness to embrace both the market and its unvarnished results, its winners and losers. Indeed, according to Kermit L. Hall, William M. Wiecek, and Paul Finkelman, *Seymour* on appeal "anticipates a modern marketplace, based on securities, speculative contracts, and other kinds of risky investments. Sudam's opinion supports such an economic environment, but at the expense of those who might enter into blatantly unfair bargains out of ignorance."[198]

A perfect illustration of the latter is the 1815 Tennessee case, *White v. Flora and Cherry*.[199] Jesse Flora inherited from Lazarus Flora a grant for 274 acres of land, but Jesse had only a general idea of where the land actually was. After a futile attempt to find the property, Flora came to White's residence and asked if he might have any idea where the land was. White claimed he did not, but after considerable persuasion agreed to help find it in exchange for half the property, should it be found. "The parties then went to an attorney to have writings drawn," according to the case report, at which time Flora acknowledged "he was illiterate, and a stranger in the country." The Tennessee Supreme Court then provides a seemingly straight-faced rendition of what happened next: "The agreement was signed…and both parties went on to Nashville, which was only a few miles, to search the register's office. White got a copy of the grant, and the next day…White found where the land was, and that it lay within or two or three miles of his own house…There is no satisfactory proof going to show that White knew where the land was situated, before he made his contract with Flora."

Perhaps only William Faulkner could do justice to the facts of this case, along the lines of his wisely comic novel, *The Rievers*, so attuned as his writing is to the cupidity of some men, the cunning of others, and the general folly of trusting in lawyers and courts to set right the damage done. Cooke, J., delivering the opinion of the court, no longer even pays lip service to the doctrine of inadequacy. First, he ruled that the appearance White may have known where the land was all along, did not consti-

197 Kermit Hall, et. al., *Legal History*, pp. 176–177.
198 Hall et al., *Legal History*, pp. 177–178.
199 *White v. Flora and Cherry*, 2 Tenn.

(2 Overt.) 426 (1815); excerpted in Presser and Zainaldin, *Law and Jurisprudence*, pp. 276–279.

tute solid proof of fraud. Second, the court states that the "mere circumstance of the sum paid being greatly inferior in value to the thing contracted to be purchased, will not, of itself, be sufficient to set aside an
agreement..." The court in *White* had no problem dispensing with the
doctrine relied upon by Kent in *Seymour.*

Cooke's language in explaining equity away is noteworthy: "The sum it
really cost White to find the land is, as we conceive, not the proper question; the bargain was clearly a risking one; it might cost only a few dollars
to find the land, or it might cost the worth of the land itself. At the time
the contract was made, it was utterly unknown to the parties, and impossible to tell which had the advantage..." The court would have been well
advised not to dwell on this part of the opinion too long. Even if they
were determined to do away with gross inadequacy of consideration as a
basis for refusing to enforce a contract, surely they would have done better
simply saying so. Instead, they accept the dubious claim that White knew
not where the land was.

Cooke concludes, "If White had in the end, been put to an expense
more than sufficient to absorb the whole value of the land, an event which
no man can say was impossible, could a court of equity have relieved
him?" Not, it would seem, this court; though one suspects that White's
attorney—especially if he is the same one who claimed to have made certain that Flora understood the agreement—would have found a way. It is,
in any event, this kind of reasoning that makes *White v. Flora and Cherry*
an especially memorable marker in the doctrinal history of the great
transformation.[200]

200 Donna Kline observes that it "was clear in the
nineteenth century that [the right to bargain
as to terms] was considered an indispensable
part of the doctrine of freedom of contract.
With the exception of the usury laws,
relatively few terms of contracts were set by
statute or by the courts [which] would enforce
contracts where the exchange was unequal,
provided that there was no coercion or fraud
and that both parties gave up something, no
matter how small." It is hard to imagine what
could be smaller than what White gave up in
exchange for half of Flora's 274 acres. "Morton
Horwitz," Kline adds, "has argued that this
rule reflected a subjective theory of value.
That is, Horwitz argued essentially that courts
permitted parties to write their own ticket
because it was generally thought that the

items of exchange have no intrinsic,
ascertainable value."
    This is precisely what the Tennessee
Supreme Court says in *White:* the assertion
that "no man can say" what the value of
White's consideration might be is as close as
you can come to claiming an item exchanged
has no knowable, or "ascertainable" value.
Nevertheless, Kline concludes: "It is perhaps
more plausible to say—and certainly more
easily supported by the cases—that the
courts believed that each person was the best
judge of the worth of an item to him....
Regardless of the theory of value involved,
it is clear that the courts felt that the state,
in the person of the judges enforcing
contracts, would be tyrannical if it were to
impose the judge's values upon the parties

Nor is *White* alone in the degree to which a market-oriented court was willing to avert its glance from purported fraud. Stanford law professor Lawrence Friedman, in his history of American contract law, cites the Wisconsin case, *Mowry v. Hill*, where a litigant claimed that a sale of railroad stock "had been induced by false statements 'that the railroad company was then in good and solvent condition, and that the capital stock thereof was then worth 100 cents on the dollar.' In fact the stock was then worth only five cents on the dollar. The court saw no 'fraud' whatsoever. 'Representations as to value,' said the court, 'have not generally been held to constitute such a fraud as would avoid the contract, even though the value was greatly exaggerated.'"[201] We are no longer dealing with a consideration doctrine which, as far as Kent was concerned, was sufficient to prevent enforcement of contracts where there is excessive profit on either side, even absent fraud; now it is a question of evisceration of the concept of fraud itself—to such a degree that the railroad's conduct in *Mowry* was not sufficiently fraudulent to actually "avoid the contract." Exaggeration, as well as speculation, now appeared to be par for the course. Buyer beware! "Nor did the statement that the railroad was 'solvent' have any legal effect," concludes Friedman; indeed, the court added insult to injury by asserting, "it 'might have been true, and still the stock have been worthless. The value of the stock of a company depends upon the value of its property over and above its debt.'"[202]

What Friedman says next about *Mowry* is crucial to our understanding of everything that was going on in American law during the transition to a capitalist market economy: "In [*Mowry*] the court was insensitive, to say the least, to the notion that a seller must deal honestly with his buyer. The court upheld the 'security of transactions'; but this does not really explain the decision. The key seems to lie in the court's idea of 'value.' 'Value' can

to the contracts" Donna C. Kline, *Dominion and Wealth* (Dordrecht, Holland: D. Reidel Publishing Co., 1987), pp. 91–92. One assumes that the phrase, "distinction without a difference" was invented for comparisons like this. Horwitz calls it a "subjective" theory of value; Kline says it is more plausible to believe that courts were saying an individual was stuck with his own evaluation of the exchange. What would one call that if not a "subjective" theory of value? More to the point, though, when one has accepted that all values are subjective, in Kline's sense, then one has destroyed the legal

category of objective values—the precapitalist community's conception of real value— against which what a person receives can be measured in order to ascertain whether the contract was fair (hence whether it should be enforced). And *that*, as both Horwitz and "the cases" make clear, is what subordinating objective or real values to market values is all about.

201 *Mowry v. Hill*, 11 Wis. 146 (1860). See Lawrence M. Friedman, *Contract Law in America* (Madison: University of Wisconsin Press, 1965), pp. 99–100.

202 Ibid., p. 100.

have a double meaning. It can refer to a (theoretical) inherent worth, based on actual input of resources, such as cash, raw materials, and labor...Another kind of value is speculative; it is the risk element, the potential capital gain that may accrue to an asset."[203]

In other words, *Seymour* on appeal, *White*, and *Mowry* all evidence a judicial commitment to Friedman's second definition of "value" and to the creation of a common law of contract which would, in effect, ratify market decisions. Judges would not only avoid interfering with the contracts of individuals and sporting with their vested rights as Sudam put it but, as Friedman indicates, they would enhance the security of commercial transactions (put plainly, they would ensure that you could actually take to the bank your market winnings). Moreover, as Friedman goes on to suggest, this change in the law responded to a genuine difficulty encountered by courts when determining exactly how to value something *in a market society* without considering market value. What Friedman refers to as "inherent worth" we can easily assimilate to what we have called "real" value, and what he calls "speculative value" to "market" value. Once courts have demonstrated that real values (inherent worth) must give way to the "risk element," it is clear that a market economy has made its presence felt within the legal superstructure of a society. *Here*, finally, Innes' blind and unconscionable market forces carry the day. In a capitalist society, what anything is worth—to borrow a phrase from the *White* decision—no man can say: it is "worth" whatever you can get for it.

In his now classic *Legal Foundations of Capitalism*, University of Wisconsin professor and social reformer John R. Commons notes this distinction between real and market value. Employing his own theory of historical stages of development, Commons concludes that each stage precipitates significant change in economics, jurisprudence, and politics. For Commons, an economist and jurisprudential materialist in the long line stretching from Adam Smith to Richard Posner, transformations in the field of economics naturally produce alteration in the ancillary terrain of politics and law. "In *economics*," he argues, the transition from an agricultural society to an industrial capitalist one "implies the expansion from use-value or 'real' values, to exchange-values, from production and consumption to buying and selling, from things to prices. The use-values, that is 'real values' of physical things proceed from the direct control of lands, chattels and human beings in both the production and consump-

203 Ibid.

tion of wealth. Exchange-values, or prices, spring up between the primary producers and ultimate consumers, through a nation-wide division of labor, a credit system and freedom in bargaining. Upon the foundation of use-value was built feudalism; upon nominal values or prices, capitalism and industrialism."[204]

Real values pushed aside by exchange values, declining employment of equitable remedies, and the rise of *caveat emptor*, judges subordinating common law to the market—these were the hallmarks of an entrepreneurial revolution that took the nineteenth-century legal system by storm.[205] State appellate decisions cut buyers loose, forced them to go it

---

204 John R. Commons, *The Legal Foundations of Capitalism* (Madison: University of Wisconsin Press, 1968), pp. 313–14. See Horwitz, *Transformation*: "The first thinker to see the relationship between the de-physicalization of property and its abstraction into market value was the great Wisconsin institutional economist John R. Commons. His penetrating—though often obscure—*Legal Foundations of Capitalism* (1924) traced the late-nineteenth-century judicial shift to a market value standard. The Rate Cases, in particular, allowed Commons to appreciate that it was the guarantee of a *future* income stream that determined the *present* value of property. 'All value is expectancy,' Commons proclaimed" (p. 162).

It is true that the Rate Cases discussed by Commons were from the last quarter of the nineteenth century; but these constitutional decisions merely put the final touches on the larger judicial project that had preoccupied nineteenth-century courts. "Finally, in the first Minnesota Rate Case, in 1890 the Supreme Court itself made the transition and changed the definition of property from physical things having only use value to the exchange-value of anything. . . . Thus Justice Field's definition of property as the exchange-value of property was approved and, therefore, the protection of that property was brought under the jurisdiction of the federal courts conformably to the Fourteenth Amendment....[T]he transition in the definition of property from physical objects to exchange-value was completed" (Commons, *Legal Foundations*, pp. 14–16). Again, the development Commons here describes, conceived broadly, is that of

the "evolution of Anglo-American systems of Value and Valuation" (ibid., p. 313).

205 "By the end of the eighteenth century," according to Bryn Mawr economist Richard B. DuBoff, "labor power and instruments of production, including land, were being transformed into commodities bought and sold in the marketplace like any others. Private property, individual mobility and acquisitiveness, and commercial exchange were all prevalent. They were powerful solvents of institutions and values incompatible with capitalist expansion (subsistence farming, religion as a guide to personal behavior, social ties based on communal or nonprice norms)" (*Accumulation and Power: An Economic History of the United States* [Armonk, N.Y.: M. E. Sharpe, 1989], p. 11). Stuart Bruchey remarks: "Although the story of profits is not necessarily the story of economic growth, abundant evidence shows that these were flourishing times, that the level of welfare of numerous economic groups was rising. In the first place, hundreds of merchants in the leading seaboard cities of the North and East appear to have taken advantage of the 'brilliant prospects held out by commerce.'...Flourishing shipping and trade also promoted urban and economic development in the northeastern states. The percentage of the population living in urban places rose from 5.1 percent in 1790 to 7.3 percent in 1810, with most of the increase occurring in the four major ports of Boston, New York, Baltimore, and Philadelphia.... Other business organizations and institutions also grew in numbers to accommodate the

alone. Purchasers had to carefully inspect whatever they bought before they paid for it. No longer were judges enthusiastic about remaking contracts for hapless litigants; no longer were courts willing to insulate the improvident, commercially inept, or simply ignorant from the rough and tumble of the marketplace.[206]

needs of the reexport and carrying trades. Among these were bill brokers and commission houses, marine insurance companies and commercial banks, the latter then being incorporated in increasing numbers because of the ease with which charters could be secured from state legislatures" (*Enterprise* [Cambridge, Mass.: Harvard University Press, 1990], p. 147).

Charles Sellers writes in *The Market Revolution* [New York: Oxford University Press, 1991]: "Economic takeoff spread from the major ports as merchant capital and government-fostered transport pushed an accelerating division of labor across the interior....As surging trade set off surging productivity, capital began shifting from commerce to more profitable wage exploitation. By the 1830s and 1840s, trade and specialization among the four port/hinterland regions were creating an integrated sectional market embracing the Northeast as a whole. Meanwhile commercial agriculture spread over the West and South; and during the second half of the nineteenth century, the Northeast market reached out to incorporate these sections into an integrated national market. By midcentury, capital and technology were converting enough central workshops into mechanized factories to convert the market revolution into a staggeringly productive industrial revolution" (pp. 20-21).

Curtis P. Nettels observes, in his foreword to *The Emergence of a National Economy* (Armonk, N.Y.: M. E. Sharpe, 1989): "By 1815—in the forty years since 1775—America had been transformed. In this brief interval, Americans had endowed themselves with a vast domain, made easy entrance into it on a freehold basis, dedicated it to internal free trade, and decreed that contracts and debts should be uniformly protected by federal law. The country had its own money of account and a national coinage; the large fund of

federal securities provided capital for business, substitutes for currency, and a safe medium for long-term investments. Modern commercial banks—in considerable part directed by the central banking of the First Bank of the United States—expanded credit for industry and trade. Thus stimulated, innovation flourished—in transportation, manufactures, insurance; at the same time, Americans, freed from the restraints of the British colonial system, pushed their commerce into many remote or once forbidden areas" (p. xiii).

Robert Heilbroner and Aaron Singer assert in *The Economic Transformation of America* (3d ed., Fort Worth, Texas: Harcourt Brace, 1994): "The first source of the expansion in the value of total output must be self-evident. It is the sheer increase in the amounts of labor and capital that enter the production process. In 1860 our total labor force was about eleven million, over five times the 1800 labor force of 1.9 million. During the period 1810—1860 the total value of manufactures increased roughly tenfold, from $200 million to just under $2 billion, while capital invested in manufactures actually grew twentyfold, from about $50 million to $1 billion. By 1860 the United States was second only to Great Britain in manufacturing" (p. 125).

206 Picking up where Harvard's David Landes left off, Emory University economic historian Rondo Cameron argues that "government can play a variety of possible roles with respect to the economy. The most fundamental function of government in the economic sphere, one that cannot be avoided or abdicated, is the creation of the legal environment for economic endeavor. This can range from a pure 'hands-off' policy to one of total state control. The cardinal sin in this area is neither intervention nor nonintervention, but ambiguity. The 'rules of the game' should be clear, unequivocal, and enforceable. They include, as a minimum, the definition of rights (property and other) and

responsibilities (contractual, legal, etc.)"
(*A Concise Economic History of the World* [New
York: Oxford University Press, 1991], p. 317).
Cameron argues not that governments should
seek to accomplish the impossible (that is,
abolish law's indeterminacy) but, rather, that
they should effectively identify a set of rules
that can be relied on to further the goals of
development under a particular economic
regime. Although Cameron is sufficiently
unorthodox that he eschews terms such as
capitalism, mercantilism, and industrial
revolution (none of which Landes, for
example, hesitates to use), his rendition of the
relationship between economic system and
legal environment is not very different than
that portrayed by Engels a century before.
Engels's observation that when politics and
economics run in the same direction then
development is rapid, whereas when politics
and its construction of Cameron's "legal
environment" lag behind economic change
then development is impeded. The remnants
of precapitalist and mercantilist legal
arrangements presented just such an obstacle
to be superseded as nineteenth-century
common law and constitutional interpretation
unfolded.

Recall, as well, Mitchell Franklin's
observation that "as the old legal order,
consecrating the old property relations is
threatened, it becomes arbitrary and
equivocal" "Legal Method in the Philosophies
of Hegel and Savigny," *Tulane Law Review*
44, (1970, p. 770). The host of doctrines at the
heart of what Lawrence Friedman, Grant
Gilmore, Presser and Zainaldin, and others
now call the "classical theory" of contract law
were specifically adopted in order to align
law's development with that of the emerging
capitalist economy, to clarify a system still
permeated with precapitalist remnants, and to
make American common law reflect what
Franklin calls the "course and outcome of the
struggle between the old and new social
forces…" (ibid.).

James Willard Hurst notes: "Of course,
businessmen's invention—and, even more,
their initiative—joined that of lawyers to
fashion instruments of dealing; and of course,
men abide by their agreements for other
reasons than fear of lawsuits. But it does not
exaggerate the role of law to see that its

procedures and compulsions were inextricably
involved in the growth of our market
economy. By providing authoritative forms
of dealing and by enforcing valid agreements,
we loaned the organized force of the
community to private planners.…For a time
the century seemed well satisfied to make
the market its central institution, and contract
set the legal framework for market dealing.
Thereby, also, the law greatly extended its
reach into the organization of the economy"
(Law and the Conditions of Freedom
[Madison: University of Wisconsin Press,
1956], p. 11–12). This is what Cameron means
by governmental construction of a legal
environment conducive to economic endeavor
and, more specifically, what Landes means
by the progressive adaptation of legal usages
to requirements of a both rational and
mobile capitalism.

"The nineteenth-century presumption,"
Hurst concludes, "always favored the exercise
of the autonomy which the law of
contract gave private decision makers. Thus,
the restrictive features of the doctrine of
consideration were offset by the general
rule that, absent such gross inadequacy of
consideration as to evidence fraud, mistake,
or duress, the courts would not make the
existence of a contract turn on the judges'
appraisal of the worth of the exchange"
(ibid., p. 12).

According to Kermit L. Hall: "In the
eighteenth century, most sales occurred in
local markets in which title to specified goods
passed from one hand to another.…The
expanding commercial market economy of
the nineteenth century changed these close
relationships.…The doctrine of *caveat emptor*
demonstrates the impact of the theory of
contract on the law of sales. *Caveat emptor*
means buyer beware. The doctrine, which had
its roots in the English common law, provided
that in the absence of fraud or breach of an
express or implied warranty, the buyer buys
at his own risk, relying on his own estimate
of the quality and suitability of goods. In
colonial America, the sound-price doctrine
undermined *caveat emptor*, and judges
subscribed to the view 'that a sound price
warrants a sound commodity.' Simply put, in
colonial America, if one paid a reasonable
price for a good that proved defective, it

In a New York case, *Seixas and Seixas v. Woods*, the plaintiffs sought to return to the seller a shipment of worthless peachum wood because it was not the valuable brazilletto wood for which they had bargained and paid a fair price. The wood had indeed been labeled and described as brazilletto in the bill of parcels.[207] The plaintiffs did not allege fraud or seek damages; they merely wished to return the wood and have their payment refunded. Judge Smith Thompson of the New York Supreme Court put the legal question at issue squarely enough by asking "whether there was an implied warranty, so as to afford redress to the plaintiffs, or whether the maxim *caveat emptor* must be applied to them." Thompson concluded that in the absence of an express warranty or evidence of fraud in the sale,

followed that *caveat emptor* would not apply" (*The Magic Mirror* [New York: Oxford University Press, 1989], p. 121).

Caveat emptor was thus held at bay by the nearly feudal constraints of the common law. Thomas Sowell observes that "[t]heUnited States, therefore, 'without any feudal past' has in Engels' words, nevertheless 'taken over from England a whole store of ideology from feudal times, such as the English common law...'" (*Marxism* [New York: William Morrow, 1985], pp. 63–64).

Thus we see a glimpse both of Adam Smith's materialist jurisprudence and of Hegel's dialectic: once the precapitalist economies of Puritan New England and the colonial period are undercut by the rise of a market society, *caveat emptor* comes to fore, while equitable theories such as the sound-price doctrine are pushed to the back. With the rise of state capitalism, in the twentieth century, an ensemble of equitable doctrines were "rediscovered," only to lose ground once again in the new legal environment of global capitalism. Materialism sheds lights on the basic fault lines, the direction of social determination, but only a dialectical approach can come to grips with change, the dynamic of contradiction, and the curious way in which each period of legal history both transcends and preserves the doctrinal past.

Classical contract, Lawrence Friedman concludes, represents a "deliberate relinquishment of the temptation to restrict untrammeled individual autonomy of the completely free market in the name of social policy. The law of contract is,

therefore, roughly coextensive with the free market. Liberal nineteenth-century economics fits in neatly with the law of contracts so viewed....[I]n a rough way, the rise and fall of the law of contract paralleled the rise and fall of liberal economics as a working philosophy. Mention of a few of the doctrines of the law of contract shows how closely the two ideological systems fit together" (*Contract Law*, pp. 20–21). Not only do legal doctrine and economic philosophy fit together but the legal superstructure and economic infrastructure of Friedman's nineteenth-century free market society fit together as well. Grant Gilmore adds a useful clarification, while commenting on this very same passage from Friedman: "I assume that Professor Friedman's 'liberal nineteenth century economics' refers to what is often described as laissez faire" (*The Death of Contract* [Columbus: Ohio State University Press, 1974], p. 106). What is important for our purposes, at this specific juncture, is simply to record the agreement between Friedman and Gilmore with respect to a certain symmetry between nineteenth-century American capitalism and the contract law which it generated and by which it was, in turn, rationalized. It was this classical law of contract, more than any other aspect of the legal system, that provided Cameron's "rules of the game" with an overarching definition of legal rights and responsibilities.

207 *Seixas and Seixas v. Woods*, 2 Cai. R. (N.Y.) 48 (1804); for case excerpts, see Hall, et al., *Legal History*, pp. 172–173.

there was nothing his court could do for the Seixases, and thus the doctrine of *caveat emptor* applied. "I see no injustice or inconvenience resulting from this doctrine," Thompson observed dryly, "but, on the contrary, think it best calculated to excite that caution and attention which all prudent men ought to observe in making their contracts."

Contemporary economists who lament the declining competitiveness of American products in the world market will no doubt be intrigued by the outcome of another contracts case, this one heard by the Supreme Judicial Court of Massachusetts in 1822. In *Goulding v. Skinner*, plaintiffs wanted their money back when they discovered that the machine cards they had purchased were of such poor quality as to be of little or no value.[208] Their legal pleadings stated specifically that the seller had warranted the cards to be good and merchantable; to prove their claim as to how the cards had been represented to them, the purchasers "read to the jury an advertisement stating that machine cards were manufactured by the defendants, warranted equal to any in America." The jury returned a verdict for the plaintiffs but the seller appealed, arguing that a "warranty that the cards should be equal to any in America cannot be considered the same with a warranty that they should be good and merchantable...The best cards in America might not be merchantable." That argument *won* on appeal and a new trial was ordered.

In the Pennsylvania case *McFarland v. Newman*, Newman had purchased a colt from McFarland.[209] It was proved that the colt had demonstrated symptoms of an incurable disease for about a year prior to being sold; at the time of sale though, McFarland claimed the horse was suffering from ordinary distemper and had been sick only a few days. The jury awarded seventy-five dollars to Newman, but McFarland appealed, and the appellate court reversed with this comment: "As the case goes back to another jury, it is proper to intimate the principle on which a correct decision of it must depend. Though to constitute a warranty requires no particular form of words, the naked averment of a fact is neither a warranty itself, nor evidence of it...." Apparently, even if a "naked averment" turns out to be a naked lie, sellers will not be held responsible for what they have said.

In a market economy, as far as these courts were concerned, a rational person apparently would trust no one. Or, perhaps, as Grant Gilmore put

---

208 *Goulding v. Skinner*, 18 Mass. (1 Pick.) 162 (1822); for case excerpts, see Presser and Zainaldin, *Law and Jurisprudence*, pp. 281–282.

209 *McFarland v. Newman*, Watts (Pa.) 55 (1839); for case excerpts see Hall, et. al., *Legal History*, pp. 173–174.

it in his candid description of an emerging classical theory of contract, the "theory seems to have been dedicated to the proposition that, ideally, no one should be liable to anyone for anything."[210]

Even the U.S. Supreme Court, whose most familiar decisions are generally confined to cases involving interpretation of federal statutes or the resolution of major constitutional issues, adopted the doctrine of *caveat emptor* in the 1817 case *Laidlaw v. Organ*.[211] Beyond the result in the case itself, however, what makes *Laidlaw* memorable is the reporter's preservation of arguments of counsel, specifically the case put forth on behalf of the defendant in error: "Even admitting that [my client's] conduct was unlawful, in *foro conscientiae*, does that prove that it was so in the civil forum? Human laws are imperfect in this respect, and the sphere of morality is more extensive than the limits of civil jurisdiction. The maxim of *caveat emptor* could never have crept into the law, if the province of ethics had been co-extensive with it. There was, in the present case, no circumvention or manoeuvre practiced by the vendee, unless rising earlier in the morning, and obtaining by superior diligence and alertness that intelligence by which the price of commodities was regulated, be such. It is a romantic equality that is contended for on the other side."[212]

Romance and fantasy! It is these twin evils, secretly harbored in the little heart of "girl number twenty," which got Sissy Jupe into so much trouble in Charles Dickens's great novel of (capitalist) manners, his fictional but realistic portrait of an emerging market society's system of values: *Hard Times*.[213] That is what the book's "fantastic" circus characters are all

---

210 Gilmore, *Death of Contract*, p. 14.

211 *Laidlaw v. Organ*, 15 U.S. (2 Wheat.) 178 (1817). Horwitz remarks: "Verplanck's essay was written as an attack on the doctrine of caveat emptor, which had then only recently been adopted by the United States Supreme Court in *Laidlaw v. Organ* (1817), one of the first cases to come before the Court involving a contract for future delivery of a commodity. The case, Verplanck wrote, raised 'the important and difficult question of the nature and degree of equality in compensation, in skill or in knowledge, required between the parties to any contract...in order to make it valid in law, or just and right in private conscience'" (*Transformation*, p. 182). Elsewhere Horowitz observes that *Laidlaw* "grew out of a futures contract for sale of tobacco purchased by a merchant who had advance knowledge that the United States and England had signed a peace treaty ending the War of 1812" (ibid., p. 331). The opinion of the Court in *Laidlaw*, delivered by Chief Justice John Marshall, stated that the "question in this case is, whether the intelligence of extrinsic circumstances, which might influence the price of the commodity, and which was exclusively within the knowledge of the vendee, ought to have been communicated by him to the vendor? The court is of opinion that he was not bound to communicate it" (*Laidlaw v. Organ*, 15 U.S. [2 Wheat.] 178, 195 (1817)).

212 *Laidlaw v. Organ*, 15 U.S. (2 Wheat.) 178, 193 (1817).

213 Charles Dickens, *Hard Times* (London: Penguin Books, 1985). There is an interesting

about. The author put them there to provide as indelible and surreal a contrast as possible with the rising class of factory owners and their sniv-elling satraps. Was it perverse frivolity, so alien to the spirit of capital and "possessed of no facts," which led late rising plaintiffs in error to rely to their detriment upon the veracity of commercial colleagues? Reread the passage just quoted, from *Laidlaw*, but pretend you do not know its source. Could Charles Dickens, the greatest nineteenth-century novelist in the English language, the creator of innumerable rising bourgeois mer-chants and managers and lawyers with ice in their veins, of estimable bankers and insufferably censorious school teachers, have written this speech any more perfectly?

Recall how much attention Max Weber paid, in *The Protestant Ethic and the Spirit of Capitalism*, to the "classical purity" of Benjamin Franklin's own version of this rhetorical style;[214] it would clearly be appropriate to cite such legal argument in a history of how the spirit of capitalism gradu-ally pervaded the legal superstructure of American society. Just as clearly, this spirit did not merely consist in getting up early, buying cheap and selling dear, regarding time as money, and the whole panoply of bourgeois homilies. There was more to it than that.

2. CONSTITUTIONAL LAW

Consider arguments of counsel in another Supreme Court case from the same period, *Ogden v. Saunders*.[215] Like *Laidlaw*, *Saunders* was a contracts

---

Masterpiece Theatre version, *Hard Times* (British Broadcasting Co., 1994), which the PBS Video cassette box information describes as "Dickens' stinging indictment of Victorian mores…" Yes, but not only that. See E. P. Thompson, *William Morris: Romantic to Revolutionary* (London: Merlin Press, 1977): "Dickens's picture may be a caricature: but it is of the best order of caricature, which delineates the essential lines of truth. Mr. Bounderby, the coarse and avaricious mill owner of *Hard Times*, the type of the earlier Industrial Revolution, was now giving way to his more sophisticated cousin, Mr. Gradgrind. Gradgrind not only has power and wealth: he also has a theory to justify and perpetuate exploitation. The Victorian bourgeoisie had constructed from bits of Adam Smith and Ricardo, Bentham and Malthus a cast-iron theoretical system, which they were now securing with the authority of the State and the Law, and sanctifying with the blessings of Religion. The laws of supply and demand were 'God's Laws,' and in all the major affairs of society all other values must bend before commodity values" (pp. 8–9).

214 Max Weber, *The Protestant Ethic and the Spirit of Capitalism* (London: Routledge, 1992), p. 48.

215 *Ogden v. Saunders*, 25 U.S. (12 Wheat.) 213 (1827). See Richard E. Ellis, "Ogden v.

case but one with a constitutional dimension as well; consequently, it attracted some of the ablest (and most prominent) legal counsel in the young nation. At a time when the United States had no federal bankruptcy act, a debtor sought to escape his contractual obligation under a New York State insolvency law. The constitutional issues included whether Congress alone had the power to legislate in this area and, further, whether New York's statute violated the Constitution's prohibition on any state's adoption of a law "impairing the obligation of contracts" (that is, the Contract Clause).[216]

Messrs. Webster and Wheaton, the creditor's lawyers, argued that the New York law did indeed violate the Constitution and, in threatening the sanctity of contracts, threatened the very institution of private property. There were both grand legal and practical political reasons why this should be so, according to Webster and Wheaton. As to the law, the Constitution "meant to preserve the inviolability of contracts, as secured by those eternal principles of equity and justice which run throughout every civilized code, which form a part of the law of nature and nations, and by which human society, in all countries and in all ages, has been regulated and upheld." Needless to say, advocate of competitive capitalism though he was, Adam Smith would have turned over in his grave had he heard it claimed that the "obligation of contracts" was characteristic of all countries in all ages.[217]

Wheaton located authority for the Constitution's contract provision in natural law. He quotes Grotius, Burlamaqui, and Vattel as sources for the proposition that the Contract Clause was not a political creation but,

Saunders," in Kermit Hall, ed., *The Oxford Companion to the Supreme Court of the United States* (New York: Oxford University Press, 1992), p. 605.

216 U.S. Constitution, Article I, Section 10, Clause 1; see Douglas W. Kmiec, "Contracts Clause," in Hall, ed., *Oxford Companion to the Supreme Court*, pp. 195–96.

217 Consider, for example, Adam Smith, *Lectures on Jurisprudence*, R. L. Meek, D. D. Raphael, and P. G. Stein, eds. (Oxford, Eng.: Oxford University Press, 1978): "We find accordingly that in the first periods of society, and even till it had made some considerable advances, contracts were noways binding. [Nicolaos] of Damascus, an author quoted by Stobaeus (where we have many passages from him very

useful with regard to the state of society in the first periods of it) tells us that among some nations in the East Indies no contract was binding, not even that of restoring a depositum, that in which the obligation seems to be strongest as the injury in the breach of it is most glaring....Aristotle tells us also that even as far down as his time, there were severall states in Greece where the validity of contracts was not acknowledged, and that both to prevent the multitude of judicial proceedings, and also because, said they, one who enters into a contract trusts to the fidelity of the person and is supposed to have trust in him. He has himself to blame therefore if he is deceived, and not the law which [does not give him redress]" (pp. 88–89).

rather, a reflection of the "nature of things" in themselves.[218] If contract law, insolvency statutes, and the like were regarded as instances of social policy, within the competence of government, private property could never be made secure in a democracy, even one that (at this point) denied the vote to most Americans. On the other hand, if the obligation of contracts, like the rights of property holders generally, somehow preexisted political society and was derived from the natural order, then political entities (such as legislatures) had no right to interfere with private commercial agreements. New York state, in particular, had no right to pass a law permitting an individual to escape his financial obligations to others. Not for nothing did Wheaton remind the justices of the Supreme Court that the obligation of contracts "springs from a higher source" than mere politics; it came "from those great principles of universal law, which are binding on societies of men as well as individuals."[219] By "societies of men"

218 Stephane Rials, a professor of law at University of Paris, traces the same line of authority as did Wheaton in his oral argument in *Saunders*, but he specifically highlights the contribution of Grotius, Locke, and Pufendorf. "And so Locke logically ends up affirming the legitimacy of resistance to oppression," Rials argues, "whenever public powers overstep the limits of their authority. Locke's emphasis on law influenced the French, but it was only elsewhere (notably in the United States) that his insistence on the limits of the will produced serious limits on legislative power" ("Rights and Modern Law," in Mark Lilla, ed., *New French Thought: Political Philosophy* [Princeton: Princeton University Press, 1994], p. 167).

Rials's essay contrasts the Grotius–Locke natural rights line of development with that of Hobbes, Montesquieu, and Rousseau; the latter he blames, for much of what he regards as defective in the modern French (as opposed to American) political process. "Nonetheless," he concludes on an upbeat note, "it is still possible to speak of a return to Locke in France today—or, if one prefers, of the victory of the American tradition of guaranteeing rights over the French" (ibid., p. 172). A quarter-century ago, it was not the "victory of the American tradition of guaranteeing rights over the French" that worried some French intellectuals but, rather,

the American tradition of guaranteeing *economic power* over the French: "Washington always tries to impose its own political decisions on foreign firms. A French automobile manufacturing company gave up the idea of installing an assembly plant in several countries because the Quai d'Orsay had been informed that the company would then lose its United States market. A French seed company gave up contracts concluded with certain countries, including Cuba, because the United States consulate informed it that its American suppliers would refuse its orders....And, needless to say, countries economically or financially dependent upon the United States lose their freedom of political and diplomatic initiative" (Claude Julien, *America's Empire*, Renaud Bruce, trans. [New York: Pantheon, 1971], p. 261).

219 *Ogden v. Saunders*, 25 U.S. (12 Wheat.) 213, 222 (1827). On the general process of anchoring rights of property and contract in natural law theory, Harvey Goldberg notes: "You must remember that over long ages from antiquity through the seventeenth century, in one successive society after another, even the governing classes and their ideologues treated private property as a social convention. In other words, as an institution which society itself had created and consequently which it could control, which it could limit, which it

he meant to indicate government, especially including state governments, which might well feel pressure to provide some lawful outlet for those suffering the most extreme form of economic hardship.[220]

Again, this was the legal argument; but there was also a policy argument, this time offered by Wesbster, a practical point whose significance was not lost upon his august listeners: "The relation between debtor and creditor, always delicate, and always dangerous whenever it divides society, and draws out the respective parties into different ranks and classes, was in such a condition in the years 1787, '88, and '89, as to threaten the overthrow of all government; and a revolution was menaced, much more critical and alarming than that through which the country had recently passed. The object of the new constitution was to arrest these evils; to awaken industry by giving security to property; to establish confidence, credit, and commerce, by salutary laws, to be enforced by the power of the whole community." This was an allusion to the difference between the American Revolution and one "more critical and alarming," one he believed, perhaps, could have happened in the United States in 1789,[221]

could even abrogate in the interest of some transcendent good—whether that be the service of God, whether it be the preservation of the social organism, whether it be the protection of the poor. But the bourgeoisie, and its liberal ideologues in the emergent capitalist societies, did not treat private property as an artificial convention. Instead, they came to treat it as what they called a natural and inviolable right. That it was an institution that predated the organization of society itself, that was born in the state of nature, that consequently conferred upon man and the uses of property a naturalness and an inviolability that made it immune to any kind of social restraint or social coercion." Harvey Goldberg, "The Ideology of Private Property," Goldberg Center History Lecture Audiotapes (Madison, Wis.: University of Wisconsin; Jan. 24, 1977).

220 See, e.g., Everett Pepperrell Wheeler, *Daniel Webster: The Expounder of the Constitution* (Littleton, Colorado: Fred B. Rothman & Co., 1986; reprint of G. P. Putnam's Sons edition, 1905): "The severe financial distress which began with the restrictions upon our commerce created by the embargo before the War of 1812, and which was intensified by the suspension of specie payments and by the

disorganized condition of the currency at the close of that war, had led many of the states to pass insolvency laws." Interestingly enough, Wheeler feels compelled to point out, during his discussion of Webster's attack on the New York law discharging debts in bankruptcy, that in 1830, three years after *Ogden v. Saunders*, "Mr. Webster wrote a letter to the Prison Discipline Society of Boston, advocating the mitigation of the laws for the imprisonment of debtors" (p.67). Thus Wheeler's Webster, we are inclined to assume, was really a pretty decent fellow after all.

221 See, for example, Stuart Bruchey, "Law and Economic Change in the Early American Republic," in *American Industrialization, Economic Expansion, and the Law* (Tarrytown, N.Y.: Sleepy Hollow Press, 1981): "As we all know, the years immediately following the ending of the Revolutionary War in 1783 were years of tension and grave social unrest....[T]he combined downward pressure on prices—i.e., the loss of both markets and specie—[made] for severe deflation throughout the decade after 1782. Prices of American exports fell in relation to those of imported goods, the terms of trade declining each year between 1784 and 1789 from an index of 112 in the former year to 88 in the

one perhaps more like the revolution that *did* happen that year in France.[222] The federal government, represented for the moment by the U.S. Supreme Court, the ultimate guardian of constitutional order, must not risk losing control over the delicate process of "discharging debts when they are to be discharged without payment,"[223] with all that such a loss of control might portend for the very fabric of society.

If an almost evenly divided Supreme Court's attempt to resolve the many legal issues raised in *Saunders* turned out to be somewhat contradictory, and did not present the ringing endorsement of constitutionally protected property rights for which Webster hoped,[224] the policy objective he

latter. The resultant burden of debt was especially onerous in Massachusetts, where taxes which Alexander Hamilton said were the highest in the nation, together with the execution of court orders for the sale of the property of delinquent taxpayers, created an explosive situation....Serious disorders followed. In Rhode Island, for example, merchants refused to accept paper, some of them closed their stores, and would-be buyers resorted to force and rioting, with farmers pledging to withhold produce from townsmen refusing to take paper at par with specie. In 1786, armed attacks on creditors and tax collectors took place in Maryland, and a large band of armed men imprisoned the legislature in New Hampshire. That same year unrest in Massachusetts culminated in Shays' Rebellion, the well-known affair in which a Revolutionary War captain led a group of farmers into revolt against the government of the state" (pp. 89–91).

222 See Lloyd S. Kramer, "The French Revolution and the Creation of American Political Culture," Joseph Klaits and Michael H. Haltzel, eds. in *The Global Ramifications of the French Revolution* (Cambridge, Eng.: Cambridge University Press, 1994), p. 26; James Miller, "Modern Democracy: From France to America," *Salmagundi* (fall 1989), p. 177; William Appleman Williams, *America Confronts a Revolutionary World: 1776-1976* (New York: William Morrow, 1976), pp. 44–58.

223 *Ogden v. Saunders*, 25 U.S. (12 Wheat.) 213, 247–249.

224 The case was decided by the slimmest of margins, 4–3, in favor of upholding the constitutionality of New York's bankruptcy law. Ellis argues that *Saunders* "was the only case where Chief Justice Marshall dissented in an important constitutional decision" ("Ogden v. Saunders," p. 605). And Maurice Baxter, in his biography of Webster, asserts that "Marshall would have liked to have incorporated Webster's argument into a majority opinion, for he found the lawyer's reasoning quite sound....Underlying his argument was a conception of natural law which, Webster explained, created the obligation of every contract even in the absence of positive law" (*One and Inseparable: Daniel Webster and the Union* [Cambridge, Mass.: Harvard University Press, 1984], p. 171).

The *Saunders* result in no way altered the rule adopted by the Court in an earlier decision that a state bankruptcy statute seeking to provide for the discharge of debts contracted *prior* to the enactment of the statute itself would necessarily run afoul of the Contract Clause. *Saunders* had presented a different situation, where the debt was contracted after the state bankruptcy statute became law and thus, presumably, its existence was a fact of which both debtor and creditor were aware. One way of reading *Saunders* is that it simply incorporated a previously existing bankruptcy law and its stipulations into the terms of a contract entered into within the jurisdiction of the bankruptcy statute. Ellis notes that in *Saunders* on reargument, Justice William Johnson joined the original dissenters to form a new majority for placing sharp limits on the applicability of state insolvency statutes, like New York's,

had staked out was unambigous. Similarly, Justice John Marshall's objective in *Saunders*, according to Harvard professor of government Robert McCloskey, had been to "forbid any state law that impaired contracts in any way, and the acceptance of such a principle would have greatly enhanced the value of the contract clause as an instrument for the protection of private rights. But at this point even his usually acquiescent brethren called a halt, and in 1827 the court voted, four to three, to uphold a state bankruptcy law as applied to the debts contracted after its passage. Marshall dissented, and it is plain that the decision bitterly disappointed him; but he had much reason for self-congratulation all the same. With the help of the contemporary bench and bar, he had transmuted a clause of modest pretensions into a broad inhibition on the commercial laws of the states."[225] And Webster perfectly represented the forces of bench and bar to which McCloskey refers.

Webster's *legal* argument in *Saunders* only repeated the one he had made in the famous case of *Dartmouth College v. Woodward* a decade earlier, when he successfully defended the college from having its board of trustees effectively taken over by the state of New Hampshire.[226] The state's Jeffersonian-Republican governor and legislature had ousted the private college's trustees and enacted into law public control of the school. This, Webster claimed, was a perfect example of state government impairing the obligation of private agreements—in this case the college's royal charter dating from before the Revolution; thus New Hampshire had violated the Constitution's Contract Clause. The legislation against which Webster's client (and alma mater) complained had sought to take property rights from the institution's trustees and hand them over to someone else (here, state government)—just the sort of sporting with vested rights which common law courts were increasingly likely to resist. A decade before *Dartmouth College*, the U.S. Supreme Court had, in fact, ruled in the case of *Fletcher v. Peck* that, under some circumstances, the federal courts could overturn state laws that interfered with private contracts.[227] But how, asks McCloskey, could the "tentative suggestion of

to out-of-state creditors.

225 Robert G. McCloskey, *The American Supreme Court* (2d ed., rev. by Sanford Levinson [Chicago: University of Chicago Press, 1984], p. 50).

226 *Dartmouth College v. Woodward*, 17 U.S. (4 Wheat.) 518 (1819); see Alfred S. Konefsky, "*Dartmouth College v. Woodward*," in Hall,

ed., *Oxford Companion to the Supreme Court* (New York: Oxford University Press, 1992), pp. 217–48. Excerpts from the decision are found in Presser and Zainaldin, *Law and Jurisprudence*, pp. 325–39, and in Kermit Hall, et. al., *Legal History*, pp. 141–46.

227 *Fletcher v. Peck*, 10 U.S. (6 Cranch.) 87 (1810); see Sandra F. VanBurkleo, "*Fletcher v. Peck*,"

Fletcher in 1810 become the confident assertion of *Dartmouth* in 1819?"[228]

McCloskey's answer is that, in the interim, lawyers and judges, had been at work molding professional opinion on behalf of the interests of businessmen and property owners in America's emerging commercial society.[229] Thus, from the *Fletcher* decision in 1810 to powerful constitutional arguments advanced in *Dartmouth College* and *Saunders*, we can trace the development of the political economy, if you will, of Contract Clause jurisprudence. In the *Charles River Bridge v. Warren Bridge* case of 1837, where the state of Massachusetts sought to interfere with the terms of a charter granted to a private corporation, it is not surprising that the latter hired Daniel Webster to present its case to the U.S. Supreme Court. Once again, Webster provided a Contract Clause argument for insulating private property rights from public regulation; but this time, in spite of his eloquence and the *Fletcher/Dartmouth College* line of cases which he could now marshal on his side of the argument, Webster lost.[230]

In the decade after the American Revolution, the Massachusetts state legislature granted the Charles River Bridge Company a seventy-five year charter to operate a toll bridge between Boston and Charlestown. In 1828, the same body authorized Charlestown merchants to build a second bridge across the Charles River; once the new bridge's owners had made back their investment, the bridge was to become state property and be operated without charge. The Charles River Bridge Company saw this as a threat to its ability to make money and sought an injunction against the Warren Bridge Company, which was slated to build the new bridge.

in Hall, ed., *Oxford Companion to the Supreme Court*, pp. 304–05.
228 McCloskey, *American Supreme Court*, p. 49.
229 Ibid.: "The explanation is that the Court's 'constituency' had been at work on its behalf in the meantime. The idea that the contract clause might serve to protect private property from the states and the corollary idea that corporate charters could be included in such protection—these embryonic ideas had caught hold in the minds of lawyers and judges, had been fostered and developed by them, and had thereby been raised to the status of mature constitutional doctrines. By 1819, they were so well entrenched that the Supreme Court needed to do little more than stamp them with its formal sanctions. The *Dartmouth* decision is important then, not for its own accomplishments but for its

acknowledgement of results already achieved. Businessmen, secure in the possession of inviolable state-granted charters, could thank their stars for 'the inner republic of bench and bar' as well as for John Marshall" (ibid., pp. 49–50). Note McCloskey's reference to "results already achieved"—that is, achieved elsewhere, outside of public legal process, as well as his description of an *inner* republic, a state within the state.
230 *Charles River Bridge v. Warren Bridge*, 36 U.S. (11 Pet.) 420 (1837); see Elizabeth B. Monroe, "*Charles River Bridge v. Warren Bridge*," in Hall, ed., *Oxford Companion to the Supreme Court*, pp. 135–36 (New York: Oxford University Press, 1992). For case excerpts from *Charles River Bridge*, see Presser and Zainaldin, *Law and Jurisprudence*, pp. 582–95, and Hall, et. al., *Legal History*, pp. 146–50.

Charles River asserted that the charter it had been granted by the state of Massachusetts provided, in effect, a monopoly over bridge-building and toll-charging between Boston and Charlestown. Such state-granted monopoly charters were a common means of encouraging economic development during the first decades of the nineteenth century; with almost thirty years left on its charter, Charles River had a lot to lose if its charter were abrogated by legislative fiat.

Nevertheless, the Supreme Court ruled that neither the Contract Clause nor any other part of the Constitution prevented the people of Massachusetts, through their elected state representatives, from authorizing construction of a competing bridge. The new Jacksonian Chief Justice, Roger B. Taney, argued that legislative grants should be narrowly construed. The Charles River Bridge Company had placed a construction upon the language of their grant which gave them rights of exclusivity not fully conferred by the original charter; they took too much for granted, in a manner of speaking. However, Justice Joseph Story bitterly criticized Taney's legal rationale and it is, in fact, Taney's candid statement of the social policy basis for the Court's decision which has earned prominence in histories of Jacksonian America as well as chronicles of the Supreme Court.[231]

The Charles River Bridge Company, according to Taney, had sought to have an implied right of monopoly over the collection of tolls read into its grant from the state legislature. To this claim of implied right, Taney responded: "Let it once be understood that such charters carry with them these implied contracts, and give this unknown and undefined property in a line of traveling; and you will soon find the old turnpike corporations awakening from their sleep, and calling upon this court to put down the improvements which have taken their place." Perhaps needless to say, the image conjured up here by Taney—of turnpike companies rising from slumber in the earth—is as vivid as those employed by Smith or Marx (or

---

231 Monroe remarks: "Justice Story insisted in dissent that the Charles River Bridge charter was a form of contract granted for valuable consideration. The proprietors had offered to build the bridge to further the public good and the legislature had conferred the right to collect tolls. Where valuable consideration was received, courts should construe public contracts in favor of the grantee. Story's broad construction of the bridge charter inferred an exclusive grant to collect tolls along the line of travel. 'If the government means to invite its citizens to enlarge the public comforts and conveniences,…there must be some pledge that the property will be safe;…and that success will not be the signal of a general combination to overthrow its rights, and to take away its profits' (p. 608)" (*Charles River Bridge*," p. 136).

perhaps even Shelley). "The millions of property which have been invested," he continued, "in rail roads and canals, upon lines of travel which had been before occupied by turnpike corporations, will be put in jeopardy. We shall be thrown back to the improvements of the last century, and obliged to stand still, until the claims of the old turnpike corporations shall be satisfied; and they shall consent to permit these states to avail themselves of the lights of modern science, and to partake of the benefit of those improvements which are now adding to the wealth and prosperity, and the convenience and comfort, of every other part of the civilized world. Nor is this all." Taney then went on to contrast the modern world of towns and railroads and booming transportation infrastructures with a bygone age dominated by "old feudal grants." In the teeth of millions of dollars invested in transportation, the inexorable advance of society, and expanding prosperity and convenience, who could kowtow to the wishes of a feudal corporation bidding a nation to stop in its tracks? *Charles River Bridge* was only superficially about competing theories of how the technical legal language of grants and charters should be construed; it was really about competing models of economic development—indeed, the paramount value of economic competition itself.

Thus, juxtaposing the Supreme Court's Contract Clause analysis in *Charles River Bridge* with an opposite approach found in the previous line of Contract Clause cases—especially *Fletcher* and *Dartmouth College*—presents the legal scholar with an intriguing contradiction, resolution of which I now pursue tenaciously, if admittedly at some length.

Princeton University political scientist Edward Samuel Corwin, whom Kermit Hall describes as the "twentieth century's foremost academic commentator on the presidency, constitutional law, and the Supreme Court,"[232] quotes a key passage from Aristotle's *Politics*. The text contrasts two ways of governing: one that places authority within the ambit of law, thereby investing it with "God and reason only," and another that places authority within the power of men, which introduces "a beast, as desire is something bestial." Corwin then develops the dichotomy between law and men, reason and desire or passion: "Nearly two thousand years after Aristotle, the sense of this passage, condensed into Harrington's famous phrase, 'a government of laws and not of men,' was to find its way successively into the Massachusetts constitution of 1780 and into Chief Justice Marshall's opinion in *Marbury v. Madison*." Corwin cites Harrington's

232 Kermit L. Hall, "Corwin, Edward Samuel," in Hall,
     ed., *Oxford Companion to the Supreme Court*, p. 200.

Oceana and Other Works for the original formulation of the famous phrase "An empire of laws and not of men"—empires evidently having gone out of style in the years separating the two men—and concludes: "The opposition which it," i.e., Harrington's terse description of the rule of law, "discovers between the desire of the human governor and the reason of the law lies, indeed, at the foundation of the American interpretation of the doctrine of the separation of powers and so of the entire American system of constitutional law."[233]

Our problem is how to reconcile this scheme with the above-mentioned juxtaposition of *Dartmouth College* and *Charles River Bridge*, of existing precedent and apparent departure from rule. One way of doing so, of course, is to assert that prior to the Court's *Charles River Bridge* decision, the Constitution must have been changed. And it *was* changed, of course, twice before *Charles River Bridge*, but the Eleventh and Twelfth Amendments were already there when *Dartmouth College* was decided and neither figured at all in *Charles River Bridge* or changed the language of the Contract Clause. So had America departed not only from an initial interpretation of the Contract Clause but perhaps even from the rule of law itself?

One could argue that *Charles River Bridge* was, in essence, what lawyers like to call "confined to its facts." The case was distinguished from those which had previously been decided the other way by Taney throughout his opinion: first, the language of state-granted charters should be narrowly construed; second, the specific charter in question, properly construed, did not grant the rights maintained by the plaintiff. McCloskey offers one version of this argument himself in his effort to iron out apparent points of divergence between the Marshall and Taney Courts. Devoting only a single paragraph to this landmark decision, he suggests that in *Charles River Bridge*, there is "no challenge to the basic principles of Marshall's contract-clause doctrine—that a charter is a contract that binds the states—nor is there evidence in later contract-clause cases that the Taney Court was reckless of property rights, as the Whigs had feared."[234] The main problem with this analysis is that the Charles River Bridge Company's charter apparently did *not* bind the state of Massachusetts—certainly not in the way the company hoped, once Taney had "construed" it. Also, McCloskey uses the word "property" with no

233   Richard Loss, ed., *Corwin on the Constitution* (Ithaca, N.Y.: Cornell University Press, 1981), vol. 1, pp. 83–84. Corwin cites Harrington, *Oceana and Other Works*, p. 37.

234   Robert McCloskey, *Supreme Court*, p. 58.

sense of nuance or appreciation for the range of meanings the term can denote, some of them radically different. More specifically, with *whose* property rights were Taney and the Supreme Court, in fact, not to become reckless? In reality the most famous constitutional decision of the Jacksonian period was less about state government versus private property than about one set of property rights versus another, as we shall soon see.

Another conventional way, however, of synthesizing the Contract Clause cases is simply to argue that Taney was not Marshall and that, as the times changed, the Court's reading of the Constitution changed. It is just this sort of reading that McCloskey, quite the Marshall Court advocate and fan, seems to have resisted at times—for example, around 1837. In a very important sense, he is right about continuity between the Marshall and Taney Courts, though not at the level he indicates. But it is worthwhile asking, right now, whether an acknowledgment that who decides matters—that changes in the composition of the Court over time are likely to lead to changes in the Court's understanding of what the Constitution means—by itself, negates Harrington's distinction between law and passion, or politics. Put more simply, do changes in constitutional interpretation, resulting from changes in Court personnel, mean that in a sense, men rather than laws govern? Even politically conservative justices and constitutional scholars have found ways of answering this question in the negative. The simple truth that "who decides matters" can in fact be affirmed in a way that does not deny Harrington's "rule of law" doctrine.

A recent illustration of this balancing act can be found in public broadcast station WETA's two-part documentary, *This Honorable Court*. The film, an historical overview of American constitutional adjudication, includes a number of conversations with sitting members of the Supreme Court—relaxed, informal, and in small groups. When journalist Paul Duke asks the justices how conscious they are of the Court's precedents, Justice Byron R. White responds: "If you didn't have some respect for precedent, the law would be in a shambles. No one would have any basis for reliance." White acknowledges that he, like most of his colleagues, often finds himself in dissent, yet he nevertheless accepts the majority position and applies that view to new cases that arise. "The next term," he adds stoically, "you may have to write an opinion based on the precedent that you didn't agree with but now you accept." Justice Antonin Scalia interjects: "Of course, it's a little unrealistic, too, to talk about the Court as though it is a continuing, unchanging institution rather than, to some extent, necessarily a reflection of the society in which it functions." Duke seizes upon this opening, asking: "If societal attitude is indeed important are you saying then that the Court follows the election returns?" The camera cuts to a shot of Justice Lewis Powell shaking his head ever so slightly from left to right with a pained expression on his face; an audible groan seems to escape from Justice White. "No, don't misstate me as having said that," Scalia objects. "I don't think societal attitude is important to my decision at all, and I doubt whether any of the other justices would think that." Glancing to left and right, at White and Powell, he adds, "Above all else, a judge is there to be a protection against at least *temporary* societal attitudes." Scalia adds a few more civics homilies on judicial autonomy before returning to what he really wanted to say: "My only point is"—he leans forward and shakes his finger at Duke—"if the society changes you are eventually going to be drawing judges from that same society, and however impartial they may try to be, they are going to bring with them those societal attitudes, in their *heads*, not because they are trying to reflect them."[235]

Here the film cuts to a series of images, from long shot down to close-ups, of a large and boisterous political demonstration in front of the U.S. Supreme Court building in Washington. The feeling is very similar to that recreated in an opening sequence from the motion picture, *The Pelican Brief*. In voice-over, Paul Duke says that "the Court may ignore the election returns but it has never gone against public opinion for long."[236]

Though this film segment lasts only a few minutes it is surely rich material. Why does the body language of White and Powell suggest that they are arrayed on the side of judicial "restraint" while Scalia's remarks suggest judicial "activism"? We are accustomed to associating judicial restraint with political conservatism and activism with liberalism. Yet, White was a Kennedy Democrat,[237] described by Kenneth Starr and Kate Stith as the last of the New Dealers or New Deal liberals,[238]—and his willingness to join the majority in *Metro Broadcasting, Inc. v. Federal Communications Commission*, narrowly decided by a 5–4 vote, was crucial

235 *This Honorable Court: Inside the Supreme Court* (Washington, D.C.: Greater Washington Telecommunications Association, 1988).

236 For an interesting new assessment of the relation between courts, public opinion, and much more, see Duncan Kennedy, *A Critique of Adjudication* (Cambridge, Mass: Harvard, 1997).

237 See, for example, Edwin Guthman, *We Band of Brothers* (New York: Harper and Row, 1971).

238 Kenneth W. Starr, "Justice Byron R. White: The Last New Dealer," *Yale Law Journal* 103 (1993), p. 37; Kate Stith, "Byron R. White: Last of the New Deal Liberals," *Yale Law Journal* 103 (1993), p. 19.

to the preservation of federally mandated affirmative action programs. (*Metro* was overruled five years later by *Adarand v. Pena* soon after White retired from the Supreme Court.)[239] Even Powell provided the closest thing possible to a majority opinion in *Regents of the University of California v. Bakke* in 1978, which held, among other things, that race *could* constitutionally be considered as part of a properly designed affirmative action program.[240] Scalia, on the other hand, is accurately perceived to be one of the current Court's most intellectual, as well as conservative, justices. Why then do their perspectives on judicial review seem to have been switched, given their substantive political histories?

Perhaps, if during the years when he was playing football at Colorado and before, White had been a little older and cast his fortunes with the early New Deal—and, like some Legal Realists, felt politically compelled to discredit the Supreme Court's philosophy of judicial restraint—then he might have been more willing to embrace the kind of insight into the nature of the system offered by Scalia. Conversely, were Scalia not part of the global capitalist generation, seeking to destabilize the structure of judicial interpretation developed from the Roosevelt days through those of the Warren Court, he might have deferred to White's admonition regarding the bedrock value of precedent.

Thus, the fundamental contradiction Corwin lays out in his commentary on Aristotle and Harrington, Marshall and *Marbury*—the dichotomy between governments of law and those of men—can be preserved, at least in appearance, even during dramatic infrastructural shifts. In the transition from one watershed period to the next, what started on the anarchic and threatening side of the law/men dichotomy—desire, passion, politics—very subtly shifts to the *other* side, safely within the patrician citadel of law, reason, and order. However unexpected it may be to incorporate into Hegelian materialist jurisprudence Scalia's "product of the times" approach to legal sociology, doing so avails us of his willingness to account for doctrinal transformation *within* a government of laws and also his acknowledgment that constitutional law is "necessarily a reflection of the society in which it functions." Scalia's notion that judges carry the new order "in their heads," rather than consciously trying to revolutionize the system, is in fact quite similar to views held by both Legal Realist Karl Llewellyn and socialist theoretician Friedriech Engels.

239 *Metro Broadcasting, Inc. vs. Federal Communications Commission*, 487 U.S.547, 110 S.Ct. 2997 (1990); *Adarand Constructors,*

Inc. vs. Pena, 115 S.Ct. 2097 (1995).
240 *Regents of the University of California v. Bakke*, 438 U.S. 265, 98 S.Ct. 2733 (1978).

Scalia's attempt to paint what he regards as a common but *false* picture of the Supreme Court—as a "continuing, unchanging institution," as he put it—fits our dialectically Smithian approach to history: the superstructure rests upon the underlying modes of subsistence or forces of economic development, but because those forces conflict, economic change transforms the law from institution into process. Scalia, who reflects the values of a rising global capitalist period, punctures the conventional judicial wisdom of White and Powell, who reflect the values of a *superseded* state capitalist period; and his gesture is no different than that of Cardozo or the Legal Realists, who reflected the values of a *rising* state capitalist period, who fifty or sixty years earlier destabilized the legal culture in place since at least the end of the nineteenth century.

This task is almost invariably accomplished within the system, through appellate argument and judicial reasoning, as Karl Renner observed in his work on legal norm and economic substratum. Thus, in the 1995 *Adarand* decision, which sharply restricted Congress's ability to sponsor minority preference programs, the dissenting justices complained that *stare decisis* was being ignored and prior case law abandoned.[241] But that, of course, is how even such landmark decisions as *Brown v. Board of Education* and the constitutionalization of school desegregation had originally come about themselves.[242] So there is an unacceptable way of saying that who decides

241 *Adarand v. Pena*, 115 S.Ct. 2097, 2126 (Justice Stevens, with whom Justice Ginsburg joined, dissenting): "The Court's concept of *stare decisis* treats some of the language we have used in explaining our decisions as though it were more important than our actual holdings." But that is the point: just as *stare decisis*, fidelity to precedent, as a mode of legal reasoning can be contrasted with "result-orientation" or policy argument (once again, law versus politics), policy differences can in fact be fought out *within* the framework of *stare decisis* simply through bifurcation of that concept into language versus holding, a kind of "doubling" of which Stevens here accuses the majority.

However much the substance of the majority opinion in *Adarand* may have distressed dissenters, or at least seemed to them to have been built upon faulty judicial foundations, the decision nevertheless almost immediately affected how the nation conducts its business. See, for example, Steven A.

Holmes, "White House to Suspend a Program for Minorities," *New York Times* (March 8, 1996): "After a long review of affirmative action, the Clinton Administration has decided to suspend, for at least three years, all Federal programs that reserve some contracts exclusively for minority and women-owned companies, officials said today. The officials added that the three-year moratorium on set-aside programs, which have proved to be the most hotly debated type of affirmative action, would include such stringent conditions for reintroducing the programs that it was doubtful they would ever return....The President ordered the review to determine whether Federal affirmative action programs are effective and if they comply with last June's Supreme Court decision in Adarand Constructors v. Pena..." (p. A10).

242 *Brown v. Board of Education of Topeka*, 347 U.S. 483 (1954). In *Brown*, the Court struck down the infamous "separate but equal"

matter (for example, "following the election returns,") which all three justices quoted above from *This Honorable Court* reject out of hand and a perfectly acceptable way of acknowledging virtually the same thing: the Supreme Court of the United States, says Scalia, cannot be a "continuing, unchanging, institution."

3. CREATIVE DESTRUCTION

The contradiction between a government of laws and of men—between, in short, law and politics—is present in the very heart of many of the contract cases just surveyed. This should come as no surprise, considering that these cases are located on the nineteenth-century legal system's equivalent of the San Andreas fault—an infrastructural shift from precapitalist to capitalist social relations. And these cases, moreover, provided a crucial mechanism for readjusting American contract law, bringing it into sync with new economic values and structures. The subordination of law to *politics*, of course, is fatal for the "rule of law" ideal, but one can subtly recharacterize the law/politics dichotomy as [doctrine/policy] versus politics, in which case politics—now "policy"—has been adroitly shifted from one side of the opposition to the other. Thus, what was impermissible becomes perfectly natural and, in the process, nearly invisible.

But what, then, constitutes the residual category "politics"? Legislation, perhaps; certainly the mob, revolution, violence, and war— but even these, in the right circumstances, can be shifted to the legal side of the dichotomy. That is the process by which supreme charters of the rule of law—constitutions and their amendments—come into being. More modestly, however, let us stick with doctorine and policy a little longer. Interestingly, the contracts cases I have discussed tend to include *both* doctrinal and policy arguments, single cases reflecting a dual approach to legal change.

Recall John Adams' diary entry about the appropriate disposition of his hypothetical case in which someone is compelled to sell everything he

doctrine—which had made its initial appearance in the case of *Plessy v. Ferguson*, 163 U.S. 537 (1896)—and further ruled that public school segregation on the basis of race violated the Constitution's guarantee of equal protection of the laws. A unanimous opinion, delivered by Justice Earl Warren, stated candidly that any language in *Plessy* which contradicted the Court's findings in *Brown* was now simply rejected.

owns at a fraction of its value in order to avoid imprisonment for debt. Adams describes legal coercion thus: "Here the seller is wronged, tho he sell [them?] voluntarily *in one sense*." As long as the coercion/voluntariness rule retains a capacity or potential for having or making *more than one sense*, then the rule can be infinitely adjusted to accommodate reconfigurations of remnant and precursor, dominant and subordinate, real and market values—in short, the redistribution of social power.

Rather than suppressing the inevitable consequences of choosing one rule over another, however, Adams plunges ahead and questions inconvenience and damage to trade, injustice and duty to neighbor, what policy best serves a new country. A lawyer's diary and a judicial opinion reflect two different legal genres; but one frequently discovers in common law and constitutional decisions both doctrinal magic (judicial acrobatics, legal irony, and so forth) and the candid acknowledgment that a rule has outlived its usefulness. Some factor external to or unrecognized within a prior line of cases, now, today, simply preempts precedent—or at least, what the losing side happens to believe that *stare decisis* commands. On occasion, courts deploy policy argument as a threat: if you do not like the doctrinal readjustment fashioned by the majority, then the judges will simply junk existing rules which no longer work, if they ever did.

Policy arguments are always close at hand. Senator Sudam on appeal in *Seymour*—which, again, involved country farms and city lots—pointed out that land values fluctuate, rendering the whole idea of "real" or, at least, stable values in that market suspect. Pleading rules to one side, attorneys for the plaintiff in *Goulding*—which involved machine card warranties—complained that common sense dictated that a "common advertisement is not to be viewed with as much strictness as a deed." Gibson, C. J., deciding *McFarland*—which involved a horse with glanders—denounced what he conceded was the existing law regarding evidence of a warranty, dismissing the view of judges whom he believed had adopted a mischievous rule "in pursuit of a phantom in the guise of a principle of impracticable policy and questionable morality...."

Examples from the common law of property tell the same story. In *Parker v. Foote*, decided by the Supreme Court of New York in 1838, appellate judges effectively overturned established common law doctrine permitting prescriptive easements for light and air.[243] Employing the sophistry that there could never be an adverse use of light and air, since

---

243 *Parker v. Foote*, 19 Wend. 309 (1838), excerpted in
Presser and Zainaldin, *Law and Jurisprudence*, pp. 293–98.

the injury suffered is "merely ideal or imaginary," the court struck down one more "obstacle to progress." While acknowledging existing precedent for the very doctrine being abandoned, the *Parker* opinion states simply that the "learned judges who have laid down this doctrine have not told us upon what principle or analogy in the law it can be maintained": the letter of the law was defeated if not by spirit then by principle and analog. And if that did not seem especially persuasive, Bronson, J., for the Court, adds that even if doctrines of ancient lights and easements for light and air had been part of the English common law, such a rule "cannot be applied in the growing cities and villages of this country, without working the most mischievous consequences." That is your central holding in the case: a snappy doctrinal argument buttressed with reference to policy. In the transition from a capitalist to state capitalist legal system in the twentieth century, which involved an equivalent retooling of common law rules and procedures, Benjamin Cardozo became grand master of this technique, the iron fist of policy in the velvet glove of doctrine.

In another property case *Van Ness v. Pacard*, the U.S. Supreme Court, taking up rather mundane business coming from the District of Columbia, transformed common law rules on waste and fixtures—doctrines that, among other things, favored traditional property interests by making it difficult, on the expiration of a lease, for tenants to remove physical improvements, such as buildings, that they had erected on leased property.[244] Such improvements, denominated "fixtures," had traditionally stayed with the land. In *Van Ness*, however, the Court claimed that a milk cellar in the basement of a home and a work bench outside in the yard, qualified the residents as workers engaged in manufacturing trades, (dairying and carpentry). Thus, a house erected by the tenant in *Van Ness* was neatly fit within the "trade fixtures" exception to the waste doctrine: defying the popular wisdom that "you can't take it with you," the tenant was allowed to do so. He disassembled his house and took it with him when his lease was up. So much for the ancient Latin maxim *Quidquid plantatur solo, solo cedit* ("Whatever is annexed to the soil becomes part thereof").[245]

Sensing, perhaps, that the facts of the case demonstrated that the house in question had been used as a family residence and, therefore, that the court's doctrinal soft shoe was not especially amusing, Justice Story

---

244 *Van Ness v. Pacard*, 27 U.S. (2 Pet.) 137 (1929), excerpted in Presser and Zainaldin, *Law and Jurisprudence*, pp. 289–300.

245 See Herbert Thorndike Tiffany, *A Treatise on the Modern Law of Real Property* (Chicago: Callaghan, 1912), pp. 535–37.

added: "The common law of England is not to be taken in all respects to be that of America. Our ancestors brought with them its general principles, and claimed it as their birthright; but they brought with them and adopted only that portion which was applicable to their situation." It is easy to guess which portion of the law Story has decided is not applicable here. "In the comparative poverty of the country," he concludes, "what tenant could afford to erect fixtures of much expense or value, if he was to lose his whole interest therein by the very act of erection?" In other words, if a country is poor enough, then the waste doctrine (and its fixtures rule) are likely to have the effect of discouraging a range of improvements or alterations to the land.

To be sure, the waste doctrine might help identify property in areas where specific, recognizable physical features served to establish boundary lines. Nevertheless, Story sought to adopt a rule that would encourage tenants to improve the land, engage in agricultural and manufacturing pursuits, and pursue entrepreneurialism; the existing common law rule just did not serve that end. He went to the trouble of trying to make the tenant's house fit an existing exception: the one for "trade fixtures." It had previously included furnaces, vats for dyers and soap-boilers, and fire engines for a colliery—but not a house.[246] So the judges—Justices in *Van Ness*—did precisely what they were supposed to do: they made sure that the development of American law, on balance, served the dominant interests of a developing economy. "The release of energy," Willard Hurst

---

246　For another case that turns on finding the right legal exception for a house (and one that clearly demonstrates that sophisticated legal reasoning did not begin with Justice Story), see Duke University professor of religion, E. P. Sanders's book, *The Historical Figure of Jesus* (London: Allen Lane, Penguin, 1993): "The prophet Jeremiah had forbidden Jews to carry burdens out of their houses on the sabbath (Jer. 17.19–27). This made festive dining very difficult, since the easiest way for friends to dine together was for each family to bring a cooked dish, and sabbaths were the only days when socializing was possible (because the demands of daily work were so heavy). The Pharisees decided that, when several houses were next to each other along an alley or around a court, they could make them all into one 'house' by joining them with a series of doorposts and lintels. They could

then carry pots and dishes from one part of the 'house' to another, and thus dine together on the sabbath. The Pharisees knew that this and other symbolic actions that altered the sabbath limits—actions that are technically called *eruvin*—had no support in the Hebrew Bible, but they made it a 'tradition of the elders' and observed it. Some Jews thought that they were transgressing the law, since they carried vessels out of what most people would call a house" (p. 45).

247　James Willard Hurst, *Law and the Conditions of Freedom in the Nineteenth-Century United States* (Madison, Wis.: University of Wisconsin Press, 1956). Morton Horwitz's specific discussion of the *Van Ness* and *Parker* cases is exemplary. "Although, technically," he writes, "*Van Ness* held only that the fixtures in question were in fact trade fixtures and thus still within the English exception,

called it.[247] Legal institutions automatically changed their function alright, sometimes even being turned inside out, yet the forms of law were preserved. In *Van Ness*, for example, the law of easements or the fixtures rule remained intact, modifications in their coverage or the scope of their exceptions, as Renner put it, "scarcely noticed."[248]

The *Charles River Bridge* conundrum, to which we now return, can itself be illuminated by an insight from Georg Lukács's *History and Class Consciousness*, mentioned earlier. Borrowing Hegel's distinction between forms of the absolute spirit (for example, art, religion, and philosophy) and forms of the objective spirit (for example, economics, law and politics), Lukács contends that even the latter "often manage to survive the demise of the social foundations to which they owe their existence. But in that event they survive as obstacles to progress which have to be swept away or by changing their functions they adapt themselves to the new economic circumstances."[249] Thus, on the one hand, with the forms of the absolute spirit, law and politics share a genuine, if socially conditioned, autonomy from the life of society; on the other hand, their *degree* of inde-

Story's decision was, as Chancellor Kent observed, part of 'a system of judicial legislation' that had 'grown up...so as to almost render the right of removal of fixtures a general rule, instead of being an exception'" (*Transformation*, p. 56). Horwitz uses *Van Ness* to illustrate the subtle process whereby rule and exception may simply switch places during periods of economic transformation. The common law rule of ancient lights, adds Horwitz, "which enabled the owner of an ancient tenement to prevent his neighbor from undertaking any building that would interfere with his own enjoyment of sunlight, rested on even more long-standing legal authority than did the doctrine of prescription in water cases....[U]nder [James] Gould's approach there could be no stopping short of transforming the whole law of prescription. And in the leading case of *Parker v. Foote* (1838), the New York court, following Gould's analysis, overthrew the doctrine of ancient lights" (ibid., p. 46).

Horwitz ties cases like *Van Ness* and *Parker* into the larger transformation of the common law of property, the latter revealing as daramatically as the common law of contract the "economic plate techtonics," in Lester Thurow's terminology, governing nineteenth-century American legal development. Horwitz concludes: "At its deepest level, the attack on prescription represented an effort to free American law from the restraints on economic development that had been molded by the common law's feudal conception of property." Horwitz also ties changes in the common law of property to the *Charles River Bridge* case and the assault on mercantilism: "By the Civil War, this [antiprescriptive] attitude had acquired such momentum that it challenged even the well-established doctrine that a right to support of buildings could be acquired by prescription. The most striking rejection of the common law assumption that long use was sufficient to create an exclusive property interest occurred in the great *Charles River Bridge* case" (ibid., p. 46).

248 Karl Renner, "The Development of Law," in *Austro-Marxism*, Tom Bottomore and Patrick Goode, ed. and trans. (Oxford: Oxford University Press, 1978), p. 269.

249 Georg Lukács, *History and Class Consciousness*, Rodney Livingstone, trans. (Cambridge, Mass.: MIT Press, 1971), p. 234.

pendence remains much less. Consequently, once they have become "an obstacle to progress," they must necessarily either be "swept away" or else reconstructed into complimentary, rather than antagonistic, social tendencies. Lukács pointedly observes that the "history of law is rich in instances of both possibilities."

Lukács identifies the system's dilemma and Karl Renner theorizes *one* of its solutions: the intricate process through which institutional adjustment to a reorganized economic substratum takes place *but within the forms of the law*. But who provides an analysis of the *remaining* alternative, the process by which recalcitrant forms of objective spirit are destroyed?

In 1971, University of Wisconsin historian Stanley Kutler published a book on the *Charles River Bridge* case: *Privilege and Creative Destruction*.[250] His examination is considerably more detailed than that found in Carl Brent Swisher's standard biography of Justice Taney.[251] Kutler's analysis emphasizes the social and historical environment surrounding the decision and he argues that a dominant view reflected in the case was one that "regarded private property as a dynamic and not static institution. An entrepreneurial rather than a *rentier* spirit was favored and Taney's opinion was the quintessence of this preference."[252] In this observation we recognize a familiar dialectic: private property conceived as having two contradictory aspects in the early-nineteenth-century landscape of American law. A dynamic/entrepreneurial view of property relations now contested an entrenched static/rentier view. Kutler's approach differs sharply from McCloskey's which treated property—and the economic relations upon which it was founded—as uniform, without contradiction; he did, after all, assert that Taney's opinion in *Charles River Bridge* not only comported with Marshall's jurisprudence but did not threaten property rights as had been feared. Taney's antimonopoly decision was threatening indeed, but to an older, static, anticompetitive notion of property rights, routinely associated with mercantilism.[253]

250 Stanley I. Kutler, *Privilege and Creative Destruction: The Charles River Bridge Case* (Philadelphia: J. B. Lippincott, 1971; repr. Baltimore: Johns Hopkins University Press, 1990).

251 Carl Brent Swisher, *Roger B. Taney* (New York: MacMillan, 1935), pp. 361–74.

252 Stanley Kutler, *Privilege and Creative Destruction*, p. 5.

253 In his standard history of economic thought, Eric Roll observes that for some economists, in defining mercantilism, the "building-up of nation-states is put in the forefront, and monetary, protectionist, and other economic devices are regarded merely as instruments to this end. State intervention was an essential part of mercantilist doctrine." Roll quickly adds, however, that "a view which makes political unification the end to which both economic practice and theory were subservient ignores the more powerful

causal influence on political institutions which proceeds from changes in economic structure."

If mercantilism can be reduced to state intervention per se, what are we to do with the view of theorists like Immanuel Wallerstein, according to which the state is invariably a constitutive element of capitalism? From this it follows that state involvement in economic affairs, in one form or another, is constant as well as critical to capitalism's reproduction—indeed, that involvement (and concomitant protection of private property) is, in Adam Smith's view, the *purpose* of law and government. Roll accounts for this objection as well: "It is not surprising that mercantilists should have clothed their views in the garb of a policy designed to strengthen the nation or that they should have looked to the state to carry out their theories. The expansion of commerce brought with it a divergence of individual trading interests. Nearly all these interests looked to a strong central authority to protect them against the claims of their rivals. The waverings of state policy during the long period in which mercantilism held sway cannot be understood without realizing the extent to which the state was a creature of warring commercial interests...." So what specific form does state intervention take under a mercantilist regime? "It is generally conceded," Roll, continues, "that mercantile capitalism preceded and prepared the ground for modern industrial capitalism. The latter, as we shall find, saw in the power of the state and in state intervention in economic matters a serious hindrance to its own development. Thus it set itself up in opposition to the political structure which its own forebear had found it necessary to create." The mercantilists, according to Roll, demanded a "state" (and, we might add here, sympathetic state legislatures and court systems in the United States) that would protect their interests and "the principle of regulation and restriction itself—now applied on a much larger scale through monopolies and protection—was an essential basis of that state."

Roll acknowledges that we "know now that monopoly, protection, and state regulation in general did not remain indispensable qualities of capitalism once it reached its full flower.

And it is symptomatic of the development of modern industry that the outcry against monopoly begins fairly soon in the field of domestic trade...." In the United States, as soon as the litigation over the Charles River Bridge. "The spectacle of capitalism," concludes Roll, "in its liberal age, attacking and destroying that which had given it birth contains a paradox only if one takes a narrow view of the development of economic doctrine" Eric Roll, *A History of Economic Thought* (London: Faber and Faber, 5th rev. ed., 1992), pp. 49–51.

Cambridge University economist, Maurice Dobb, describing the tension between static and dynamic conceptions of property rights as one of the essential features of capitalist development in Europe, argues: "In the period of the system's adolescence, this contradiction was generally displayed in the form of a conflict between the interests of an older generation of capitalists, already entrenched in certain spheres of trade and usury where capital had earliest penetrated, and the interests of a new generation who had become investors in newer trades or industries or in newer methods of production....In the seventeenth century the contradiction found expression in the conflict between rising industrial capital and the merchant princes with their chartered monopolies; in the early nineteenth century in the challenge that the new class of factory-capitalists threw down to the Whig aristocracy and the whole Mercantile System" (*Studies in the Development of Capitalism* [New York: International Publishers, 1947], p. 219–20).

A contradiction, extending Dobb's observation, that found expression in early nineteenth-century America as well, in the challenge that a new generation of entrepreneurs threw down to the existing system of mercantilist privilege. The rise of a competitive market society held profound implications, and not only for the few "owners of stock, most of them Bostonians," who had a stake in preserving the Charles River Bridge monopoly. Counsel for the Warren Bridge Company, on oral argument before the Supreme Court, were themselves among the first to make the point: "The proprietors of the Charles River Bridge were in no worse condition, John Davis declared, and had no

The capitalist economy that began to take shape after the American Revolution remained a mercantile one, as Louis Hacker, William Appleman Williams, Douglas Dowd, and many other commentators on the period have contended for some time.[254] And the Supreme Court's

higher claim to indemnity than other losers by public improvements. Railroads took traffic from highways near which they were built, thus depriving the latter of tolls which had been anticipated, and reducing the value of stages, wagons, and other property. Some communities were deprived of business and the value of their real estate depreciated, but there could be no legal indemnity for such losses, and, since public convenience demanded such improvements, they could not be obstructed from such causes" Swisher, *Roger B. Taney*, pp. 362, 370–71. Nor could an American capitalism be further obstructed, save by the stubborn survival of that peculiar institution upon which the wealth and power of the southern agrarian system was based.

254   Louis M. Hacker, *American Capitalism* (repr. Huntington, N.Y.: Robert E. Krieger, 1979): "A key to the capitalist development of the United States before the Civil War is to be found in the fact that business enterprise was still largely in the mercantile stage. The businessman was a merchant, usually an undifferentiated one, who combined the functions of trader, 'manufacturer,' banker, and speculator.…The golden period of the American carrying trade lasted from the founding of the Republic until the mid-1830s" (p. 40).

"Though it signified the rise of manufactures to a position of parity, the division of the congressional Committee on Commerce and Manufactures in 1819 also symbolized a breaking apart of the integrated thought of mercantilism. Having been nurtured by mercantilism, manufacturing was about to become a faction and step forth as a spokesman for laissez faire. A similar meaning was implicit in the translation and publication in America of the works of Jean Baptiste Say, a French economist who carried the ideas of Adam Smith and the early physiocrats to their logical conclusion. Say argued that complete freedom of trade and unrestricted enterprise would produce welfare and happiness for everyone" (William Appleman William, *The Contours of American History* [repr. New York: W. W. Norton, 1988], pp. 201–02). See also "The Age of Mercantilism: An Interpretation of the American Political Economy, 1763 to 1828," in *History as a Way of Learning* [1958] (New York: Franklin Watts, 1973), pp. 243–66.

Economist Douglas Dowd argues: "Among our very first steps after Independence was the creation of our own mercantilist system. Alexander Hamilton was the most productive and influential economic thinker of the new nation, issuing one *Report* after another. His *Report on Manufactures* (1791), revolving around the need to develop industry and to protect it in its "infant" stages, set the stage for a coherent and tight protectionist trading policy, with subsidies mixed in where needed" (*U. S. Capitalist Development Since 1763* [Armonk, N.Y.: M. E. Sharpe, 1993], p. 358). Underscoring the same contrast between static/rentier and dynamic/entrepreneurial property brought forward by Kutler, Roll, and Dobb, Dowd adds that the "emergence of laissez-faire capitalism depended upon the abolition of State mercantilism. What [Adam] Smith had correctly viewed as obstacles to the full increase of productive powers in the mercantilist era was also a system of protections and privileges.…Laissez-faire capitalism placed individuals' and enterprises' fates in the hands of impersonal market forces, forces which changed swiftly and at times violently. In the absence of the protections and privileges of labor and capital of the mercantile era, such had to be obtained (if at all) through private efforts. It was a contest the powerless could not win" (Ibid., pp. 63–64). To the mercantile era, Dowd adds three more periods that correspond quite closely to mine: "The upshot, for the first half-century of our existence as a nation, was far from laissez-faire capitalism. Here we may note very briefly…four different periods regarding the role of the State in United States economic life. The first has just been noted, as the United States period of limited, Hamiltonian mercantilism. The second period, replacing mercantilism after Jackson's presidency, amounted to the beginnings of United States–style laissez-faire capitalism. It came to its roaring climax in the decades after the Civil War, called by Marx Twain the Gilded Age, and by Vernon Parrington the Great Barbecue. The third phase, a response to both the instabilities and beckoning possibilities of maturing industrial capitalism, began to develop as this century opened, and it found coherence during Wilson's presidency. It involved increased concentration of State power in Washington....Although the 1920s saw a decade-long detour from that evolving 'neomercantilism,' the depression of the 1930s (and FDR's 'New Deal') and World War II combined to renew the broadening and deepening of the role of the State in almost all aspects of United States economic life, well beyond the policies of the Wilson years....The fourth phase began in the late 1970s and the 1980s and became a tidal wave of efforts seeking to remove the regulatory role of the State from the economy and its protective role from the society" (ibid., p. 76).

The elimination of mercantilist monopoly and protection, along with elimination of colonial dependence and precapitalist economic formations, reflect what I have described as the transition from first to second periods in American legal history. Dowd is right to emphasize the Civil War and its impact on the development of American capitalism during the Gilded Age. I extend this period up to Roosevelt's New Deal, despite Martin Sklar's important work on the maturation of industrial capitalism (and governmental involvement in the "private sector") during the Progressive era. I am more impressed by the *difference* between Wilson's sending American troops to Russia to overthrow Lenin's regime and Roosevelt's immediate recognition of the Soviet Union, which would become our crucial ally in the world historical struggle against authoritarian capitalism. Certainly, Dowd is correct to point out that the "broadening and deepening of the role of the State" during the 1930s and 1940s went "well beyond the policies of the Wilson years." Finally, he places the rise of global

capitalism and its deregulatory regime slightly later than I do, since I emphasize such marginally earlier events as Barry Goldwater's capture of the Republican Party, the Kennedy assassination, and the Vietnam War.

Herbert Hovenkamp observes: "Until the late 1930s the prevailing economic ideology on the Supreme Court was that of the classical political economists, who also had a strong bias in favor of the 'unregulated' market. The result was a general judicial hostility toward state and federal regulation. A far-reaching revolution in economic theory in the 1930s was followed, however, by a Supreme Court that was much less trusting of markets and more tolerant of regulatory intervention than it had previously been" ("Capitalism," in Hall, ed., *Oxford Companion to the Supreme Court*, pp. 117, 118).

Margit Mayer and Margaret Fay, describing how the new political apparatus established by the Constitution insured achievement of the public good, add that this "public good, in principle, corresponded to the interests of no single class in American society; and the internal structure of the governing apparatus sought to perpetuate and realize in practice the effective representation of a manifold diversity of interests. But, given the world market conditions of those times, the national interest inevitably coincided with, and depended on, the interests of merchant capital. Consequently, as long as the political structures of the U.S. nation-state guaranteed the sifting-out of the public good, the merchants were assured of the state's support and promotion of their interests *without themselves having to participate directly in the government*. Contrast this with the period before Independence, when the only way that any economically dominant group could ensure public protection and support was to exercise direct control over the provincial legislatures by usurping the leading political positions. Later when the conditions for the accumulation of capital changed, the same structures of the U.S. state-apparatus, which in and of themselves had promoted the interests of mercantile capital in the eighteenth century, performed the same function for the development and domination of industrial capital in the second half of the nineteenth century and the twentieth century.

decision in *Charles River Bridge* was a watershed event in that system's demise at the hands of a vigorously competitive or entrepreneurial capitalism.[255] Yet this subordination of a mercantilist approach to development—along with termination of colonial dependence, the elimination of precapitalist economic formations, and eventually the Civil War itself—

The capacity of the nation's political structures to operate in this way, without the dominant economic group itself exercising direct control over these structures, is what we mean by the relative autonomy of the capitalist state" ("The Formation of the American Nation State," in *Kapitalistate* [fall 1977], p. 70–71).

255 "Jacksonian insurgency against disruptive enterprise ended by making free enterprise a constitutional principle. Chief Justice Taney's first major decision, in the 1837 Charles River Bridge case, struck down chartered monopoly for the sake of free competition" (Sellers, *The Market Revolution*, pp. 352–53). Kermit L. Hall remarks: "Beneath these prosaic actions a political, legal, and economic storm raged....Daniel Webster, appearing for the old bridge company, argued that, if legislators went back on their promise to investors, no one would invest in future improvements. Property rights had to be strictly protected or economic development would collapse. Justice Taney, however, offered for the Jacksonian majority on the Court a different vision of how to achieve economic progress....Only by preventing established capital from entrenching itself could economic growth based on new corporate development occur....Recognizing that the Charles River Bridge Company had an implied monopoly over bridge building on the Charles River would be bad economic policy" (*The Magic Mirror* [New York: Oxford University Press, 1989] p. 118).

For Sellers, the holding in *Charles River Bridge* was less a gloss on established methods of interpreting the language of state grants and charters than a bold announcement that free enterprise was an idea whose time had come. For Hall, the case reflected neither victory nor defeat for property rights but, rather, a resounding triumph for one particular set of property rights as against

another—the interests of new corporate development prevailed over those of entrenched capital. This was no threadbare legal reading producing bad economic policy but an emergent market system and its economic policy mandating sweeping reformulation of legal doctrine. Free enterprise, as Seller suggests, was provided the status of constitutional rule.

See also Robert Heilbroner and Aaron Singer, *The Economic Transformation of America* (3d. ed., Fort Worth, Texas: Harcourt Brace, 1994): "As chief justice, [Taney's] decisions encouraged free enterprise and individual economic opportunity....'The object and end of all government,' he wrote in the famous *Charles River Bridge v. Warren Bridge* case (1837), 'is to promote the happiness and prosperity of the community by which it is established....' By engraving free, fair, and open competition as the economic hallmarks of the Court, the judiciary further buttressed economic development" (p. 144). But it was not just any kind of development; it was specifically competitive capitalist rather than mercantile development which was now to be favored as the primary beneficiary of public policy in the United States. Morton Horwitz notes: "The *Charles River Bridge* case represented the last great contest in America between two different models of economic development," between, in short, protectionism and the market which Horwitz sees, respectively, as bases for two different conceptions of property (*Transformation*, p. 134).

Stuart Bruchey quotes this same passage from Horwitz and adds: "Another possible view of the matter, however, is that the contest was not between two different models of economic development at all, but rather between a model of development and an effort by an older elite to hold back the forces of change in the interests of preserving its place in a more stable society" (*Enterprise*, p. 212). It is important to understand that mercantilism was, of course, a distinct model of economic development but, like all models of development, it became little more than a facade for reactionary social forces once its time had passed. This is necessarily the fate of all political philosophies and economic programs that fall behind decisive infrastructural transformation.

In America, the bitter defeat of domestic mercantilism meant little more than that lawyers like Daniel Webster, ranked at the top of their profession, began to lose big cases. However, in authoritarian capitalist countries such as Germany, the consequences following from sectors of the bourgeoisie aligning themselves with "feudal remnants" were enormous. Although "government, nobility, and military have traditionally been considered the forces dominating the German Empire in its early years," writes historian Andreas Dorpalen, "with the bourgeoisie trying not very successfully to change conditions, [East German] authors consider the bourgeoisie even at that time a determining factor in the fate of the empire. The bourgeoisie's impact is traced to its very inaction; its responsibility is seen in its abdication of its leadership function in the capitalist order." The German bourgeoisie's "tolerance of reactionary domestic conditions in return for economic concessions," is condemned precisely because it led to a settlement that "reconciled both clerical and capitalist concerns (anti-Socialist legislation, protective tariffs) but also reinforced the predominance of the state and curbed the competitive structure of capitalism" (*German History in Marxist Perspective* [Detroit, Mich.: Wayne State University Press, 1988], pp. 240–41).

If East German historians rightly criticize the German bourgeoisie for its historical failure to fulfill its "class mandate"—the establishment in the nineteenth century of a genuinely bourgeois, liberal capitalist regime—no historian can fault America's ruling class for such a failure. In the hands of Jacksonian Chief Justice and free marketeer Roger B. Taney, the stock certificates held by hapless investors in the Charles River Bridge were drained of their value in the name of

progress and public interest. So much for mercantilism.

Taney himself, author of the infamous *Dred Scott* decision, was eventually caught on the wrong side of history's dialectic and discarded. "There was no sadder figure to be seen in Washington during the years of the Civil War," wrote one of Swisher's sources, Mrs. J. A. Logan, "than that of the aged Chief Justice. His form was bent by the weight of years, and his thin, nervous, and deeply-furrowed face was shaded by long, gray locks....He had outlived his epoch, and was shunned and hated by the men of the new time of storm and struggle for the principles of freedom and nationality" (Swisher, *Roger B. Taney*, pp. 574–75). Taney, whose *Charles River Bridge* opinion was regarded as the great charter of economic liberty, who "argued for an end to slavery" and had "also freed his own slaves around 1820," thought he *had* fought a "struggle for the principles of freedom"; Sidney Ratner, James H. Soltow, and Richard Sylla, *The Evolution of the American Economy* (2d ed., New York: Macmillan, 1993), p. 233. But the transition from precapitalist to capitalist legal systems required not only the creative destruction of state-granted monopolies and privileges but also that of the slave South and there Taney's jurisprudence missed the mark. So much for Taney.

So much for laissez faire, too, when its time came around, as William Appleman Williams insightfully observes in his own remarks on *Charles River Bridge* and beyond: "Honoring the identical faith [in laissez faire], Chief Justice Roger B. Taney, who had served earlier as Jackson's attorney general, rendered a militant decision against monopolies in the Charles River Bridge case. Declaring that restrictive charters delayed progress, and that the country would be 'thrown back...to the last century and be obliged to stand still' if they were not destroyed, he announced the new political economy and opened the market place to all competitors. But Taney's opinion also confirmed the corporation as a legitimate unit of competition. And that aspect of the court's decision amounted in the long run to a death sentence for individualized laissez faire, for the independent businessman proved incapable of holding his own against the corporation" (*Contours*, p. 248).

were rites of passage from the first to second periods of American legal development. Only by this tumultuous and often violent route did a liberal, competitive capitalism finally emerge as not only the dominant econony but also the essential infrastructural base upon which a new legal system could be constructed.

Returning, then, to McCloskey's argument, was the Taney Court reckless of property rights or not? It certainly was if one believes the Whig interpretation of the *Charles River Bridge* opinion. The Whigs, as Swisher notes, "were distressed and disapproving." A Boston reporter expressed the belief, upon reading the Taney Court's decision, that federal "restraint would be removed from state legislatures, and investments in corporate property would have no guarantee or legal protection." The *North American Review* went so far as to suggest that the new Supreme Court majority had adopted an economic doctrine likely to cause "subversion of the principles of law and property."[256]

The Whig response was correct, up to a point. In *Charles River Bridge*, the Supreme Court *had* permitted a state legislature to escape the provisions of a previously binding grant of monopoly privileges; but it did so not in the name of state's rights but, rather, that of enhanced economic competition. Investments in corporate property *could* lose judicial protection but only where that investment reflected a rentier, as opposed to entrepreneurial spirit. Or, in Kutler's reference, a static rather than dynamic approach to economic development. It did not follow that private property *itself* was being subverted—on the contrary, it was merely the property rights of a dying class or, perhaps, "Whig aristocracy" as Dobb put it in the English context, which were subject to abuse.

Is it too much to refer to this "older elite of original investors" as an expendable estate, in contrast to a rising social class with its own economic interests and, therefore, corresponding set of "ideas"? "The preservation of attractive privileges," says Columbia University business historian Stuart Bruchey, "even of monopoly rights, was justifiable when savings were limited and the risk of loss a pronounced one, for otherwise private individuals would not have been willing to invest their money and government would have been forced to resort to taxation, then as now a highly unpopular alternative, to raise the funds required."[257] What changed the situation from one in which savings were negligible to some-

---

256 Carl Brent Swisher, *Roger B. Taney*, pp. 376–77.   257 Stuart Bruchey, *Enterprise*, p. 211.

thing quite different was the emergence of an entrepreneurial social class. Savings per capita, again according to Bruchey, "were surely far more abundant by the time of Taney than they had been in the later colonial years. And the people doing the saving were far more numerous than earlier wealthholders."

Were these new holders of wealth a rising bourgeoisie? "Their numbers and affluence," concludes Bruchey, "had increased not only with the opening of opportunities in trade, privateering, and land speculation during the Revolution, but probably even more as a result of those created during the wars of the French Revolution and Napoleon (1793–1815) and, after their conclusion, those in banking, early industry, and agriculture, especially the growing of cotton." By the time the case pitting Charles River and Warren Bridge companies against each other came before the Supreme Court, these litigants were merely stand-ins for a class struggle between owners of the old and new property. "By the mid-thirties," of the nineteenth century, concludes Bruchey, "new entrepreneurs were beating on the doors of legal privilege and demanding equal investment opportunity before the law."[258]

In a sense, then, the editors of the *North American Review* were quite wrong when they suggested that the *Charles River Bridge* decision threatened to subvert the principles of law and property. The case, in fact, upheld the first principle of American law in relation to property: subordination of legal rule to the relentless dialectic of social change emerging from transformation in the mode of subsistence and corresponding relations of production. This point is elegantly underscored in the work of an economist upon whom we can rely for a compelling account of that process by which outlived forms of law and economy are, in fact, swept away.

Recall the title of Wisconsin historian Stanley Kutler's definitive work on the Charles River Bridge case: *Privilege and Creative Destruction*. According to Elizabeth Monroe, writing in the *Oxford Companion to the Supreme Court*, "Taney fashioned his opinion [in *Charles River Bridge*] to justify creative destruction of old property in order that new ventures might prosper."[259] The association of the Taney opinion with "creative destruction," subsequent to Kutler's having fused the two in his account, became sufficiently familiar that Monroe did not even have to drop a footnote to Kutler in her Oxford entry, though her bibliography, at the

---

258 Ibid, pp. 211–12.   259 Elizabeth Monroe, "Charles River Bridge," p. 136.

end, included just one book: Stan Kutler's. So from whence did Kutler derive this arresting notion? In the "bibliographic essay" which concludes his book on *Charles River Bridge*, after citing the work of Willard Hurst and acknowledging the importance of Hurst's "release of energy" theory, Kutler states that he "derived the corollary theme of 'creative destruction' from Joseph Schumpeter's *Capitalism, Socialism and Democracy*."[260]

There, Schumpeter writes: "The opening up of new markets, foreign or domestic, and the organizational development from the craft shop and factory to such concerns as U.S. Steel illustrate the same process of industrial mutation—if I may use the biological term—that incessantly revolutionizes the economic structure *from within*, incessantly destroying the old one, incessantly creating a new one." Schumpeter's depiction of relentless creation and destruction within the economic infrastructure of society certainly invites comparison with Hegel's dialectical method. "This process of Creative Destruction," concludes Schumpeter, "is the essential fact about capitalism. It is what capitalism consists in and what every capitalist concern has got to live in."[261] No wonder Kutler chose to draw upon Schumpeter's impressive body of work, however less well known that work may be to legal historians than to economists, for a concept as crucial to the development of capitalism as that of creative destruction.[262]

---

260 Stanley Kutler, *Creative Destruction*, p. 180.

261 Joseph A. Schumpeter, *Capitalism, Socialism and Democracy* (3d. ed., New York: Harper and Brothers, 1950); pp. 9–10. The U.S. Steel Company, specifically cited by Schumpeter in 1950, had to live with this same process, a process by which the entire U.S. steel industry was effectively, if "creatively," destroyed. See Jeffrey A. Hart, "A Comparative Analysis of the Sources of America's Relative Economic Decline," in Michael A. Bernstein and David E. Adler, eds. *Understanding American Economic Decline* (New York: Cambridge University Press, 1994) p. 199. See also Michael Barratt Brown, *Models in Political Economy* (2d ed., London: Penguin, 1995): "Abandoning text-book theory of tendencies toward equilibrium in marginal demand....Schumpeter in his great work on *Capitalism, Socialism and Democracy*, described a real world of 'Creative Destruction.'... Price competition in itself and resulting profitability cannot create the

innovation in new products, new processes and new forms of organization that make for survival in the capitalist system. Schumpeter believed in the role of the individual entrepreneur in the system's success. His Japanese disciples extended this to collectivities of entrepreneurial activity" (p. 95).

262 See also "Critics of Marxism," in Tom Bottomoe, ed., *A Dictionary of Marxist Thought* (Oxford: Basil Blackwell, 1983), p. 105; Robert Heilbroner, "Schumpeter's Vision," in *Behind the Veil of Economics: Essays in the Worldly Philosophy* (New York: W. W. Norton, 1988) pp. 165–84; and John Kenneth Galbraith, *Economics in Perspective* (Boston: Houghton Mifflin, 1987): "The entrepreneur of traditional economic theory ages and is replaced as to both capital and its direction by newcomers riding new waves of innovation. This is the process—'the gales of creative destruction'—that was made famous by Joseph Schumpeter" (p. 279).

Returning, then, to McCloskey's analysis of these events one more time: in what sense was he actually right with respect to his claim of continuity between the Marshall and Taney Courts? Not, I think, with regard to the doctrine of state-federal relations, nor at the level of Contract Clause jurisprudence. Was Marshall among the justices prepared to decide against the Massachusetts legislature and in favor of the Charles River Bridge monopoly when the case was first argued before the Supreme Court and Marshall was still alive? Commentators disagree.[263] Nevertheless, despite McCloskey's underestimation of the threat the Taney Court's ruling posed to entrenched property interests, the Charles River Bridge decision can still be seen as vindicating McCloskey's claim of consistency between the Marshall and Taney courts. Consider the following observation from Gustavus Myers's *History of the Supreme Court*:

> So far as the State rights issue was involved, the Supreme Court's policy under Taney, although exactly the reverse of what it had been under Marshall, produced in one respect the same result in effect. The Charles River Bridge Case was a striking instance of this.…[The] decision again effectually stamped into law the doctrine then proclaimed as immutable by aggressive capitalism, and consequently by statesmen, universities, editorial sanctums and legislative halls—the doctrine that 'competition is the life of trade.' A companion edict to Marshall's decision in the Livingston steamboat monopoly case, the decision demolished the last stand of the old, archaic, feudal aristocracy and gave the new industrial and transportation aristocracy unlimited opportunities for competitive expansion and individual and corporate development.[264]

Myers's conclusion reveals a degree of class analysis which initially seems on a par with Charles Beard and the Progressive historians: "This decision," Myers states flatly, "freshly demonstrated that the Supreme Court of the United States continuously and accurately reflected, both in personnel and in spirit, the needs and demands of the dominant sections of the ruling class, and incarnated those requisites into constitutional law."[265] What distinguishes Myers's approach, however, is its dialectical hard edge. Not until Mitchell Franklin do we again find such close scrutiny of doctrinal law accomplishing so effectively the primary aim of legal theory: the concrete analysis of a concrete situation.

263 Swisher, *Roger B. Tanty*, pp. 363; contrast Kutler, *Creative Destruction*, pp. 172–79.
264 Gustavus Myers, *History of the Supreme*

Court of the United States (Chicago: Charles H. Kerr, 1912); p. 397.
265 Ibid., p. 397.

Here we must pause for a moment and draw a parallel between the transformation to global capitalism (which would eventually come to dominate the late twentieth century) with the transformation to laissez faire I have been describing. Following an Hegelian approach, we might reasonably expect to encounter this contradiction between mercantilism and laissez faire, or something uncannily like it, once again. And indeed we do, in the global capitalist assault on state capitalism. The transition from third to fourth periods presents us with analogous kinds of rhetoric and mental constructs. To be sure, the emergence of capitalist social relations constitutes what appears, from our present vantage point at the end of the twentieth century, to be an irreversible change in the structure of societies; precapitalist legal arrangements never again appear as more than remnants among the debris of social history. But that would not prevent mercantilism, for example, from functioning later as (at least) an interesting metaphor for state capitalist regimes of social and legal regulation.

William Appleman Williams, explaining Supreme Court Justice Stephen J. Field's crucial role in adjusting constitutional doctrine to the liberal capitalism rising from the ashes of Civil War, argues that Field's laissez faire views were adopted by New York's high court as it reviewed a challenge to the state's authority to regulate "the atrocious conditions of cigar manufacturing." According to Williams, the New York judges "explicitly raised the specter of a return to mercantilist doctrine on social property. Such ideas—'from those ages when governmental prefects supervised…the rate of wages, the price of food, and a large range of other affairs'—were declared archaic. They disturbed the 'normal adjustments' of the market place…"[266] And, indeed, the retooling of constitutional law itself aligning it with an entrepreneurial victory over entrenched rentier interests, should be seen as one more "normal adjustment" to the market and its alternative structure of social relations.

The constitutional transformation—which Williams, McCloskey, and other legal historians have described as taking place in the decades between the Civil War and the century's end[267]—represented a sharp rejection of the social and economic philosophy to which Justice Morrison Waite gave voice in the Granger cases.[268] Waite specifically

266 Williams, *Contours*, p. 329.
267 See, for example, Robert McCloskey, Constitutional Evolution in the Gilded Age: 1865–1900," in McCloskey, *Supreme Court*, pp. 67–90.

268 "The Granger decisions did not settle the question of laissez faire.…A contemporary article in *Nation* said that no machinery any state can create will be half as likely as the managers themselves to promote the best

invoked mercantilist precedents, Williams argues, and claimed that "property does become clothed with a public interest when used in a manner to make it of public consequence, and affect the community at large."[269] However, this view lapsed into minority sentiment once Field and his cohorts on the Court had managed to take command of the judicial high ground.[270] Their high ground, too, of course, eventually gave way with the shifting economic infrastructure beneath it. By the Great Depression of the 1930s, enough had changed for constitutional doctrine, once again, to go through a period of radical reinterpretation. Thus, the Supreme Court's 1934 decision in *Nebbia v. New York* includes language very similar to that employed by Justice Waite, language that had been discarded years before—or so it seemed. In *Nebbia*, McCloskey reports, "the Court upheld a state law fixing minimum and maximum prices for

interests of the public. They are controlled by the *laws of trade*, which enforce themselves more thoroughly than any administration could. The common law doctrines of the majority opinions had grown up when everything was regulated. Hence, many of these principles are now seen to be folly. Arthur T. Hadley, a leading economist of the period, also endorsed the idea of economic law as a limit to the principle of the decision. In 1885 he wrote, 'By the time the Supreme Court published the Granger decisions the fight had been settled, not by constitutional limitations, but by industrial ones'" Benjamin R. Twiss, *Lawyers and the Constitution: How Laissez Faire Came to the Supreme Court* [Princeton: Princeton University Press, 1942], p. 90). Thus, in the area of constitutional law, we see the same kind of subordination of existing law to market or to "industrial" exigency that we saw in the transition from real values to market values in contract. From local courts deciding mundane issues of adequate consideration in private agreements to the Supreme Court of the United States ruling on the constitutional right of railroads to due process protection against governmental interference with corporate profits and decision-making, the law generally came to be seen primarily as a mechanism for ratifying market results.

269 *Contours*, p. 310.
270 See, for example, Loren P. Beth, "Stephen Johnson Field," in Hall, ed., *Oxford*

Companion to the Supreme Court; "Field was thus the leader of the Court's movement toward reading laissez faire into the Constitution—a movement that reached its apogee in Harlan's opinion in *Smyth v. Ames* (1898), Rufus Peckham's opinion in *Lochner v. New York* (1905), and in various decisions of the Taft Court in the 1920s" (p. 291). Harold J. Laski remarks: "No one can examine the mind of Mr. Justice Peckham, as it was revealed in his opinion in *Lochner v. New York*, or note the long years in which Mr. Justice Field maintained that the Court prevents 'dangerous changes in the good society,' without concluding that, by substituting their private social philosophies for that of the legislatures whose statutes they sought to strike down, both of them were confusing the function of a judge with that of a legislator" (*The American Democracy: A Commentary and Interpretation* [New York: Viking, 1948], p. 113). Laski's real difference with Peckham and Field, of course, was not over philosophies of the judicial function but, rather, over what constituted "the good society." See also Carl Brent Swisher, *Stephen J. Field, Craftsman of the Law* (Chicago: University of Chicago Press, 1969), which, like his biography of Taney, was originally published in the 1930s; and Arnold M. Paul, *Conservative Crisis and the Rule of Law: Attitudes of Bar and Bench, 1887–1895* (Ithaca: Cornell University Press, 1960).

milk, and took the occasion to announce that 'there is no closed category of businesses affected with a public interest.'" Another stumbling block "in the path of the regulatory movement was cleared away."[271]

Economist Douglas Dowd refers to the same regulatory movement, in its initial progressive stage as well as its more mature New Deal and Second World War manifestations, as "neomercantilism." It is what I refer to as state capitalism. And, again, Dowd identifies a "fourth phase" in the development of American capitalism, very much like our fourth or global capitalist period of legal history, as one beginning around the time of the Vietnam War and which, under Reagan, "became a tidal wave of efforts seeking to remove the regulatory role of the State from the economy and its protective role from society."[272] Defending this "tidal wave," and the global capitalist system which it keeps afloat, international trade economist Jeffrey Sachs argues that the "cement that will ultimately hold the world system together is not markets per se, but the international rule of law." This is a particularly interesting observation given that international law and legal institutions have always presented a steep challenge to the autonomy and authority of individual sovereign states, especially with respect to their ability to judge for themselves the lawfulness of their own conduct. When the nation state and, crucially, its military apparatus provides a primary mechanism for extending the power and influence of concentrated economic forces, then international law is ignored. But in the midst of a reconfiguration of familiar political patterns and alignments, like that accompanying the emergence of a post–Cold War, global capitalism, where the sovereign state is increasingly perceived as a potential obstacle to economic development, then international law seems an attractive, transnational system of institutional values and arrangements which can help rationalize effective rule by global capital itself.

Sachs, of course, is well aware of this tendency within contemporary economic and legal history. He observes that in public debate over the GATT treaty, "the leading charge against it was that international rules of the [World Trade Organization], especially its new binding dispute settlement process, would deprive the United States of sovereignty." If the United States turns its back on a new world order based upon global circuits of trade and finance, warns Sachs, "Americans will find themselves quickly descending into a swamp of *mercantilism* and trade conflict...."[273]

271 McCloskey, *Supreme Court*, p. 108.
272 Douglas Dowd, *Capitalist Development*, p. 76.

273 Jeffrey D. Sachs, "Consolidating Capitalism," *Foreign Policy* (Spring, 1995) p. 64, (emphasis added).

So, as a legal structure specific to the global capitalist period of historical development is pieced together and, in the process, conflicts between the economic exigencies of multinational firms and the traditional prerogatives of the nation state make their appearance, international law is elevated within the canons of jurisprudence and, even more surprisingly, official government policy. The transition from the Reagan administration's hostility to international law (accompanied by a public threat to send the United Nations packing) to that legal regime's embrace by George Bush's administration (apparently convinced that UN authorization was more important than that of Congress when sending U.S. troops to fight in the Gulf) was nothing short of astonishing. Who would have predicted, even a few years earlier, the degree of unanimity which characterized U.N. Security Council voting on Gulf War resolutions?[274]

Just as Sachs presents a quagmire of governmental interference and mercantile residuum as a potential threat to the rising global system, former Reagan aide Edward Luttwak, in a pointed commentary on the current development of what he calls turbo-charged capitalism, retrieves terminology from an earlier tectonic shift. Workers at Boeing aircraft corporation, Luttwak asserts, have every reason to be anxious about their jobs because "Boeing has joined other American businesses, large and small, in firing employees not only en masse when hard-pressed, as they always did of necessity, but even in prosperity, as a matter of deliberate choice, every day of the week." Nothing in the UN Charter about that. "In theory," says Luttwak, "it is just the objective force of technology-driven *creative destruction* that is at work: more efficient modes of produc-

---

274 See Malcolm N. Shaw, *International Law* (Cambridge: Cambridge Univ. Press, 3rd ed., 1991): "[T]he changing relationship between the two superpowers and the new era of co-operation ushered in by the late 1980s suggested an increasing reliance upon the United Nations. This developing possibility was speedily concretised following the invasion of Kuwait by Iraq on 2 August 1990. Resolution 660 (1990), adopted unanimously the same day by the Security Council, condemned the invasion and called for an immediate and unconditional withdrawal.... The armed action commenced on 16 January 1991 by a coalition of states under the leadership of the United States can thus be seen as a legitimate use of force authorised by the UN Security Council under its enforcement powers....It is, in fact, an example of how the Security Council was intended to function from the start, with the proviso that it had been hoped initially that the Council would have had at its disposal UN-dedicated units rather than having to rely upon member-states to organise the logistical and operational aspects of the action. This operation constitutes therefore a watershed in UN history." (pp. 710–11)For an analysis of the UN's use of force against Iraq less sanguine than Shaw's, by a diplomat who participated in the Security Council debate, see Fidel Castro and Ricardo Alarcon, *U.S. Hands Off the Mideast! Cuba Speaks out at the United Nations* (New York: Pathfinder, 2nd ed., 1990).

tion displace less efficient ones....”[275] Now Sachs and Luttwak come at the issues confronting contemporary globalism from different perspectives and both, certainly, would be at odds with Douglas Dowd in their critique of capitalism's performance. But my purpose here is limited to drawing out of these writers and their texts the familiar rhetoric of mercantilism vs. laissez faire, insulation from the rigors of the market vs. creative destruction, and so forth, which so effectively shaped our critique of an earlier conflict in the emergence of nineteenth-century American legal and economic relations. What goes around, comes around, or so it would seem in the dialectical unfolding of American legal history.

Rather than further anticipate a discussion of global capitalism and its legal structure, with which we will end the next chapter, it makes sense here to conclude our commentary on the transition to liberal capitalism itself in the nineteenth century. With the effective elimination of British political domination, precapitalist economic formations, and mercantilist domestic policies, what still remained at midcentury, as a barrier to the realization of a uniform national market economy organized on the basis of capitalist social relations, was the slave South.[276] Here we might turn

275   Edward Luttwak, "Turbo-Charged Capitalism and Its Consequences," *London Review of Books* (Books, Nov. 2, 1995 p. 6. (emphasis added).

276   "[T]he postwar pattern remained mixed. The Northwest Ordinance of 1787 did ban slavery from this region. And the matter of the slave trade was much debated in the Constitutional Convention. The famous compromise, a total abolition of the slave trade to come into effect 20 years later (in 1808), had the important side effect of pushing slavery 'deeper into the South.' Seventy years later, in 1857, Chief Justice Roger Taney would declare in the Dred Scott decision that, as of 1787, the Blacks 'had no rights which man was bound to respect.' As Litwak says, this was 'less a sign of moral callousness than an important historical truth.' The 'inalienable rights' of the colonists did not yet include Blacks" (Immanuel Wallerstein, *The Modern World-System* [San Diego, Cal.: Academic Press, 1989], vol. 3, p. 236).

Contemporary Supreme Court Chief Justice William Rehnquist disagrees with the proposition that the result in *Dred Scott* expressed an "important historical truth," at least with respect to that portion of Taney's reasoning which justified the result on private property grounds. The "*Dred Scott* opinion," Rehnquist writes, "falls short of that minimum degree of plausibility that should be required before a court declares any act of Congress unconstitutional. The Constitution expressly gave to Congress the authority to make rules and regulations for the territories of the United States, and Taney's opinion relies on no provision in the Constitution that would even arguably make the Missouri Compromise fall outside this general grant of power. The opinion is based almost entirely on the sense of the unfairness to southerners of preventing them from bringing with them their peculiar institution when northerners were allowed to bring property of all descriptions. But a sense that a law is unfair, however deeply felt, ought not to be itself a ground for declaring an act of Congress void" William H. Rehnquist (*The Supreme Court: How It Was, How it Is* [New York: William Morrow, 1987] pp. 144–45).

Contrast the reading of *Dred Scott* by James W. Ely, Jr., who contends: "substantive due process first appeared in federal jurisprudence

our attention to Charles Beard's critique of the Civil War, which addressed large economic forces rather than the narrow financial interests he saw behind the shaping of the Constitution,[277] and also to the work of

in the controversial 1857 *Dred Scott* decision. Chief Justice Roger Taney interpreted the due process clause as placing substantive limitation on the power of Congress with respect to slave property in the territories. The *Dred Scott* decision was effectively superseded by the Civil War and the Fourteenth Amendment, but the concept of substantive due process was destined for a robust rebirth in a later generation. After the Civil War, both federal and state courts vigorously employed substantive due process to safeguard economic liberty from legislative control" (*The Guardian of Every Other Right: A Constitutional History of Property Rights* [New York: Oxford University Press, 1992], pp. 79–80). Contrary to Rehnquist, Ely regards Taney's opinion in *Dred Scott* to have been motivated not by a general sense of unfairness but, rather, by a view of the Constitution as guaranteeing the private property rights of all American citizens, including those who happened to make their living from the southern plantation economy.

African-Americans had no rights, not even a property right in their own person, according to Taney; but white slave owners had a constitutionally protected right against invasion of their property interests by the federal government. This is exactly the same philosophy ("substantive economic due process") that animates much of the Supreme Court's laissez faire jurisprudence of the capitalist period, right up to and including the Court's resistance to Roosevelt's New Deal. Taney relied upon the due process clause of the Fifth Amendment; after the Civil War, the Court would be able to rely upon the due process clause of the Fourteenth Amendment—an especially useful addition to the Constitution, since it permitted application of substantive due process values to the states and, therefore, to efforts by progressive state legislatures to interfere with the prerogatives of industrial America's growing corporations. What changed between *Dred Scott* and the later substantive economic

due process cases was simply the definition of what kind of property the Constitution would protect. Rehnquist fails to make these connections, and his interpretation of *Dred Scott* turns out to be rather pedestrian. For a range of views on both the economics of slavery as well as the history of the Supreme Court during this period, see Robin Blackburn, *The Overthrow of Colonial Slavery 1776-1848* (London: Verso, 1988); Thomas Bender, ed., *The Antislavery Debate: Capitalism and Abolitionism as a Problem in Historical Interpretation* (Berkeley: University of California Press, 1992); Arnold M. Paul, *Conservative Crisis and the Rule of Law*, previously cited; Twiss, *Lawyers and the Constitution*; Hall, *The Magic Mirror*; John Hope Franklin and Alfred A. Moss, Jr., *From Slavery to Freedom: A History of African Americans* (7th ed., New York: Knopf, 1994).

277 Richard Hofstadter remarks: "What probably left the deepest impress on Beard's readers was his brilliant interpretation of the Civil War as the Second American Revolution....He saw the whole catastrophe as America's counterpart of the Puritan revolution or the French Revolution—an inevitable battle of rival social classes ending in a transit of power, a 'social cataclysm in which the capitalists, laborers, and farmers of the North and West drove from power in the national government the planting aristocracy of the South.'... With the power of the slaveholders shattered, the Northern capitalists were able to impose their economic program, quickly passing a series of measures on tariffs, banking, homesteads, and immigration that guaranteed the success of their plans for economic development. Solicitude for the freedman had little to do with Northern policies" (*The Progressive Historians* [New York: Knopf, 1968], pp. 303–04).

See also, Harold J. Laski, *The American Democracy* (New York: Viking Press, 1948): "[W]ithin the framework of the American situation compromise was quite impossible. Costs had begun so to eat into prices that it

a host of later scholars from across several disciplines who have followed Beard's lead in this regard.[278] In fact, an understanding of the Civil War

was only the exceptional man who, by the eighteen-fifties, was effectually solvent. The Southern economy was so rigidly geared to its unique institution that it could no more break with the system of ideas it imposed than France could break with the *ancien regime*, or Russia with Tsarism, without a revolutionary catastrophe. That is why Beard is so inescapably right in insisting that the Civil War was, in fact, the second American Revolution" (p. 462).

278   Louis Hackert, after listing the goals of Lincoln's Republican Party, adds that many "of these intentions were incorporated into the Republican Party platform of 1860. The defeat of Southern slavery in the Civil War made possible the carrying out of the program; industrial capitalism then was launched in the United States and moved ahead to its great successes of capital accumulation and higher standards of living generally....It was during the Civil War that the basis for the industrial growth of the United States was laid" (*American Capitalism*, pp. 52–53). Representing a younger generation of historians, the authors of *Generations of Americans* write: "The Republican economic package passed readily because the personal interests of Republican leaders—most of whom had substantial fortunes and extensive business interests—predisposed them to view it favorably. Furthermore, they believed it would promote the kind of modern industrial progress (as opposed to plantation agriculture) that the war, in part, was being fought to achieve. In fact, signs of the new order abounded as fortunes were made in government securities, army contracts, gold speculation, slum housing, retail merchandising, real estate, and railroads. In 1864, the year of Cold Harbor and the March to the Sea, a single New York department store cleared $5 million. The war years produced, in sum, both high profits and a network of laws and institutions that would assist business in the decades to come. On this, if not on race relations and the reconstruction of the nation, Republicans could agree" (Polakoff et al., *Generations of*

Americans [New York: St. Martin's Press, 1976], p. 375–76).

For another view, see Heilbroner and Singer, *Economic Transformation of America*: "[N]ot only was the North openly opposing the crucial institution of slavery on which the plantation system depended, but for all the contrary efforts of southern congressmen it was evident that the industrial interests in the nation were clearly rising to dominance over the agricultural. To put it bluntly, the North was rich and growing richer, and the South by comparison was poor and growing poorer....In 1860, not counting its slaves, the South possessed about a quarter of the nation's population, but only a tenth of its capital. Worse was the seemingly unbreakable hold of agriculture, especially cotton, over the southern economy. Central to this fatal involvement was the plantation aristocracy. Unlike its commerce-minded forebears, the great planters had increasingly distanced themselves from business. They complained endlessly about their dependence on Yankee middlemen and resisted rather than welcomed capitalist attitudes in their daily affairs. Perhaps this reflected the fact that their investment in slaves—about $4 billion— represented half the value of all the assets in the cotton region of the South. Slavery is not a capitalist institution, and it is not surprising that as the South found itself ever more dependent on slavery, at least in its cotton economy, it also found itself more and more hostile to a capitalist way of life" (pp. 37–39).

Richard B. DuBoff, *Accumulation and Power: An Economic History of the United States* (Armonk, N.Y.: M. E. Sharpe, 1989): "The history-making developments of the last three decades of the nineteenth century had their origins in the 1850s. Structural trends in the economy were probably unaffected by the bloody 1861–1865 conflict—'the red business,' Walt Whitman called it—although the triumph of industrial capitalism would not have been so complete without the institutional shifts the war effected. The demise of slavery marked a turning point in national politics, and it removed the last

along the lines of Richard Hofstadter's reading of Beard's work has become the conventional wisdom. Consider, for example, the following passage from a popular magazine essay:

When the United States was established, the North and the South accepted each other as effectively two distinct economic and ideological entities based on antagonistic systems of property: the North was industrial, liberal-bourgeois, and capitalist, while the South was agricultural, aristocratic, paternalis-

---

obstacle to northern industrial hegemony and the expansion of the capitalist mode of production to continental dimensions" (p. 28).

Michel Aglieta, *A Theory of Capitalist Regulation: The U.S. Experience*, David Fernbach, trans. (London: Verso, 1979): "The American Civil War was the final act of the struggle against colonial domination. This is why it is legitimate to see it as the origin of the modern epoch in the overall trajectory of the American capitalist revolution. The slave form of production in the South owed its existence and its prosperity to its total integration into an English-dominated international trade. It blocked the unification of the American nation at every level, and threatened to put an end to the frontier expansion....What was at stake in the Northern war effort was thus simultaneously the direct penetration of capitalism to the entire territory of the Union, the establishment of tariff protection, and the political and ideological unification of the nation under the leadership of the industrial and financial bourgeoisie" (pp. 77–78).

Ratner, Soltow and Sylla, *Evolution of the American Economy*: "The southern economy was not stagnant in the antebellum years, and its slave labor system, however deplorable on other grounds, apparently contributed to the South's overall economic prosperity. It was a prosperity, however, that was much less evenly shared than it would have been without slavery....The nearly four million slaves of 1860 were owned by fewer than 400,000 persons. Less than one-third of southern families, in fact, held slaves. The slaveholders were greatly outnumbered by small, nonslaveholding planters and yeoman farmers. Slaveholders, nevertheless,

dominated the economic, political, and social life of the South and exercised great power in national affairs. This resulted from their inherited wealth, social position, and control of southern policies, but it was also based on incomes and wealth that continued to increase throughout the antebellum years as the result of a cotton boom unique in history" (pp. 147–49).

Dowd, *U.S. Capitalist Development*: "[B]y the 1820s [the South] was the leading sector in the U.S. economy, with its King Cotton. Its economic needs and its social system gave it a viewpoint on matters of the State profoundly different from that coming to be held by the manufacturers, merchants, and financiers of the North. But up to the Civil War, the South on balance held the largest part of the strategic posts in the State system: Supreme Court justices, heads of congressional committees, cabinet posts, and the presidency....[O]ne can gain useful insights into what those involved in a struggle wanted most by seeing what those who won did with their enhanced power. The slaves were freed, of course. But within a few years, the promises of 'forty acres and a mule' were discreetly shelved; more important and at least as revealing, arrangements were made between the triumphant North and the defeated South to allow the latter to regain full sway over its *internal* (including its racial) politics in exchange for northern control of the federal government and easy access to the investment possibilities of the resource-rich South—in railroads, timber, land speculation, minerals, and the like. The new State system rapidly removed all obstacles to the full realization of industrial capitalism in the United States" (pp. 437–38).

tic, and anticapitalist....As the North's power and ambitions grew, it was unwilling to abide by arrangements based on a previous and obsolete calculus of relative strength, while the South was not satisfied with merely a diminishing respect for its view. It wanted to determine its own future without being subordinate to or dependent on an opposing, and increasingly threatening, ideology and political economy. In the end the North's vision—of a powerful centralized state, a "Yankee Leviathan," deemed necessary for capitalist development—emerged as the nation's....Our separatist conflict was followed not, as Yankees assert, by national reconciliation but by military occupation to impose a new political and economic order on the defeated land...."[279]

The "North's vision," of course, is that of the classical theory of contract: the free labor, free market philosophy of an emerging entrepreneurial class that managed to translate its vision of social reality into the dominant legal and political structure of American life.[280] With final comple-

279 Benjamin Schwarz, "The Diversity Myth: America's Leading Export," *Atlantic Monthly* (May 1995), pp. 64–65. Similarly, John Agnew, a geographer and director of the Social Science Program at Maxwell Graduate School of Syracuse University, argues that "America was settled by Europeans as it was incorporated into the world-economy. It also became the first 'settler-state' after achieving its political independence from Britain. Within its original territory along the Atlantic coast it also contained contrasting, and ultimately incompatible, modes of socio-economic organization: a plantation agriculture based on slavery in the South and classic capitalist or 'free' enterprise in the North" ("The United States in the World-Economy," Bertell Ollman and Jonathan Birnbaum, eds., in *The United States Constitution* [New York: New York University Press, 1990], p. 29).

280 Richard H. Abbott observes: "Slavery, they claimed, was at war with northern values and institutions and threatened to strangle the economic development of the whole nation. These Boston businessmen were bound together by a passionate commitment to a free-labor economy. To them, free labor meant more than the literal freedom of a worker to earn his own living. It represented the opportunity of all men to advance their personal welfare by their own efforts. Free labor in their minds was associated with institutions that enhanced opportunity for self improvement...[a]nd it depended heavily upon the existence of free, democratic political institutions. In the minds of the Boston free-labor advocates, slavery, and the insidious southern political influence it generated, which they called the Slave Power, threatened all of these things" (*Cotton and Capital: Boston Businessmen and Antislavery Reform, 1854-1868* [Amherst, Mass.: University of Massachusetts Press, 1991], p. 5). Assessing defects in the free-labor argument, he adds: "Some historians have wondered how northerners could attack slavery as oppressive and at the same time be blind to the deficiencies of their own wage-labor system. It would appear that critics of slavery failed to acknowledge these deficiencies at least in part because they regarded slavery as a far worse form of labor exploitation. Their goal was to give the slave the same freedom as the free white worker; then blacks, like whites, would be free to rise or fall to the level they deserved" (ibid., pp. 7–8). John R. Commons and Richard T. Ely typified the reforming economists who, early in the twentieth century (during the rise of state capitalist critique of the dominant legal system) attacked this particular "defect" in free labor

tion of that project which history seemed to have set for northern market forces, the transition from precapitalist to capitalist society was now secure. Yet this enterprise could not have become firmly enshrined in law, and would not have produced concrete constitutional alterations, were it not for the massive deployment of military force to crush southern resistance. Violence was the key to a realization of legal and economic transformation.

The "Civil War Amendments," as they are frequently designated, were quickly added to the Constitution in the years following Appomattox.[281] Ratified in 1868, the Fourteenth Amendment contained clauses that would become among the Constitution's moar famous: a due process clause, the equal protection clause, and so forth. However, much these clauses might have been used to benefit newly emancipated African-Americans in succeeding decades, that would not be their primary purpose for many years to come; on the contrary, there were other, more "substantial" interests waiting in line to receive the kind of benefits that only law could provide. "As every educated person knows," Barrington Moore wrote in 1966, "the Fourteenth Amendment has done precious little to protect Negroes and a tremendous amount to protect corpora-

theory: legal equality in contract, including employment contracts, simply masked the real inequality of social condition.

Tony A. Freyer remarks: "By the 1850s the process was sufficiently advanced that the values of personal independence rooted in the traditional producer economy increasingly were amalgamated with capitalist values in a new order premised on free labor. [Virginia Supreme Court Justice Peter] Daniel's response to the rise of free-labor ideals was characteristically defiant. Increasingly dominated by capitalist values, the North by 1850 was, he believed, incapable of producing 'any thing' that was 'good and decent.' As for a society based on the free-labor ideology, he could 'scarcely imagine a greater slavery, or any condition more absolutely vulgar, unrefined and unrefining than the scuffle and the selfish contention' it engendered in even the most mundane affairs of life....Finally, of course, the conflict between free and slave labor could not be contained within the constitutional order, and Daniel, like most southerners, supported secession" (*Producers*

Versus Capitalists: Constitutional Conflict in Antebellum America [Charlottesville: University of Virginia Press, 1994], p. 201).

William Appleman Williams notes: "[T]he advocates of antislavery laissez faire insisted that no one who did not accept their version of the axioms of laissez faire should be permitted to share the territorial empire. As far as they were concerned, slavery was a violation of those principles. For them, at any rate, the arrival of the Age of Laissez Nous Faire meant that the Constitution had to be interpreted—that is, rewritten—in the light of this outlook. Since the divergence of opinion ultimately defined *the* question, the basic cause of the Civil War was the Weltanschauung of laissez faire. Unwilling to compete within the framework and under the terms of the Constitution, northern antislavery advocates of laissez faire finally undertook to change the rules in the middle of the game—and in the middle of the continent—by denying the south further access to the expanding market place" (*Contours*, p. 286).

tions."[282] The historically crucial clause of the Fourteenth Amendment, which many educated people seem never to have read, states: "neither the United States nor any State shall assume or pay any debt or obligation incurred in aid of insurrection or rebellion against the United States, or any claim for the loss or emancipation of any slave; but all such debts, obligations and claims shall be held illegal and void."[283] Far from being a

---

281   See Hall, *Magic Mirror*, 144–45; Richard B. Bernstein with Jerome Agel, "Redefining the Union: The Civil War Amendments," in *Amending America* (New York: Times Books, 1993), pp. 94–116; Franklin and Moss, *From Slavery to Freedom*, pp. 220–46; Eric Foner and Olivia Mahoney, *America's Reconstruction* (New York.: HarperCollins, 1995); Donald W. Rogers, ed., *Voting and the Spirit of American Democracy* (Urbana: University of Illinois Press, 1990), pp. 55–81.

282   Barrington Moore, Jr., *Social Origins of Dictatorship and Democracy: Lord and Peasant in the Making of the Modern World* (Boston: Beacon Press, 1966), p. 149.

283   *The U.S. Constitution and Fascinating Facts About It* (Green Farms, Conn.: Tiger Publishing Group, 1993), p. 37. See also George Olshausen, "Socialism is Constitutional," *Monthly Review* 11 (1960): "There is another approach to the question whether socialism (as defined above) would be constitutional under the present United States Constitution. Setting up socialism means substituting a new economic system for the existing one. The reason for believing that this can be done within the present framework of government is that a previous economic change of comparable magnitude was accomplished with virtually no modification in the form of government. The pre–Civil War system of chattel slavery differed from private wage capitalism at least as much as private wage capitalism differs from socialism" (pp. 454–55). While Olshausen's last point is debatable, the observation with which he concludes his essay is not: "Under a constitutional amendment, moreover, private property may be taken without compensation, if desired. This was done for the first time by the Fourteenth Amendment. It is one of the ironies of American constitutional history that the Fourteenth Amendment, which provides in its *first* section that no person may be deprived of life, liberty, or property without due process of law, should provide in its *fourth* section that, 'neither the United States nor any state shall assume or pay…any claim for the loss or emancipation of any slave; but all such debts, obligations and claims shall be held illegal and void.' It all depends on whose ox is gored" (pp. 456–57).

Richard Epstein worries that "private property may be taken without compensation" even *without* a constitutional amendment: "The weaknesses of modern law apply to both the ends and the means. Today judicial accounts of the police power are said to embrace virtually any kind of concern. To block the view of a neighbor and to fill in a ditch on one's own land are treated routinely as private wrongs that the state may prevent as of right, without payment of compensation. On matters of means, the most fanciful connections between an individual act and some ordinary harm may limit the use of private property.…Just as the tort law can operate properly only with a narrow conception of compensable harms, so too the constitutional law must embrace that conception to prevent the police power exception from swamping the basic substantive protection of property rights" (*Simple Rules for a Complex World* [Cambridge, Mass.: Harvard University Press, 1995], pp. 133–34).

Epstein is right about the nature of law but wrong to think that the law's inherent capacity for reflecting shifts in the structure of economic power, evaluation of which usually depends on whose ox is gored, is a "weakness of *modern* law" (whatever period of legal history that adjective is intended to delimit). No doubt, southern slave owners regarded the constitutional philosophy of northern capitalists as "swamping the basic substantive

due process or equal protection clause, this was the clause that explicitly set forth how capitalist legality really works. In his constitutional history of the right to property, *The Guardian of Every Other Right*, Vanderbilt legal historian James W. Ely, Jr., states bluntly that the "property interests of slave owners were eliminated without compensation, an instance of massive government interference with existing economic relationships to achieve societal goals."[284] Here was creative destruction with a vengeance: the old South was destroyed precisely in order to eliminate those "existing economic relationships" which interfered with—from the northern perspective—*America's* rise to power.

Furthermore, while many constitutional scholars have argued that the Fourteenth Amendment served the goals of economic rather than human liberty, it very clearly reflected what the Civil War was fought over. This point was stated succinctly by government attorney and legal commentator William Seagle more than half a century ago:

> In American constitutional law there has long raged a celebrated controversy whether the Supreme court of the United States perverted the intentions of the framers of the Fourteenth Amendment to the Federal Constitution, which, to protect the recently liberated slaves in the enjoyment of civil rights, guaranteed to all 'persons' due process of law and the equal protection of the laws. The Court held that the word "person" applied also to corporations and protected them against "discriminatory'" legislation. The merits of the controversy are almost irrelevant; the result was predetermined by the whole course of modern legal evolution and all the dominant tendencies of legal theory. The corporation was bound to be held a person as water is bound to flow downhill; otherwise the free market, *to ensure which the Civil War was fought*, would have been stultified at its birth.[285]

They are creating law, they are founding property, said Anatole France's Bulloch of the murderous penguins. And he was right. Nothing could illustrate more perfectly than the material surveyed here the little-acknowledged fact that law and property are ultimately founded in violence; and, by extension, profound shifts in social and economic power—represented by the kind of earth-shaking infrastructural transformations I have been discussing—are necessarily accompanied by resort

protection of property rights." But that's capitalism for you.

284 Ely, *Guardian of Every Other Right*, p. 83.

285 William Seagle, *The Quest for Law* (New York: Knopf, 1941), p. 268 (emphasis added).

to arms. Quoting Sir Thomas Erskine Holland, Ian Brownlie remarks that war has even been regarded as a form of "judicial procedure involving also execution and punishment; it was looked upon as the 'litigation of nations....'"[286] The Civil War "was a holocaust of death and destruction. The North lost some 360,000 men; the South 260,000—more, together, than the nation's total fatalities in all other wars combined."[287] *All* other wars combined. Nevertheless, phoenixlike, from the killing fields of America's greatest civil disorder, a new regime of law emerged. Just as "policy" can adroitly shift sides in the law/politics dichotomy, even violence and war can shift to the "law" side of the ledger during extraordinary periods of constitutional crisis. And that was exactly the situation when southern plantation owners refused to acquiesce in the expropriation of billions of dollars worth of their property.[288]

But what then remained of the rule of law? With not only *stare decisis* and the famous system of checks and balances on the left side of the law/politics opposition, but now policy, social engineering, even civil war, all recruited to the "law" side, what remained of the far pole, the "government of men" side of the antinomy, the world of desire, passion and politics, to which law might still bravely oppose itself? As we shall see in the next chapter, the violence of liberal capitalism would be deployed in

286   Ian Brownlie, *International Law and the Use of Force By States* (Oxford: Oxford University Press, 1963), p. 21.

287   Polakoff, et al., *Generations of Americans*, p. 370.

288   "In the late eighteenth century slavery in North America was under siege. Many of the ex-colonies had adopted constitutions banning slavery even when they had no slaves to ban, and slavery was outlawed in the Northwest Territory. Furthermore, demand for tobacco, a leading slave crop, was stagnant. These conditions have led historians to argue that but for the appearance of cotton, slavery might have become economically unsuitable and withered away. Instead three generations later tens of thousands died in the Civil War and billions of dollars were spent in the effort to eradicate slavery from North America. Clearly southerners were not prepared to relinquish their 'peculiar institution' willingly" Atack and Passell, *A New Economic View of American History* (New York: W. W. Norton, 1994), p. 326. The authors conclude, that "despite sharp

and sometimes acrimonious debate over the nature of slavery and its consequences, Robert Fogel and Stanley Engerman's estimate that slaveowners earned about 10 percent on the market price of their bondsmen and women has gone almost unchallenged for two decades. The issue now seems fairly settled: Slavery was profitable....Estimates of sustained slave profitability from at least the 1830s suggest that southern slaveowners were unlikely to have freed their working slaves voluntarily" (ibid., p. 330). As Laski suggested, the Civil War was as essential to American history as the French Revolution was to that of France, for both brought into being what was, indeed, a "new regime": see Isser Woloch, *The New Regime: Transformations of the French Civic Order, 1789-1820s* (New York: W. W. Norton, 1994).

289   See *Webster's New Universal Unabridged Dictionary* 2d ed., (New York: Simon and Schuster, 1979), p. 798. *Merriam-Webster's Collegiate Dictionary* (10th ed., Springfield, Mass.: Merriam-Webster, Inc., 1993), p. 510.

the first half of the twentieth century on an unprecedented scale, against the forces of authoritarian capitalism, precisely in the name of the rule of law and, indeed, in behalf of what Churchill would call, to the astonishment of excluded Germans, Western Christian civilization.

But the nineteenth century was more than just an another episode in the history of legal adjustment to real social change. Just as William Seagle speaks of water running downhill and Lester Thurow of economic plate tectonics, we may draw upon one further geological metaphor. Webster's dictionaries refer to a principal mountain watershed—specifically, the Rocky Mountains—as the Great Divide. More generally, the term can refer to death, an important crisis, or a significant point of division. The transformation from precapitalist to capitalist civilization in the United States involved all of these meanings. The earliest recorded date of usage in English is listed as 1868—the same year that the Fourteenth Amendment, with its triumphant legitimation of the spoils of war, was incorporated within America's fundamental law.[289]

CHAPTER IV

WAKE OF
THE FLOOD

By which time, arrival of the twentieth century keenly anticipated. A curious dialogue among law professors about motivation in history is briefly analyzed, then set to one side. Philosophical reflections on the German Ideology, the like not to be found in any light French romance. Materialist approach to distinguishing American and German legal development adopted, with strict liability and fault standards in tort law given particular emphasis. Bismarck makes an appearance; legal, political, and economic continuity among three Reichs proposed; Barrington Moore's critique of all this, once again, relied upon. The New Deal and emergence generally of state capitalism are pictured as part of a "left of center" strategy deployed to preserve a liberal capitalism which rose from the ashes of Sherman's March to the Sea. Various factors eventually producing a new synthesis, global capitalism, contribute to the demise of the New Deal order. Law, once again (as it had first with capitalism's prise de pouvoir *and then, later, under the influence of Roosevelt liberalism) turns somersaults and the end of the nation state is predicted without enthusiasm.*

> *While American anticolonialism was to have a great impact on the*
> *Third World countries, the biggest impact on Europe was the*
> *American ideology personified by Roosevelt and the New Deal.*
> *Virtually the entire communist movement from America to Russia*
> *to the European and Asian parties believed that America was*
> *coterminous with Roosevelt and the New Deal. Ho Chi Minh was*
> *so taken with America that he made the American Declaration of*
> *Independence the model for Vietnam's own declaration of*
> *independence from France.*
> FRANZ SCHURMANN[290]

> *The following must also be considered, gentlemen. In all history*
> *there has never been a coalition composed of such heterogeneous*
> *partners with such totally divergent objectives as that of our*
> *enemies. The states which are now our enemies are the greatest*
> *opposites which exist on earth: ultra-capitalist states on one side*
> *and ultra-Marxist states on the other; on one side a dying*
> *empire—Britain; on the other side a colony, the United States*
> *waiting to claim its inheritance. These are states whose objectives*
> *diverge daily....If we can deal it a couple of heavy blows, this*
> *artificially constructed common front may collapse with a mighty*
> *thunderclap at any moment.*
> ADOLPH HITLER[291]

The market approach to social organization, and its corresponding set of legal relationships, generated substantial criticism, even before the nineteenth century ended; the emergence of a Progressive critique of the system during the twentieth century fed directly into a reorganization of state and society once the Great Depression set in and the market seemed increasingly to depend upon outside intervention simply for its own survival. "After a generation of nibbling away at the Classical system," Robert Gordon writes, "the Progressives brought it crashing down in the New Deal"[292]—hence, the rise of state capitalism.

The state capitalist approach to managing economic crisis itself lasted only a few decades and never threatened to exceed the boundaries or limits of capitalist social relations. The resurrection of laissez faire ideology

290 Franz Schurmann, *The Logic of World Power* (New York: Pantheon, 1974), pp. 67–68.
291 Adolph Hitler's address to his generals, December, 1944, quoted in Gabriel Kolko, *The Politics of War* (New York: Pantheon, 1990), p. 37.

and antistatist social policy today seems to retrieve the classical economic orientation of an earlier period; at the same time it forges a new synthesis, a further permutation of social forces, if not presaging Fukuyama's end of history. The transition from precapitalist to capitalist society in the nineteenth century, to be sure, represents *the* "great transformation," and alteration and adjustment of legal doctrine in the twentieth century stands in the shadow of the one really big change.

Having said that, however, interesting questions about modern society and its politics remain. How, for example, could both the world communist movement (according to Franz Schurmann) and a host of influential postwar American historians see the modern United States almost entirely in terms of New Deal liberalism while, at the same time, the leader of German fascism (Adolph Hitler) saw the same national culture in terms of a dramatic divergence of interest between capitalism and communism? Overemphasizing the left-of-center character of twentieth-century American capitalism may have misled leftwing militants then and academic historians later, whereas over-emphasizing right-of-center interests may have led Hitler into a false optimism about World War II's possible outcome, even as late as the end of 1944. With this in mind, I will try to avoid these twin errors of historical and political judgment as I conclude my outline of American legal development.

I. MOTIVE

> *Marx and Engels made a fundamental contribution to historical*
> *thinking with this distinction between the subjective motivations*
> *of historical actors and the transforming factors underlying*
> *the observable course of events.... To accept what the historical*
> *actors say or believe as the actual cause of historical events in a*
> *given epoch is to "share the illusion of that epoch."*
> THOMAS SOWELL [293]

Judge Richard Posner devotes a full chapter of his book, *Overcoming Law*, to the work of Harvard legal historian Morton Horwitz. While Posner

---

292 Robert W. Gordon, "The Elusive Transformation," *Yale Journal of Law and the Humanities* 6 (1994), p. 143.

293 Thomas Sowell, *Marxism* (New York: William Morrow, 1985), pp. 62–63.

describes Horwitz's main thesis as arresting and clearly argued—not only plausible but "a formidable synthesis of historical materials and a powerful if partial vision"—he nevertheless registers a critical reservation to Horwitz's explanation of why American law developed as it did. He charges Horwitz with having "overlooked efficiency justifications for legal doctrines," and asks pointedly, "if the judges had been bent on putting one over on the public, why had the great 'redistributive' decisions been so forthright in grounding legal doctrine on economic policy rather than just on the usual obfuscatory talk about rights, justice, precedent?"[294]

We need not return to a chapter and verse recital of language from the common law contract cases we have already examined to discover an enormous amount of extremely artful obfuscatory talk about rights, justice, and precedent, specifically employed in behalf of judicial decisions which dramatically readjusted common law doctrine to fit new economic realities. Whether the courts *intentionally* sought to engage in redistributive decision-making seems beside the point; in any case, no one could seriously assert that the transition from precapitalist to capitalist society could be accomplished without "redistributive" consequences. Rather, Posner's main point (contra Horwitz) is that the judiciary was not engaged in some sort of elaborate confidence game. Judges were hardly timid about acknowledging what was going on: they openly grounded their legal decisions in economic policy explanations. Posner's primary objection, then, seems to be the notion that courts were "bent on putting one over on the public"—in which case, the difference between these two writers amounts to very little. Perhaps it is a question of the relative degree of consciousness they ascribe to the individual judges who were engaged in adapting the law to new social realities. Perhaps they differ as to whether judges were motivated by a desire to foster efficient economic growth, or simply to enhance the social and political power of entrepreneurial capitalists. Reading between the lines, one can even argue that Posner and Horwitz are really just disagreeing about whether the kind of capitalist economic development the United States underwent in the nineteenth century was, on balance, good or bad. More important than their differences is what they—and I—hold in common: a conviction that law has responded in important ways to the unfolding economic history of the nation; that there are, in fact, "transforming factors underlying the observable course of events," as Thomas Sowell has put it. Whatever their

294 Richard Posner, *Overcoming Law* (Cambridge,
Mass.: Harvard University Press, 1995), pp. 272–73.

ultimate political differences might be, Posner cannot resist acknowledging what he regards as the primary strength of Horwitz's scholarship, specifically the way that Horwitz's second volume of legal history remains grounded in the first. Posner singles out, in his critique, what he regards as a "theme better documented, less conjectural, and more closely connected to the earlier book. This is the story of the struggle to adapt legal categories to changed social or economic conditions." That was Adam Smith's story. It was Friedrich Engels' story, too. "This is the kind of story," Posner concludes, "that Horwitz tells well."[295]

That there is an underlying commonality to the accounts provided by Posner and Horwitz is not a unique insight. Historian and law professor Herbert Hovenkamp, who has established himself as one of the most knowledgeable interpreters of the relationship between economic and legal development in American history, argues that "Horwitz's positive theory of wealth-transferring 'subsidies' is more compatible with Posner's historical explanations than it appears at first. Professor Horwitz never maintains that judges intended to use common law rules to transfer wealth. He argues merely that early nineteenth century jurists began to adopt certain 'utilitarian' or 'pro-developmental' principles," and that the adoption of such rules eventually (and inevitably) had redistributive consequences.[296]

Legal historian Robert Gordon, writing in the *Harvard Law Review*, comments that Horwitz's thesis "seems to me perfectly correct if taken as a proposition about judicial ideology: it's what the judges repeatedly said they wanted to do."[297]

However, professor of law and political science at the University of Toronto Jennifer Nedelsky seems to take just the opposite tack: "Morton Horwitz has convincingly shown that in the decades before the Civil War, the courts were actively engaged in reshaping the rules of the common law." Some of Horwitz's claims, she states, "are disputed, but generally not those about the extent—as opposed to the dates and purpose—of

295 Richard Posner, *Overcoming Law*, pp. 285–86.

296 Herbert Hovenkamp, "The Economics of Legal History," *Minnesota Law Review* 67, (1983), p. 676. See also Herbert Hovenkamp, "Capitalism," in *The Oxford Companion to the Supreme Court of the United States* pp. 117–25 (New York: Oxford University Press, 1992); Herbert Hovenkamp,

Enterprise and American Law 1836–1937 (Cambridge, Mass.: Harvard University Press, 1991); Victoria A. Saker, "Between a Doctrine and a Hard Place," review of Hovenkamp's *Enterprise and American Law* in *Reviews in American History* 21 (1993), pp. 279–84.

297 Robert W. Gordon, Book Review, *Harvard Law Review* 94, (1981), p. 907–17.

the transformations in the common law."[298] Thus, whether the common law was transformed to secure capitalist efficiency (Posner), to subsidize a rising class (Horwitz), or simply to secure economic development (Hovenkamp) is left up for grabs. "The most problematic parts of Horwitz's argument," Nedelsky comments in a footnote, "are about in whose interests these changes were made and how self-consciously." The part of what has come to be called "Horwitz's thesis" which Gordon finds "perfectly correct" (the ideological argument) is the very thing that Nedelsky regards (or believes most critics regard) as "most problematic." With reference to the actual motivations of individual legal actors on the nineteenth-century historical stage, Nedelsky specifically says that her own argument "does not rely on the claims of class bias."[299]

My particular account of history—of American legal history—is organized around the way in which alterations in the forces and relations of production produce corresponding, broad-brush changes in law and society, over quite extended periods of time.[300] The unfolding of such powerful forces invariably have large-scale human consequences: great events—the sweep of history—tend to transcend our capacity to provide an intimately detailed human portrait, a novelistic depiction of historical "motivation," if what is meant by that is something along the lines of a human psychology.

Historians may well profit, in the end, from devoting their (necessarily limited) time and energy to observable social causes and consequences, in lieu of the much less transparent categories like ideology or motivation. I take my cue from no less than the "queen of crime" herself, P. D. James, who writes in *Unnatural Causes*: "Admittedly she had no apparent motive. But what did that matter? Despite what he had said to his aunt that morning Dalgliesh knew perfectly well that motive was not the first concern. The detective who concentrated logically on the 'where,' 'when,' and 'how,' would inevitably have the 'why,' revealed to him in all its pitiful inadequacy."[301]

298 Jennifer Nedelsky, *Private Property and the Limits of American Constitutionalism* (Chicago: University of Chicago Press, 1990), p. 226.
299 Ibid., p. 319.
300 See historian Harvey Goldberg's reference to Karl Kautsky, "the original armchair Marxist. This is a man who never saw the street, never saw a barricade, and who never has people when he writes history, only movements and trends" ("Rosa Luxemburg," Goldberg Center History Lecture Audiotapes [Madison: University of Wisconsin, Feb. 9, 1976]). Kautsky provides the example of how writing like mine can go wrong.
301 P. D. James, *Unnatural Causes* (New York: Charles Scribner's, 1967), p. 88.

2. THE GERMAN IDEOLOGY

It has not occurred to any one of these philosophers to inquire into the connection of German philosophy with German reality, the connection of their criticism with their own material surroundings.
MARX AND ENGELS, *The German Ideology*[302]

On a micro-level as it were, or segmentarily, we may look at the differences within modern civilization just as we do at differences between it and nonmodern cultures. Precisely such contrasts within Germany have often been insisted upon, especially that between the most rapid industrial development and the continued existence of archaic features in the society.
LOUIS DUMONT, *German Ideology*[303]

In the same review essay where he discusses questions of judicial motivation during the transformation of nineteenth-century American common law, Robert Gordon raises a comparative issue regarding the transformation of German private law during the same period. He asks, "why Germany responded to industrialization by imposing strict liability on railroads and industrial concerns for accidents by way of exception to a preexisting fault standard," while a systematic generalization of the fault principle itself appeared to characterize the American response.[304]

A fault standard for determining civil liability focuses on whether an individual causing harm or injury was negligent in his conduct. If he was negligent—if he is found, that is, to have acted carelessly—then he is regarded as liable for the damage he caused and must compensate those on whom he has inflicted injury.[305] A strict liability standard on the other hand, tends to impose liability on those who caused injury whether or not they were actually at fault or acted carelessly: they are held "strictly" liable and are not allowed to defend themselves by arguing that though they

---

302 Karl Marx and Friedrich Engels, *The German Ideology* (3d ed., Moscow: Progress Publishers, 1976).

303 Louis Dumont, *German Ideology: From France to Germany and Back* (Chicago: University of Chicago Press, 1994), p. 18.

304 Robert Gordon, Book Review, p. 907.

305 "[N]ineteenth century judges adopted a highly moralistic rhetoric, allowing recovery only if defendants were morally culpable and victims wholly innocent" (Richard L. Abel, "Torts," in David Kairys, ed., *The Politics of Law: A Progressive Critique* [rev. ed., New York: Pantheon, 1990], p. 328).

may have caused injury, they nevertheless exercised a reasonable degree of care. They have to pay damages even though their conduct may well have been free of carelessness or negligence.[306] Obviously, the fault approach places emphasis on an actor's conduct, whereas the strict or absolute liablity approach subordinates blameworthiness to presumedly a more pressing concern with who will pay injured victims for harm suffered. Strict liability avoids, as much as possible, the problem of injured yet "uncompensated plaintiffs."

Yale professor Robert Gordon puts squarely in question the doctrinal disparity between nineteenth-century German and American tort theory: Why did industrialization, he wants to know, produce a fault approach in the U.S. and yet its seeming opposite, a strict liability approach, at about the same time in Germany? This is an excellent question and one, I suspect, few American law professors would think to ask. Yet it is just the sort of genuinely insightful query one expects from a serious intellectual historian like Gordon.

Most American law professors are not comparativists and Gordon understandably provides a footnote for his colleagues indicating where this bit of information extracted from German legal history has come: the first, or 1950 Oxford edition, of F. H. Lawson's standard *Negligence in the Civil Law*.[307] The year after Gordon's review was published, Oxford University Press brought out Lawson's and, Cambridge colleague, B. S. Markesinis' co-written sequel to *Negligence in the Civil Law*. In the revised text, they cite changes in the "industrial and economic environment" as a coherent explanation for changes in legal doctrine and, further, observe that although "lawyers and judges have, on the whole, avoided mentioning these factors in public and, instead, have chosen to conduct their argument on the basis of abstract concepts…they are there nonetheless."[308]

---

306 See, e.g., Judith Jarvis Thomson, "Remarks on Causation and Liability, Saul Levmore, ed." *Foundations of Tort Law* 103, 104 [New York, N.Y.: Oxford Univ. Press; , 1994]: "What we are concerned with here is not blame, but only who is to be out of pocket for the costs (p. 104).

307 Gordon, Book Review, p. 907n16 cites "F. Lawson, *Negligence in the Civil Law* pp. 45–46 (1950)."

308 "With the passage of time, however, the vagueness if not outright artificiality of these

distinctions became an asset which judges were prepared to utilise in response to the exigencies of a changed economic and social environment. The use of the 'implied license' concept thus became the 'most palpable fiction ever employed in order to impose legal responsibility,' and recently Lord Denning openly admitted the utility of such fictions as a means of avoiding the rigidity of the old law" (F. H. Lawson and B. S. Markesinis, *Tortious Liability for Unintentional Harm in the Common Law and Civil Law*. Cambridge,

Referring, again, to the "exigencies" of economy and society in determining the development of private law, the authors cite work by Lawrence Friedman and Jack Ladinsky which dramatically brings to light "environmental factors influencing the development of the law of torts."[309] Professor Lawrence Friedman (at Wisconsin, later Stanford),[310] to whom the authors refer, in conjunction with Lawson and Markesinis themselves,[311] and accompanied by a long list of preeminent economic and

Eng.: Cambridge University Press, 1982], vol. 1, p. 58): Here the authors juxtapose realist and materialist critiques in an admirable exposition of British legal development, even going so far as to find in Lord Denning's "open admissions" the equivalent of Judge Posner's jurisprudence of candor. They also assert: "Though there is clearly a considerable overlap between this and the previous policy factors, in this present type the emphasis is not so much on 'moral' or 'value' considerations as on the exigencies of the economic environment. Once again, lawyers and judges have, on the whole, avoided mentioning these factors in public and, instead, have chosen to conduct their argument on the basis of abstract concepts and legal doctrine. But unexpressed though these considerations may be, they are there nonetheless. Indeed, few are the cases which, once stripped of their legal technicalities, do not reveal the environmental forces that dictated their outcome" (ibid., p. 57). For these scholars, the superstructure does not simply reflect or correspond to the base; rather, the economic environment *dictates* legal outcomes.

309   "The law related to industrial accidents and workers' compensation can provide us with our last example of environmental factors influencing the development of the law of torts. In the rise and fall of the doctrine of 'common employment' we can find a neat illustration of these forces at work" (ibid., p. 58). For the specific citation, ibid. 203-n72. See also, Lawrence M. Friedman and Jack Ladinsky, "Social Change and the Law of Industrial Accidents," in *Foundations of Tort Law* (New York, N.Y.: Oxford Univ. Press; Saul Levmore, ed., 1994, pp. 205-15).

310   "Every legal system tries to redress harm done by one person to another. The industrial

revolution added an appalling increase in dimension. It manufactured injury and sudden death, along with profits and products of machines. The profits were a tempting and logical fund out of which the costs of the dead and the injured *might* be paid. Moreover, the industrial relationship was impersonal. No ties of blood or love prevented one cog in the machine from suing the machine and its owners. But precisely here (to the 19th century mind) lay the danger. Lawsuits and damages might injure the health of precarious enterprise. The machines were the basis for economic growth, for national wealth, for the greater good of society....In the mind of the 19th century, absolute liability might have been too dangerous; it might have strangled the economy altogether. If railroads, and enterprise generally, had to pay for all the damage done by 'accident,' lawsuits could drain them of their economic blood. Ordinary caution became the standard" (Lawrence M. Friedman, *A History of American Law* [New York: Simon and Schuster, 2d ed., 1985]. pp. 468–69).

311   F. H. Lawson and B. S. Markesinis: "With the growing mechanisation of the second half of the last century and the resulting multiplication of accidents, this kind of approach came more and more under scrutiny. The moral and educative basis of the fault system was also increasingly questioned. With some 35,000 deaths and 2,000,000 injuries in industrial accident in the U.S.A. alone from about 1900 onwards, the idea of leaving all these victims uncompensated became morally intolerable and politically unwise and the same was true in the more advanced countries of Western Europe. But these doubts, on their own, could not have altered the system if changes in the economic environment did not also favour some reappraisal of the problem.

legal historians, writing both before,[312] and after Friedman,[313] have per-
suasively argued, at least in outline, for the social and economic character
of a transformation in the rules of American tort law in the nineteenth
century. Lawson and Markesinis readily acknowledge in their 1982 pref-

For by that time industry was standing on its own feet and the protectionist spirit which had brought it to maturity was becoming less relevant. And, with the help of rapidly increasing insurance protection, business concerns were more and more capable of carrying such losses" *Tortious Liability*, p.143.

312 See, for example, Charles Gregory, "Trespass to Negligence to Absolute Liability," 37 *Virginia Law Review* 359 (1951), excerpted in *Law and Jurisprudence in American History* Stephen B. Presser and Jamil S. Zainaldin, eds., 1995). pp. 306–312. (St. Paul, Minn.: West Publ. Co.; 3rd ed., 1995). Willard Hurst argues that "[t]ort cases evidenced a similar caution against creating indefinite risks of liability, especially during the rise of new industries in the first half of the century; for example, early difficulties of raising capital for railroads underlined the hazard of throttling promising beginnings by imposing too heavy financial burdens. Of course, it was also true that the functioning of a market-oriented, division-of-labor society rested on the maintenance of an assured framework of justifiable expectations as to other people's behavior. At some point, this emphasis was inconsistent with relieving entrepreneurs from damage liability. However, the extent of the inconsistency did not become clear until the enormous expansion of the use of machinery in the last quarter of the century" (James Willard Hurst, *Law and the Conditions of Freedom in the Nineteenth-Century United States* [Madison: University of Wisconsin Press, 1956], p. 20).

313 See, for example, Morton J. Horwitz, *The Transformation of American Law, 1780–1860* (Cambridge, Mass.: Harvard University Press, 1977) pp. 85–108; Stuart Bruchey remarks in *Enterprise* (Cambridge, Mass.: Harvard Univ. Press, 1990): "In the 1842 case of *Farwell v. The Boston and Worcester Railroad Corporation*, Chief Justice Lemuel Shaw of the Massachusetts Supreme Judicial Court laid down a principle of common law with respect to the responsibility of an employer for

accidents which governed the course of law for much of the remainder of the nineteenth century....By compelling workers themselves to bear the cost of those injuries, the fellow-servant rule unquestionably relieved employers of large sums in compensatory payments, thus encouraging investment in industrial enterprises. When Shaw wrote in the early 1840s, the human consequences of rapid technological change were unforeseeable. By the last decade of the century, though, the quickened pace of industrialization was bringing in its train thousands of deaths and perhaps as many as 2 million injuries every year" (p. 367).

Charles Sellers writes in *The Market Revolution* (New York: Oxford University Press, 1991): "So that the onward spirit of the age could have its way, common-law principles of liability were steadily eroded. To encourage men to take risks in the interest of productivity, American judges began to insist that injured parties demonstrate illegality or negligence by the person (or corporation) causing the injury. The new American law of damages 'held that every man of mature age must take care of himself,' according to its most influential interpreter. 'He need not expect to be saved from himself by legal paternalism....When he acted, he was held to have acted at his own risk with his eyes open, and he must abide the appointed consequences'" (pp. 52–53).

Kermit L. Hall writes in *The Magic Mirror: Law in American History* (New York: Oxford University Press, 1989): "Antebellum judges devised rules that shaped the law of tort for the remainder of the nineteenth century and well into the twentieth. They accepted that some injuries would go uncompensated and that a fault standard (removed from jury supervision) would facilitate economic development by insulating entrepreneurs from the costs of accidents. Tort principles fell with special harshness on the growing industrial work force, although judges in cases involving

ace that the second book "has its origins" in the first.[314] And if we look at the pages in the earlier edition, to which Professor Gordon refers the readers of his review, we can already see an interest in social causation of negligence law emerging within Lawson's legal theory. Contrasted with developments in American tort law, the German developments outlined by Gordon may appear, at least at first, somewhat surprising. Yet Lawson replies that "[i]t is indeed not altogether surprising that the first serious inroad on the principle of no liability without fault was made by the Prussian Railway Law of 1838, which introduced strict liability for certain

public transportation accidents showed some solicitude to passengers" (p. 126).

Hall et al. observe: "The emerging tort law made tortfeasors generally liable for the harms they caused others. However, four rules evolved that undermined the likelihood of injured parties recovering damages. 'Contributory negligence' prevented an injured person from winning damages if the defendant could prove that even a small part of the accident was caused by the injured party. The rule against 'wrongful death' suits prevented the families of persons killed in accidents from recovering damages. The fellow servant rule…prevented most workers from recovering damages for job-related injuries. Finally, courts refused to hold tortfeasors responsible for damages resulting from 'remote causation.' These rules tended to aid the new nineteenth-century industries, especially the emerging railroads and steamboat companies" (Kermit L. Hall, William M. Wiecek, and Paul Finkelman, eds., *American Legal History: Cases and Materials* [New York: Oxford University Press; 1991], pp. 179–80).

Even some practicing tort lawyers have gone to the trouble to write about nineteenth-century developments in their particular area of professional specialization. Stuart Speiser writes: "As industry and the railroads expanded, they left accident victims in their wake by the hundreds of thousands. The old tort law that made the injuring party absolutely liable was an inconvenience to the Industrial Revolution, so the early-nineteenth-century courts changed it, first in England, and then in the young United States. The new concept was: fault had to

be proved before there could be any payment of damages. This seemed fair enough. But the captains of industry knew that jurors in accident cases would probably be more sympathetic to injured people than to big business; so something had to be done to prevent juries from impeding industrial progress by compensating its victims too freely. The defense lawyers and the judges who were persuaded by these arguments were equal to the task. They erected an obstacle course designed to wear down or eliminate all but the hardiest accident claimants and their lawyers" *Lawsuit* [New York: Horizon, 1980], p. 124).

Last but not least, see Edward A. Purcell, Jr., *Litigation and Inequality: Federal Diversity Jurisdiction in Industrial America, 1870–1958* (New York: Oxford University Press, 1992): "Scholars have debated the extent to which nineteenth-century negligence law helped 'subsidize' business enterprise by narrowing liability and allowing corporations to avoid much of the cost of industrial accidents.…[This study] shows that in one relatively large class of claims—those held by individuals against foreign corporations—late nineteenth- and early twentieth-century practice gave defendants advantages that enabled them to impose on others a substantial part of the costs of industrial accidents.…Given the creation each year of hundreds of thousands of potential new claims against foreign corporations, the aggregate result of the system's operation was to save them large sums of money" (pp. 256–57).

314 F. H. Lawson and B. S. Markesinis, *Tortious Liability*, p. xiii.

accidents; *for the Industrial Revolution had hardly begun in Prussia by that date and power was still in the hands of the landowning classes.*"[315]

Gordon has just been discussing, in his review, the systematic generalization of the fault principle within American tort law during the second half of the nineteenth century. But Lawson is addressing the initial inroad of the fault principle in Germany, *in 1838*.[316] Lawson specifically argues that the German developments are not altogether surprising for two reasons: first, unlike the situation in Britain and the United States, the industrial revolution had hardly begun; and second, power was still in the hands of the landowning classes. Unlike Jennifer Nedelsky, who suggests that "claims of class bias" do not inform her argument about the development of American property law, Lawson incorporates questions of class relations and class power into his account of a developing Prussian tort law. Indeed, even in the first book, in 1950, he was willing to acknowledge Germany's political and economic late modernization, the status of being an industrial "latecomer," as a foundation for the story historians need to tell about German legal development.[317]

315   F. H. Lawson, *Negligence in the Civil Law*, p. 45 (emphasis added).

316   In the context of German railway development, the difference between 1838 and even the 1840s, let alone the 1880s, is important: Tom Kemp writes in *Industrialization in Nineteenth-Century Europe* (2d ed., London: Longman Group, 1985): "The early reception of the railway by the Prussian and other state governments was not encouraging. Only its disadvantages were seen and the early lines were hedged around with many restrictions; speculative excesses were especially feared. The conservative opposition to novelty began to weaken in the course of the 1840s when the estate owners began to realize that the new form of transport could expand the market for their crops and thus increase their revenues. At about the same time the military men began to understand the strategic significance of the railway. In the years following the restrictive Prussian railway law of 1838, the attitude of the state became much more encouraging and trunk lines were built with a state guarantee of interest" (p. 93).

317   "No doubt the virtual economic standstill which Germany experienced as a result of the Thirty Years War, and even more the political divisions which the Peace of Westphalia (1648)

consecrated, account in large measure for the growing lag between Germany and the neighboring regions in western Europe. In respect of social structure and political regime the German states in the eighteenth century stood nearer to Tsarist Russia than they did to the West. Within the autocratically governed states of kings, princes and dukes social relations remained feudal or semi-feudal in character. This was most evident in the Hohenzollern lands of eastern Germany where the estates of the military landowning caste, the *Junkers*, were cultivated with the compulsory labour services of peasant serfs" (ibid., p. 79).

Where Kemp characterizes Germany as an industrial "latecomer," Rondo Cameron uses the descriptive term "laggard": "Germany was the last of the early industrializers. Indeed, a case can be made that it was something of a laggard. Poor and backward in the first half of the nineteenth century, the politically divided nation was also predominantly rural and agrarian. Small concentrations of industry existed in the Rhineland, Saxony, Silesia, and the city of Berlin, but they were mostly of the handicraft or proto-industrial variety. Poor transportation and communications facilities held back economic development, and the

After discussing the emergence of strict liability in German tort law, explaining it in terms of the *specificity* of Germany's social and economic history, Lawson adds two further examples from the time frame of interest to Gordon, the 1870s and 1880s. He states that the railway act of 1838 provided a model for the "more far-reaching *Reichshaftpflichtgesetz* [imperial law of liability] of 1871, which applied to the whole Reich," and points out that the "other great occasion for applying a theory of strict liability, workmen's compensation, was dealt with by Germany in the 1880's on other lines, by making the concerns in each industry combine to insure their employees against industrial accidents."[318]

This second example involving the protection of injured workers also appears to be at odds with American practice, especially considering Lawrence Friedman's frequently quoted description of how nineteenth-century American courts "invented new and more cunning traps for injured plaintiffs. One of these traps was the doctrine of contributory negligence. Another was the fellow-servant rule and its fellow traveler, the doctrine of assumption of risk."[319] How, one wonders, did German legislation protecting injured workmen actually get passed during the final decades of the nineteenth century? It is difficult to imagine such a solution being embraced in Germany, or anywhere else, without consent from the economically and politically powerful. But why wouldn't employers seek the cheapest sort of market solution, cutting liability back to the bone? Whether in the law concerning railroad accidents or injured workmen, why were the kind of doctrinal solutions described above imposed in Germany during the 1870s and 1880s? In other words, why where "restrictive" rules (Tom Kemp's adjective) enforced not simply prior to German industrialization but after it was in full swing?

"The conditions which prevailed before *and during* Germany's industrial emergence," Kemp notes, "gave capitalism in that country its special character. This comprised, in short, a high concentration of economic power in the advanced industries, a close association between industry and the banks and the combination of an archaic, traditional, institutional framework with the most developed forms of capitalism. It was a dynamic, not to say explosive, mixture."[320] Strict liability can be seen as a

numerous political divisions with their separate monetary systems, commercial policies, and other obstacles to commercial exchange further retarded progress" (*A Concise Economic History of the World* [New York: Oxford University Press, 1989], p. 240).

318 Lawson, *Negligence*, pp. 45–46.
319 Lawrence M. Friedman, *A History of American Law* (New York: Simon and Schuster, 1973), pp. 411–12.
320 Kemp, *Industrialization*, p. 78 (emphasis added).

quite modern legal instrument or conversely as a profoundly "archaic, traditional" doctrine that characterized actions for trespass in the English common law for centuries prior to the rise of industrial civilization.[321] So the question is not why Germany embraced strict liability in the nineteenth century while American courts were adopting the fault concept but, rather, what was specific to German capitalism during this period that led it to a different legal solution than the one embraced in the United States?

"The growth of the economy" in Germany during the nineteenth century had, in Kemp's view, "brought into being a larger middle class with its balance now shifted toward business. Its goals were to be found in material success and accomodation with the powers that be rather than in the visions of the intellectuals of the 1848 revolution."[322] This German

321   "Civil liability in the common law was originally based on a fairly simple concept—trespass. The King's Court in early England issued the writ of trespass to any litigant who could show that he had sustained a physical contact on his person or property, due to the activity of another. If this litigant-plaintiff could then convince the court that the defendant had intentionally brought about this contact, he had judgment for damages because of the trespass—unless the defendant could justify his act. But if the plaintiff could not establish intent, then in order to recover he had to go ahead and show that he had sustained some actual damage....[T]his ancient concept of trespass had reference to any contact achieved as the consequence of one's conduct against the interest of another, no matter under what circumstances it occurred, as long as the defendant's causative conduct was his voluntary act" (Gregory, "Trespass to Negligence," p. 306).

322   Kemp, *Industrialization*, p. 95. For a range of complimentary views, see Hans-Ulrich Wehler, *The German Empire 1871–1918*, Kim Trayner, trans., (Providence, R.I.: Berg Publishers, 1985): "Over seventy years ago the American sociologist Thorstein Veblen gave a penetrating analysis of the configuration of factors at this time: in a largely traditional society, only partially adapted institutionally between 1866 and 1871 and still ruled over by pre-industrial elites, the most advanced Western technology forced itself through with

unprecedented speed and accelerated social change" pp. 9–10.

Koppel S. Pinson writes in *Modern Germany: Its History and Civilization* (2d ed., New York: Macmillan, 1966): "The failure to regulate cartels during the Second Reich should not be taken as an expression of *laissez faire* policy. The tradition of *laissez faire* in German economic policy was very weak and, except for a brief heyday in the 1850's and 1860's, was soon overshadowed by much more vigorous governmental policy. Reference has already been made to the state nationalization of railroads in 1879. Even more of community control and regulation was displayed in the municipalities. Here electrical power plants, gas works, water works, traction companies, slaughterhouses, and other utilities were taken over by the municipal governments from private enterprise" (pp. 238–39).

In *Modern Germany: Society, Economy and Politics in the Twentieth-Century* (Cambridge, Eng.: Cambridge University Press, 1982), V. R. Berghahn notes: "[P]russian agriculture never embraced capitalism with unbridled enthusiasm, and older traditions of economic conduct lingered on. These conditions made the *Junker* vulnerable to the vagaries of the market which they supplied with a single crop: grain....Especially in rural Prussia, many of the patriarchal structures of the pre-industrial period had survived, supported by legal rights which put the landlord in a very powerful position" (pp. 5–6).

solution to the problem of social change was just the opposite of the American solution, namely the gauntlet which Lincoln and the Republican Party threw at the feet of the slave south.

We must pause here, in the midst of Professor Kemp's critique of German developments, to reflect upon the view of writer Shelby Foote, whose perspective on American history largely structures the story Ken Burns relates in his now famous public television documentary on the Civil War. That bloody conflict was especially tragic, in Foote's view, "because we failed to do the thing we really have a genius for which is compromise. Americans like to think of themselves as uncompromising; our true genius is for compromise. Our whole government's founded on it and it failed."[323] Such a view is utterly misguided. What shaped nineteenth-century American social history, especially in contrast to that of Germany and Japan, was the *rejection* of compromise—not failure to achieve it; the avoidance of any accommodation or compromise with

Arno J. Mayer observes in *The Persistence of the Old Regime: Europe to The Great War* (New York: Pantheon, 1981): "As agrarians and businessmen sought each other out, it became evident that in the logrolling between them the agrarians had the upper hand and secured the greater benefits....In Germany, even though the tariff of 1879 consecrated the collaboration of the masters of rye and of steel, it also confirmed the political subordination of the claimant bourgeoisie. Moreover, after Bismarck's fall the removal of Chancellor General Count Leo von Caprivi in 1894 reaffirmed the resolve of the protectionist agrarians not to permit any dilution of the feudalistic element in political society, notably in the executive branch of the imperial government" (p. 33).

In *From Kaiserreich to Third Reich: Elements of Continuity in German History, 1871–1945*, Roger Fletcher, trans. (London: Allen and Unwin, 1986), Fritz Fischer writes: "In terms of its social ideas and its distribution of political power so monarchic and feudal in structure, this in 1870 still predominantly agrarian German Empire developed in two waves (1850–1873 and 1896–1914), and on a scale and tempo bearing comparison only with the development of North America, into a modern industrial state. The new industrial bourgeoisie had established itself

as the economically dominant force no later than the onset of the boom period beginning in 1896, but it had been quite unable to acquire for itself a commensurate share in political power. One of the most significant results of Bismarck's conservative policy was his success in reconciling these two social elites by means of his post-1878 economic and social policies, indeed promoting the assimilation of the new industrial big bourgeoisie by the agrarian-feudal forces. This alliance of 'steel and rye', of the manor and blast furnace...persisted as the hard core of reaction within German society and continued to play a decisive role, despite manifold divergences, in 1933" (p. 40).

This "notorious alliance of rye and steel," Avraham Barkai grimly concludes, would leave "its stamp on Germany's state and society for a long time." Barkai, *Nazi Economics* (New Haven: Yale University Press, 1990), p. 73.

323 Shelby Foote, speaking in Ken Burns, *The Civil War, Episode One: The Cause*, 1961 (Pacific Arts Video/PBS Home Video, 1990). For extended critiques of Burns's *The Civil War*, see Jeanie Attie, "Illusions of History: A Review of *The Civil War*," 52 *Radical History Review* 95–104 (1992); Brian Henderson, "*The Civil War*: Did it not seem real?" *Film Quarterly* 44 (no. 3, spring 1991) p. 2.

either slavery or the reactionary social and economic system which the South represented was crucial. "To sum up with desperate brevity," says Barrington Moore, "the ultimate causes of the war are to be found in the growth of different economic systems leading to different (but still capitalist) civilizations with incompatible stands on slavery. The connection between Northern capitalism and Western farming helped to make unnecessary for a time the characteristic reactionary coalition between urban and landed elites and hence the one compromise that could have avoided the war."[324]

The only compromise which could have been reached that would have avoided the Civil War would have been exactly the sort of "reactionary coalition" that precipitated "revolution from above" in both Germany and Japan during the nineteenth century and led to the development, in the twentieth century, of fascism. Had the United States succeeded in finding a compromise between the industrial North and slave South, what would the consequences have been? The United States might well have modernized along lines more like those of Germany and Japan. Had such an accommodation been found, then the "United States," according to Moore, "would have been in the position of some modernizing countries today, with a latifundia economy, a dominant antidemocratic aristocracy, and a weak and dependent commercial and industrial class, unable and unwilling to push forward toward political democracy."[325] Had a power-

324 Barrington Moore, Jr., *Social Origins of Dictatorship and Democracy: Lord and Peasant in the Making of the Modern World* (Boston: Beacon, 1966), p. 141.

325 In the chapter tilted "Revolution from Above and Fascism" Moore contrasts the politics of reactionary coalition with those of assertive liberalism, arguing that the "second main route to the world of modern industry we have called the capitalist and reactionary one, exemplified most clearly by Germany and Japan. There capitalism took hold quite firmly in both agriculture and industry and turned them into industrial countries. But it did so without a popular revolutionary upheaval. What tendencies there were in this direction were weak, far weaker in Japan than in Germany, and in both were diverted and crushed. Though not the only cause, agrarian conditions and the specific types of capitalist transformation that took place in the countryside contributed very heavily to these

defeats and the feebleness behind any impulse toward Western democratic forms" (Moore, ibid., p. 433).

See also Wehler's observation: "Shortly after the French Revolution the Prussian minister von Struensee had informed the French ambassador that 'the salutary revolution' which in France had proceeded 'from below upwards' would 'gradually develop above downwards in Prussia.' By a policy of limited concessions the explosive revolutionary potential would be defused and a salutary transformation brought about by peaceful means. This 'revolution from above' had also been advocated in outline relatively early by Clausewitz....[A]s his contemporary Gneisenau put it: 'Wise laws designed to forestall the outbreak of revolution are like detonating a mine laid under our feet from which we have removed the explosive bit by bit....That is why Bismarck, with a self-confidence that came

ful, thoroughly native, American version of authoritarian capitalism aligned itself (or even exercised its genius for compromise) with Germany and Japan in the 1930s, where would we be today?

Kemp concludes that the German middle class's nationalism "outweighed its liberalism....A rapidly growing and advanced industry was combined with an archaic political framework and a society still dominated by men who belonged to the old regime."[326] Could Germany's social and economic situation provide a more strikingly different context for legal development than that which characterized the United States during the same period, the final third of the nineteenth century?

Some readers may well complain that this was anticipated earlier in my introduction, already present in my discussion of Barrington Moore's dis-

---

from many years of practising 'revolution from above,' took the view that 'in Prussia only kings make revolutions'" (Wehler, *German Empire*, pp. 28–29).

Although Germany and Japan exemplified the authoritarian capitalist road to modernization, Italy too fits this paradigm. "Italian fascism," remarks Moore, "displays the same pseudoradical and propeasant features found in Germany and Japan" (Moore, *Social Origins*, p. 451). The ideology of Italy's conservative modernization was perfectly captured in Giuseppe Tomasi Di Lampedusa's *The Leopard*, Archibald Colquhoun, trans. (New York: Knopf, 1960).

For the long-term consequences of the Italian approach to "revolution from above," see Patrick McCarthy, *The Crisis of the Italian State: From the Origins of the Cold War to the Fall of Berlusconi* (New York: St. Martin's, 1995): "After Unification, Benito Mussolini's seizure of power in 1922, and the Republic created after his fall, a new regime was struggling to be born. By sweeping away the political and administrative elite and demonstrating how most other elites had collaborated, the Milan magistrates were unwittingly preparing the ground for the fourth attempt to refound the Italian state....All this does not mean that the bid to create a new regime will succeed or that it will mark an improvement. On the contrary it has been argued that it will fail, as did the three others....This view, which is associated with

Giuseppe Tomasi Di Lampedusa's novel, *The Leopard*, underestimates the changes in previous shifts of regime...." (p. 8). (Referring to the Italian version of the familiar homily "the more things change, the more they stay the same," McCarthy adds in a footnote that the "Italian name for it is *gattopardismo*" (ibid., p. 199).

The latter notion, though "associated with...*The Leopard*," in contemporary Italian political culture, is distinguishable from the one expressed by Di Lampedusa, who pointed out that ruling elites must embrace change in order to preserve their status (that is, prevent *real* change)—hence the strategy (practiced by Bismarck) of reactionary modernization. By contrast, the Italian Communist Party provided Italy with its greatest opportunity for change from below, rather than above, in this century: see Eric Hobsbawm, "The Dark Years of Italian Communism," *Revolutionaries* (New York: New American Library, 1975), pp. 31–42.

In language reminiscent of Di Lampedusa's, Immanuel Wallerstein writes: "I believe that the period after liberalism is a period of major political struggle more consequential than any other of the past five hundred years. I see forces of privilege who know very well that 'everything must change in order that nothing change,' and are working skillfully and intelligently to bring that about" (*After Liberalism* [New York: New Press, 1995], p. 3).

326 Kemp, *Industrialization*, 95.

tinction between liberal and authoritarian capitalism and the different paths of development they represent.[327] Furthermore, it is there in Andreas Dorpalen's critique of East German historiography,[328] as well as

327 See, for example, Michael Mann, *The Sources of Social Power*, vol. 2: *The Rise of Classes and Nation-States, 1760–1914* (Cambridge, Eng.: Cambridge University Press, 1993). Mann writes: "But despite their differences, liberals and their critics offer alternative versions of the same underlying scenario. Both see the semiauthoritarian *Kaiserreich* emerging as a compromise between two power actors: an old regime and a rising bourgeoisie. Liberals see the old regime dominant, the bourgeoisie forced to compromise. The critics see old regime and bourgeoisie agreeing to divide the spoils: the old regime to control politics; the bourgeoisie, economics. Liberals see militarism as old regime, unstable, and doomed, for modern capitalism is in the end liberal. The critics see militarism as joint: the old regime as warlike, but the bourgeoisie favoring repression of the working class. Sharing the pessimism of much recent Marxism, Blackbourne and Eley see this as a viable track of capitalist development: 'The orderly reproduction of capitalist productive relations could be guaranteed within a form of state which fell considerably short of pure representative democracy.' It was a 'bourgeois revolution from above,' [Barrington] Moore's 'conservative modernization from above' occurring here and in Meiji Japan and Risorgimento Italy...." (pp. 306–7).
   In spite of their overarching similarity, the main difference between these two perspectives, in Mann's view, is that the liberal historians and sociologists tend to view "the *Kaiserreich* as a developmental aberration, seeing Anglo-Saxon and French liberalism as the normal track of capitalist development," while "Marxists have attacked this liberal view of the *Sonderweg*" (ibid., pp. 305–6). The argument can certainly be made that it was Marx himself who founded what Mann characterizes as the "liberal view"—that it was the liberal rather than authoritarian route to capitalist development which represented (according to Marx) "the really revolutionary,"

apparently prototypical, way capitalist societies emerge (see, for example, Kohachiro Takahashi, "A Contribution to the Discussion," in *The Transition from Feudalism to Capitalism*, [London: Verso, 1978], pp. 87–97).
   Nor am I sure that either Moore or his colleagues, Herbert Marcuse and Otto Kirchheimer, believed that "modern capitalism is in the end liberal." See, for example, Moore's observation: "On this score, Germany and Japan are not of course unique. Since the Second World War, Western democracy has begun to display more and more of the same traits for broadly similar reasons that, however, no longer have much to do with agrarian questions. Somewhere Marx remarks that the bourgeoisie in its declining phase reproduces all the evils and irrationalities against which it once fought" (*Social Origins*, pp. 442n8). More than a decade later, Herbert Marcuse said nearly the same thing to Jürgen Habermas: "Bourgeois democracy, insofar as it is at all possible after fascism, is worth striving for in the face of fascism as an existing danger. But it seems that precisely this bourgeois democracy has been dismantled and maimed continuously by the bourgeoisie itself and by big capital..." ("Theory and Politics," *Telos* 38 [1978–1979], p. 148). I nevertheless agree with Michael Mann that historians and sociologists have provided broad support for the liberal versus authoritarian capitalist dichotomy as a useful way to inventory modern social and economic development.

328 Andreas Dorpalen writes: "On the governmental level, East German scholars see the significance of these shifts in the changing basis of Bismarck's Bonapartist regime, which from [1878–1879] on rested on, apart from the army, the class *alliance* of bourgeois industrialists and Junker agrarians and was reinforced by the continuing class *compromise* between these groups and those segments of great and middle bourgeoisie that were opposed to protective tariffs but that, once

in our commentary on how the German ideology prevented even Hegel from developing either a rigorously materialist or systematically democratic social and political philosophy.[329]

"The first essential point," Georg Lukács reminds us, "is that Hegel perceives civil society as a unified whole. This is undoubtedly a consequence of Germany's economic and social backwardness." At the same time, however, in France and England, "great class struggles" compelled philosophers and social theorists "to dig deeply into the objective economic roots of class conflict."[330] Thus, the politically progressive and socially materialist orientation of European liberalism and classical political economy mirrored the more advanced economic situation prevailing in those societies where a modern social philosophy emerged.[331]

Alternatively, other readers may find the distinction between American and German social and economic development convincing yet not necessarily see exactly how it explains the development of German law—especially Bismarck's social legislation—in contrast to that of the United States, during the last quarter of the nineteenth century.

In other words, why was the German solution, that of an authoritarian capitalist society, apparently just the opposite of the one legal historians effectively identify as having been adopted during the same time frame in

---

again from fear of the working class, did not dare to turn against Bismarck's Bonapartist dictatorship" (*German History in Marxist Perspective: The East German Approach* [Detroit: Wayne State University Press, 1988], p. 253).

329 I specifically cited Lukács's grim but accurate invocation of Germany's "graveyard stillness" in the wake of the French Revolution. It is worth adding here his grudging recognition that "given the economic, social and political situation in Germany at the time, a great and all-embracing philosophy such as Hegel's could not possibly have been created on radical-democratic foundations" (*The Young Hegel: Studies in the Relations between Dialectics and Economics*, Rodney Livingstone, trans. [Cambridge, Mass.: MIT Press, 1976], p. 369).

330 Ibid., p. 366.

331 One might ask how Marx was able to make such good use of Hegelian philosophy if it was the product of such retrograde social circumstances. Karl Korsch argues in *Marxism and Philosophy*, Fred Halliday, trans. (London:

NLB, 1970): "Hegel wrote that in the philosophic systems of this fundamentally revolutionary epoch, 'revolution was lodged and expressed as if in the very form of their thought.'" Note well: in the *form*, not in terms of practical consequences. Korsch concludes by arguing that Hegel regarded this revolution in the form of thought "as an objective component of the total process of revolution" and, yet, again quoting Hegel's *Lectures on the Philosophy of History*, if the "principle swept Germany as thought, spirit and concept; in France it was unleashed in effective reality." Korsch then adds that "Marx fully adopted and consciously developed this view of Hegel's on the division of roles between the Germans and the French within the general process of the bourgeois revolution. Compare all his early writings which contain such formulations as: 'In politics the Germans have thought what other peoples have done', 'Germany has only shared the development of modern peoples through the abstract activity of thought,'" and so forth. Korsch, *Marxism*, pp. 38–39.

the United States? I am convinced that it was precisely the special circumstances prevailing in Germany, collected and dissected by Barrington
Moore, Fritz Fischer, and many others, under the heading of "authoritarian capitalism," which provide the answer. Indeed, Max Weber argued
that Germany's ensemble of social circumstances produced a characteristically German political solution. In his lecture at Freiburg in 1895,
according to Princeton historian Arno Mayer, Weber acknowledged that
although Germany's industrial magnates had gained economic concessions from the Junker agrarians, "preindustrial elites" nevertheless had
succeeded in "maintaining themselves by containing and manipulating
the thrust for popular participation and by co-opting members of rising
counterelites."[332] Containing and manipulating competing forces within
the context of an authoritarian capitalist system of social relations was,
perhaps, the paramount political task shouldered by Bismarck and his
successors. Substituting strict liability for fault in cases of railway accidents, or directly instituting broad schemes of insurance protection which
more effectively secured similar ends, are perfect examples of Bismarck's
efforts to manage and control the contending social forces which threatened to tear Germany apart.

It would be a mistake to suggest that the emergence of strict liability in
German tort law was a simple matter. As Lawson initially observes, even
during the preindustrial 1830s the Prussian Railway Law only "introduced
strict liability for certain accidents" and "formed the model for the more
far-reaching *Reichshaftspflichtgesetz* of 1871."[333] Lawson and Markesinis
later retain the social class and preindustrial explanation for the Prussian
Railway Law's formulation while slightly altering the characterization of
the 1871 statutory regulation. The early Railway Law now provides a
"model for the subsequent, *and in most respects*, more far-reaching
Imperial Law of Liability (*Reichshaftspflichtgesetz*) of 7 June 1871 which
applied to the whole Reich."[334] The legislation of June 1871, officially
styled as a statute concerning the obligation to compensate for deaths and
physical injuries caused in the conduct of railways, mines, and so on,
states in its first section that "[i]f in the conduct of a railway a human
being is killed or suffers bodily injury, the entrepreneur (the undertaking)
is liable for the damage arising therefrom except in so far as he proves that
the accident was caused by *force majeure*, or by fault of the deceased or

332 Mayer, *Persistence of the Old Regime*, p. 296.
333 Lawson, *Negligence*, p. 45.
334 Lawson and Markesinis, *Tortious Liability*,
     p. 158 (emphasis added).

injured person."[335] Given the manipulability of legal language, the uncertainty of what practical meaning attaches to phrases like *force majeure* and "damage arising therefrom," it is not clear just how much protection this law provided those killed or injured by, for example, railway mishaps. Also note the seeming availability, under the German statute, of a contributory negligence defense, the same sort of legal escape clause so effectively deployed in American courts to insulate defendants from potentially crippling economic liability.[336]

Nevertheless, the statute of 1871 does appear, on its face, to preserve a strict liability standard with respect to railway accidents: absent contributory negligence, the enterprise is liable. But since this was the case *in 1838*, prior to German industrialization, exactly how did the 1871 law broaden or extend liability? Closer examination reveals that it actually *confined* strict liability to railways. Indeed, the second section of the 1871 statute reads: "[a]nyone who carries on a mine, quarry, pit, or factory is, if an authorized agent or representative or anyone employed in the direction or supervision of the undertaking or of the workmen causes, by a fault in the carrying out of the service arrangements, death or bodily injury to a human being, he is liable for the damage arising therefrom."[337] In other words, those who direct or supervise factories and mines are liable where they cause injury *and are themselves shown to have been at fault*. It certainly appears that the first section of the 1871 statute, applying to *railway accidents*, retains elements of strict liability, whereas the second section, applying to all other *industrial accidents*, retains the simple negligence approach—the one that, according to Gordon and most American legal historians, came to predominate during the second half of the nineteenth century in the United States.[338] In Germany, after 1871, then, the entrepre-

---

335 *Reichshaftpflichtgesetz, ss. 1, (June 7, 1871)*, reprinted in Lawson, *Negligence*, pp. 195–96.

336 Lawrence Friedman writes: "The basic idea of contributory negligence was extremely simple. If the plaintiff was negligent himself, ever so slightly, he could not recover from the defendant. This was a harsh doctrine, but extraordinarily useful. It became a favorite method through which judges kept tort claims from the deliberations of the jury. The trouble with the jury (it was thought) was that pitiful cases of crippled men suing giant corporations sometimes worked on their sympathies. Even people who respect general rules find it hard to resist bending them once in a while, especially if the victim hauls his battered body into the courtroom, or a widow and orphans stare into the jury box. For jurors—amateurs all—every case was a one-time cause. Business and its lawyers were convinced that juries were incorrigibly plaintiff-minded; that they were loose with other people's money; that they had a deep-dyed tendency to stretch facts to favor a suffering plaintiff. But if plaintiff was clearly negligent himself, there could be no recovery; there were no facts to be found, and a judge could take the case from the jury and dismiss it" (*History of American Law*, p. 470.)

neur is liable for railway accidents, unless employee negligence or *force majeure* are present; in all other industrial accidents, though, it is essential to prove fault on the part of the owners or their agents.

Otto Pflanze, in his monumental three-volume social and political biography of Bismarck, tells us that Bismarck, like many of his contemporaries, "was shocked into a renewed awareness of working class discontent by the communard revolution in Paris during April and May 1871,"[339] and that he regarded social unrest as a kind of disease infecting Europe. While pursuing a policy of repression by tightening the screws on socialist organizations and advocates of radical political change, Bismarck also laid out a broad program of social reform intended to draw working-class support away from revolutionary alternatives. Concretely, Bismarck proposed a "series of legislative and administrative measures derived from the most diverse areas of political and economic life and directed toward the effective removal of obstacles standing in the way of the earning capacity of the unpropertied classes."[340]

In his initial list of Prussian "welfare chests regulated by the state," Pflanze includes the same legal innovations cited by Lawson and Markesinis, specifically "accident insurance companies (the latter necessitated by an imperial statute of 1871 establishing liability of railway, mine, and factory companies for work-related accidents and deaths)."[341] Pflanze, however, is much less interested in the 1871 liability statute than in Bismarck's subsequent social insurance legislation of the 1880s; Lawson, too,[342] and he and Markesinis later specifically direct their readers' attention to this social legislation. Close on the heels of the 1871 statute, "followed Bismarck's social legislation...introducing accident, health, and

---

337 *Reichshaftpflichtgesetz, ss. 2 (June 7, 1871),* reprinted in Lawson, *Negligence,* p. 196.

338 On the significance of Justice Shaw's decision in the 1850 Massachusetts Supreme Court case of *Brown v. Kendall,* 6 Cush. (60 Mass.) 292 (1850), Hall et al. write under the heading "The Emergence of Negligence" in *American Legal History:* "*Brown v. Kendall* is central to the development of tort law. Charles Gregory, echoing an earlier assessment of Oliver Wendell Holmes, asserts that Chief Justice Shaw's opinion was a 'marked departure from the past,' which led to 'the establishment of a consistent theory of liability for unintentionally caused harm.' Morton

Horwitz argues that scholars have given 'an exaggerated significance' to the case, but he does accept the argument that before the 1850s 'negligence' did not apply in tort actions and that all actions for trespass were based upon strict liability. Whoever is right in this debate, *Brown v. Kendall* is an important case, as either a major new precedent or the best summary of the law as it already had developed" (p. 183).

339 Otto Pflanze, *Bismarck and the Development of Germany* (Princeton: Princeton University Press, 1990), vol. 2, p. 293.

340 Ibid., p. 301.

341 Ibid., p. 302.

342 F. H. Lawson, *Negligence,* p. 46.

old age insurance, thereby making the concerns in each industry (*Berufsgenossenschaften*) combine to insure their employees against various forms of industrial hazards."[343] Before turning to this social program, however, consider Pflanze's commentary on the Imperial Liability Law itself.

Theodore Lohmann, an undersecretary of state in Bismarck's Ministry of Commerce who had experience drafting industrial social legislation, proposed a bill "drastically extending the liability of employers for industrial accidents"; according to Pflanze, this infuriated Bismarck. The proposed law was "the fruit of years of agitation for reform of the 1871 statute on accident liability, culminating in a Reichstag resolution of 1878.... *The statute of 1871 had placed upon the worker the burden of proving the employer's liability. The reform would have obligated the employer to report accidents that resulted in injuries and have compelled him to prove the worker at fault.* Such a statute would have forced the employer to establish insurance chests, whose premiums would have been paid equally by employer, employee, and regional poor relief associations...."[344]

This sounds like an effort to extend the strict liability provisions of the Imperial Liability Law's first, or railway, section to the wide spectrum of industrial employment. Thus, not only did the statute of 1871 *not* extend strict liability to industrial concerns but its failure to do so seems to have produced an explicit backlash.

Lohmann's proposed reform bill, in response to the Reichstag resolution of 1878, "aroused Bismarck's ire" not simply because it extended strict liability but also because of its reliance upon a private, rather than statist, legal solution. It was Christian individualism, not a market orientation, that motivated Lohmann's opposition to a "state socialist solution to the problem with its centralization, bureaucratic control, and public financing..."[345] However, Lohmann's motivations made no difference to Bismarck since he was the arch-advocate of authoritarian capitalist reform: Bismarck attacked Lohmann's reform proposal as hostile to industry and "the product of liberalism."[346] An alternative "plan for accident insurance appealed to the chancellor, because it held out the prospect of a direct role for the Reich in social security, a role clearly visible to workers whose votes and loyalty he coveted."[347]

---

343 Lawson and Markesinis, *Tortious Liabaility*, p. 158.

344 Pflanze, *Bismarck and the Development of Germany*, vol. 3, p. 153n31

(emphasis added).

345 Ibid., p. 153.

346 Ibid., p. 153n31.

347 Ibid., p. 153–54.

Rodney Livingstone and Otto Kahn-Freund,[348] as well as historians like Sebastion Haffner and Gordon Craig, Arno Mayer and Koppel Pinson, Hans-Ulrich Wehler and Hajo Holborn, all identify the same pattern, the same portrait of Bismarck's desire to utilize the legal system generally, and social insurance legislation specifically, to steer industrial workers away from socialism and liberalism and toward a "sacred union" with the parties of reaction inside an authoritarian capitalist state.

So Bob Gordon certainly was on the right track. The real contradiction, however, was not so much between negligence and strict liability (both of which make their appearance at times during German and U.S. legal history) but, rather, between American market and German statist solutions during the latter part of the nineteenth century—between, in short, liberal and authoritarian capitalism and the legal and political superstructures they hammered out, at a time of spectacular (and crucial) industrial development within both societies. Certainly the American

---

348   Bismarck's strategy was not new in Germany. Rodney Livingstone writes: "The attitude of the government was inspired by conservativism of the public service. Radowitz, for example, had hoped to pursue a paternalistic policy designed to drive a wedge between the workers and socialism. Traces of this attitude can be found in the law of May 16, 1853, banning work for children under 12 and restricting the hours worked by children from 12 to 14 to 6 hours per day (at a time when 8 was the minimum age for child workers in England and France). Measures like this were passed by the conservatives in face of bitter opposition by the liberals who regarded them as unduly restricting the right to work" (Introduction, in Karl Marx and Friedrich Engels, *The Cologne Communist Trial*, Rodney Livingstone, trans. [London: Lawrence and Wishart, 1971], pp. 15–16).

Lawson, as well as Lawson and Markesinis, cite Otto Kahn-Freund as a source for the proposition that German statutory protection of industrial accident victims was inspired, in part, by voluntary programs organized by British trade unions (Lawson, *Negligence*, p. 46n2, Lawson and Markesinis, *Tortious Liability*, p. 229n75). Otto Kahn-Freund's comments on the German system of welfare provisions for workers are quite interesting: "[T]he

social-conservative view, as advanced by Bismarck, for example, rejects collective action just as much as does liberalism, only with the difference that the conservative affirms the paternalist idea of welfare provision which the liberal rejects (Otto Kahn-Freund in Roy Lewis and Jon Clark, eds., *Labour Law and Politics in the Weimar Republic*, [Oxford: Basil Blackwell, 1981], p. 124). Lewis and Clark, in their introduction to Kahn-Freund, writing, summarize the suppression of social democratic political agitation as well as the deployment of criminal law to regulate trade unions in the period 1878–1890. They then add that this "deliberate use of state power by Bismarck in order to prevent the growth of independent working-class organization was complemented by the introduction of a state system of social security for individual employees. Bismarck was quite explicit about the aim of this dual strategy, namely to 'heal social wrongs not just by the repression of social democratic excesses but simultaneously by positively advancing the well-being of the workers.' By 1889 Germany had the most advanced national insurance system in the world....However, this strategy failed to stem the growth of the labour movement" (Roy Lewis and Jon Clark, "Introduction," in Otto Kahn-Freund, *Labour Law*, pp. 20–21).

state apparatus would become increasingly implicated in systems of civil liability and capital–labor relations as the new century unfolded. And Germany's economy remained, of course, a capitalist one, however carefully regulated by Bismarck's bureaucrats, integrated as it was within a worldwide capitalist market as well.[349] But the differences between these two fundamental approaches to capitalist social organization (German and American) were real and would lead to world war twice within the next six decades.

Extending my application of the German ideology thesis,[350] I briefly draw the reader's attention, again, to Lukács's first essential point:

---

349 See, e.g., Hans-Ulrich Wehler, *German Empire:* "Bismarck, in common with countless entrepreneurs, held the view that industry should not be seriously handicapped if it were to maintain its competitiveness in international markets. Not only was his social policy, as it affected companies, put on ice. The 'furtherance of the entrepreneurs' immediate interests' was, in Schmoller's view, 'the very essence of social policy' for Bismarck" (p. 132).

350 Louis Dumont, *directeur d'etude* at France's *Ecole des Hautes Etudes en Sciences Sociales*, writes in his book, *German Ideology*, that "a culture never exists in isolation but should always be seen in relation to its environment." The same proposition, according to Lawson and Markesinis, is true of legal doctrine, specifically including tort law, constantly shaped as it is by the social and economic environment. This stark reality is overlooked, according to Dumont, "every time text is piled upon text and author added to author without acknowledging the existence of a sort of collective entity to which they all belong" (Louis Dumont, *German Ideology*, p. 28; F. H. Lawson and B. S. Markesinis, *Tortious Liability*, pp. 57–61).

A virtually identical observation deserves to be made with respect to legal scholarship, certainly when it is constructed by piling case upon case without acknowledging the existence of what Karl Llewellyn called "period style" or what we have characterized as the fundamental social and economic division of American legal history. Llewellyn writes: "There is a further cluster of conditioning and steadying factors in the

work of the appellate courts (and commonly at the same time of other branches of legal work) which has been curiously disregarded. It is the general and pervasive manner over the country at large, at any given time, of going about the job, the general outlook....It's slowish movement but striking presence remind me of shifting 'types' of economy ('agricultural,' 'industrial,' e.g.) and of the cycles or spirals many sociologists and historians discover in the history of political aggregations or of whole cultures" (Karl N. Llewellyn, *The Common Law Tradition: Deciding Appeals* [Boston: Little, Brown, 1960], pp. 35–36).

On the one hand, the notion of *German ideology*—our shorthand expression for a contradiction manifested both internally, within Germany society (between industrial modernization and political archaism) and externally, between German (authoritarian) and American (liberal) capitalism—is utilized by Dumont to help explain the development of German culture. On the other hand, it can also be employed, as we have suggested here, to help explain differences between the unfolding of German and American legal and political institutions.

Within the field of German cultural history, even in those analyses which Dumont feels insufficiently emphasize context, the "environment will figure...as an external event, or series of events, to which the German authors will be seen to react." The Germany ideology—and the specifically authoritarian capitalist route to the modern world which fosters that ideology—can be seen as the crucial environmental feature

"Hegel's philosophy is an idealism nourished on the economic base of the undeveloped class antagonism of Germany." In other words, Germany's late industrialization (on which Lawson and Markesinis rely for their explanation of the "early" introduction of strict liability concepts within Germany railway law), and the subsequent failure, as the East German historians put it, of the German bourgeoisie to carry out its "class mandate" and make a liberal democratic "revolution from below," account for—or are themselves derived from the same contradiction responsible for—Hegel's idealism and his inability to see the state as a creation of class conflict. "It is from here," Lukács writes, "that we have to understand the birth of Hegel's doctrine of the state as the realization of 'reason': this is the vantage-point from which the state can appear as standing apart from the conflicts of civil society."

At just this point in his critique of the limitations of Hegel's economic thought, Lukács warns us that Hegel's idealism will have implications for his jurisprudence as well: "it is methodologically necessary for Hegel to put law above economics. Whereas historical materialism regards the 'higher' fetishism of law as proof of its secondary, derivative character, for Hegel the opposite is the case: the transformation of economic into juridical categories represents a higher, more spiritual form of 'externalization,' a force closer to the realm of spirit."[351]

Although certainly for different reasons, many historians and law professors today repeat Hegel's error, methodologically (in scholarship) or pedagogically (in the classroom) placing "law above economics," failing to adequately emphasize the "secondary, derivative" quality of legal doctrine. In Kermit Hall's *The Magic Mirror*, the author (as we have already seen) generally endorses the notion that the development of American tort law in the nineteenth century cannot be understood simply by looking at legal doctrine, standing alone. The social environment shaping accident law, for example, remains an essential aspect of Hall's story. "Accidents associated with the advent of new technology," asserts Hall, "such as the application of steam power to transportation by railroad and steamboat, created potentially debilitating costs. One way to reduce those costs in an already capital-scarce economy was to relieve risk-taking entrepreneurs of responsibility for them."

against which the United States was compelled to react in the twentieth century. And that reaction, as we shall see, shaped the transition from capitalist to state capitalist society in America during the New Deal and Second World War. (Louis Dumont, *German Ideology*, p. 28).

351   Lukács, *Young Hegel*, pp. 366–67, 385.

Here Hall reflects, again, the general social analysis of tort law's development we have already encountered in the work of Hurst and Gregory, Friedman and Ladinsky, Lawson and Markesinis, Sellers and Bruchey, Horwitz and Purcell. Hall adds, nevertheless, that "[h]istorians differ sharply about which of these groups—capitalists or victims—benefitted from judicial mediation of disputes among them arising out of accidents,"[352] and he further suggests that "Gary Schwartz, for example, has found that for the jurisdictions of New Hampshire and California, the trial and appellate judges often showed great solicitude for the victims of accidents, especially passengers."[353] The only specific reference Hall makes (in either footnotes or bibliographic essay) to work by dissenting historians of American accident law is to this one law review article.

Now it is fine for Schwartz to suggest, as Hall indicates, that railroad passengers in two states who became accident victims were rarely denied recovery because of the contributory negligence rule. But such an assertion, one should point out right away, does not a history of nineteenth-century American tort law and policy make.

The legal history casebook Kermit Hall published two years after *The Magic Mirror* reflects just such an awareness. Discussing an oft-cited, mid-nineteenth-century accidental injury case, Hall and his co-authors, William Wiecek and Paul Finkelman, state that "*Brown v. Kendall* is central to the development of tort law. Charles Gregory, echoing an earlier assessment by Oliver Wendell Holmes, asserts Chief Justice Shaw's opinion was a 'marked departure from the past'"; the authors add that in "articulating a theory of contributory negligence, Shaw gave a great boon to America's industries. For the rest of the nineteenth century, and well into the twentieth, railroads and other industries often avoided paying tort damages because of the doctrine of contributory negligence."[354] Conspicuously absent are any references to solicitous judges in a few states, or even to Schwartz's *Yale* essay.

Schwartz argues that there was in fact no rise of negligence in the nineteenth century—that the fault doctrine did not effectively eliminate a previously existing absolute or strict liability approach.[355] Second, he

352 Hall, *The Magic Mirror: Law in American History*, p. 123.

353 Ibid., 125, citing Gary T. Schwartz, "Tort Law and the Economy in Nineteenth-Century America: A Reinterpretation," *Yale Law Journal* 90 (1981), p. 1743.

354 Kermit L. Hall, William M. Wiecek, and Paul Finkelman, *American Legal History: Cases and Materials* (New York: Oxford University Press, 1991), pp. 183–84.

355 Gary Schwartz asserts: "Part I of the article analyzes that literature and traces the processes by which the negligence standard received recognition in nineteenth-century

asserts that tort cases *do not* provide evidence that nineteenth-century American judges devised rules that would "facilitate economic development by insulating entrepreneurs from the costs of accidents," as Hall puts it, or provide industry with a subsidy and thus protect capital reserves.[356] "In all," he concludes, "there is nothing in the New Hampshire record during this half century that confirms Horwitz's view that American judges consciously intervened to overthrow a solid, general rule of strict liability. Nor is there a single New Hampshire tort opinion that bears the stamp of the dynamic, utilitarian reasoning that Horwitz believes was characteristic of that period's judiciary"[357]

Because the historians he has challenged have employed hundreds of cases from many states (especially those centrally involved in the process of nineteenth-century capitalist industrialization), Schwartz feels compelled to explain why California and New Hampshire are especially useful for intensive research: California, he asserts, is notable because "its judiciary has been so influential in the elucidation of tort doctrine in the twentieth-century" and New Hampshire because its "textile mills placed it in the forefront of nineteenth-century industrialization...." Since his article is primarily about nineteenth-, not twentieth-century tort law, the latter rationale is more persuasive. But even it is undercut by Schwartz's candid acknowledgement: "I advance no claims about the general representativeness of my two jurisdictions."[358]

Is Schwartz right when he claims that there is not a single New Hampshire tort opinion that bears the stamp of the dynamic, utilitarian reasoning that Horwitz believes was characteristic of a nineteenth-century instrumentalist judiciary? In fact, Schwartz indicates that there is only one New Hampshire case with any sort of "general discussion of industrial or economic policy" at all. And that case, *Brown v. Collins*,[359] reached the conclusion that "a rule of strict liability did not seem

New Hampshire and California. It finds the claims of strict liability subversion largely unwarranted" ("Tort Law," p. 1720). Somewhat later he writes, "It is true that during the nineteenth century the negligence standard acquired a new prominence and publicity; but to conclude, as subsidy writers suggest, that the emphasis on negligence entailed the dramatic or deliberate overthrow of an ambitious prior rule of strict liability requires a reading of the historical record that is unsubtle at best and inaccurate at

worst" (ibid., p. 1773).

356 Hall, *Magic Mirror*, p. 126. "In general, the New Hampshire and California case law resists the claim that the nineteenth-century negligence system can properly be characterized or disparaged as an industrial subsidy" (Schwartz, "Tort Law," p. 1773).

357 Ibid., p. 1731.

358 Ibid., p. 1719.

359 *Brown v. Collins*, 53 New Hampshire 442 (1873).

justified."[360] Now the reader might be forgiven for thinking that was just Horwitz's point. But, apparently, in Schwartz's opinion, the only case which would count on Horwitz's side of the debate would be one which not only rejected strict liability, like *Brown v. Collins*, but, further, did so for reasons of industrial or economic policy and also reflected dynamic, utilitarian reasoning to boot. Consider, then, language from *Brown v. Collins*, where the court discusses traditional rules of strict liability: "It would not be singular if these rules should be spontaneously produced at a certain period in the life of any community. Where they first appeared is of little consequence in the present inquiry. They were certainly introduced in England at an immature stage of English jurisprudence, and an undeveloped state of agriculture, manufactures, and commerce, when the nation had not settled down to those modern, progressive, industrial pursuits which the spirit of the common law, adapted to all conditions of society, encourages and defends."[361]

Strict liability had been "introduced when the development of many of the rational rules now universally recognized as principles of the common law had not been *demanded by the growth of intelligence, trade, and productive enterprise....*"[362] Haven't we heard this sort of language before? Is it not, after all, precisely the sort of "dynamic, utilitarian reasoning" which characterized such cases as *Parker v. Foote*, *Van Ness v. Pacard*, indeed, *Charles River Bridge* itself? Rather than *Brown* overturning Horwitz's industrial policy thesis, it would seem Horwitz could have made it the centerpiece of his argument.

Schwartz simply observes that what he understands *Brown v. Collins* to be saying is not that enterprises should be immunized from civil damages but, rather, "in light of the nineteenth century's hardly deniable public interest in economic development, liability should not be imposed when there is no proper 'legal principle' or 'legal reason' for doing so."[363] In other words, the law will not impose liability upon enterprises where the law does not impose such liability. We can do better than that. The real question remains: did the court impose liability or not, and if not, why not? As Judge Posner candidly acknowledges, there is almost always a "legal principle" or "legal reason" at hand, prepared to serve whatever purpose a court happens to have in mind. Clearing up any possible confusion on the matter, the court in *Brown v. Collins* specifically says that it is the public

---

360 Gary Schwartz, "Tort Law," 1733.

361 *Brown* at 450.

362 *Brown* at 450, emphasis added.

363 Gary Schwartz, "Tort Law," 1733.

interest in economic development which *demands* a common law rule
which can take into account new "conditions of society."

If readers are genuinely to be persuaded that nineteenth-century New
Hampshire tort jurisprudence placed legal reasoning above social policy,
law above economics, *Brown v. Collins* seems to be the last case one would
invoke to prove the point. This seems especially true if one leans heavily,
as does Schwartz, on the assertion that, at any rate, courts did not "consciously intervene" in the transformation of tort law or cause the "deliberate overthrow" of previous doctrine.[364] That appears to be just what the
Brown court regards as a task appropriately shouldered by the common
law, where circumstances warrant. And that would be no less true, with
respect to the long-term function of common law adjudication, had the
court in *Brown* betrayed less self-consciousness or been any less straightforward in explaining the social and economic philosophy it was seeking
to put into practice. On this point, as mentioned earlier, we find both
legal realist and dialectical materialist in agreement.[365]

Schwartz's previous argument, about the consistency of nineteenth-
century tort law with earlier legal doctrine, appears even more tenuous
than his subsequent claim about subordination of social policy and social
relations to legal autonomy. To bolster his position, Schwartz points out
that "[James Barr] Ames expressed the view that strict liability asserts an
'unmoral standard,' and [James Bradley] Thayer recorded his agreement
with the fundamental proposition of the common law which links liability to fault." But the fact that such legal notables as Ames and Thayer,

---

364 Gary Schwartz, "Tort Law," 1731, 1773.
365 See, e.g., Karl Llewellyn, *Common Law*:
"Meantime the inarticulateness of the vast
body of appellate judges about how they do
their work and why—their inarticulateness
even to themselves—leaves them man by man
somewhat soul-troubled, albeit their
consciences are clear (p. 43)." See also,
Friedrich Engels, "Letter to Conrad Schmidt
in Berlin; London, Oct. 27, 1890," in *Karl
Marx and Friedrich Engels: Selected
Correspondence* (Moscow: Progress Publishers;
I. Lasker, trans., S. Ryazanskaya, ed., 2nd rev.
ed., 1965): "The reflection of economic
relations as legal principles is necessarily also a
topsy-turvy one: it goes on without the person
who is acting being conscious of it; the jurist
imagines he is operating with *a priori*
propositions, whereas they are really only

economic reflexes; so everything is upside
down (p. 423)." Compare the commentary in
Karl Korsch, *Marxism and Philosophy*
(London: Verso; Fred Halliday, trans., 1970):
"Elsewhere Hegel formulated this principle
in a more general way, when he wrote that
every philosophy can be nothing but *'its own
epoch comprehended in thought.'* Essential in
any event for a real understanding of the
development of philosophical thought, this
axiom becomes even more relevant for a
revolutionary period of social evolution....
In the middle of the nineteenth century
[the *bourgeois class*] ceased to be revolutionary
in its social *practice*, and by an inner necessity
it thereby also lost the ability to comprehend
in *thought* the true dialectical interrelation
of ideas and real historical developments...."
(p. 40).

Dean and Professor at Harvard Law School, respectively, regarded fault as moral or, at least, natural and, conversely, strict liability as immoral or just wrong does not tell us much about the rise and fall of these doctrines, or about their particular rhythm of historical development. The contention that strict liability was subverted, in the nineteenth century, by the rise of a negligence or fault system represents, for Schwartz, a notion generated by modern Marxist or populist conspiracy theories of legal history. For that very reason, one would think he would be especially interested in the perspective of James Barr Ames, for example, regarding the issue Schwartz characterizes as that of "timing."[366] Ames, after all, far from subscribing to Marxism, was not only a proponent of the negligence principle but, in addition, was an author of one of the first, if not *the* first, casebooks on torts used in an American law school. Indeed, the first edition of Ames's torts casebook was published the year after *Brown v. Collins* was decided.[367]

Schwartz quotes from Ames' most famous essay on common law liability and moral values for the purpose of documenting his estimate of fault's moral credentials. Yet he declines to fill us in on Ames' view of the incandescent timing question. Here is what Ames says, in that same essay:

[T]he doctrine of civil liability for accidental damage caused by a morally innocent actor was very persistent.... There were, however, from time to time certain intimations from the judges that in the absence of negligence, an unintentional injury to another would not render the actor liable, and finally in 1891 a case was brought in the Queen's Bench which required the court to decide whether the old rule of strict liability was still in force or must give way to a rule of liability based upon moral culpability.[368]

Ames observes that the case he is reporting, *Stanley v. Powell*,[369] resulted in adoption of a moral, or negligence, as opposed to strict liability rule; had been anticipated in Massachusetts by *Brown v. Kendall* forty

366   Gary Schwartz, "Tort Law," pp. 1720n16, 1734, 1773.

367   See *The Centennial History of the Harvard Law School 1817–1917*, pp. 181, 290 (Cambridge, Mass.: Harvard Law School Association, 1918).

368   James Barr Ames, "Law and Morals," *Harvard Law Review* 22 pp. 98–99 (1908);

reprinted in James Barr Ames, *Lectures on Legal History and Miscellaneous Legal Essays* 436–37 (Cambridge, Mass.: Harvard University Press, 1913). See also Francis H. Bohlen, *Studies in the Law of Torts* (Indianapolis: Bobbs-Merrill, 1926), pp. 352–59.

369   *Stanley v. Powell*, [1891] 1 Q.B. 86.

years earlier; and, finally, that the *Brown* precedent had spread to other states. He then, rather dramatically, concludes:

> So that to-day we may say that the old law has been radically transformed. The early law asked simply, 'Did the defendant do the physical act which damaged the plaintiff?' The law of to-day, except in certain cases based upon public policy, asks the further question, 'Was the act blameworthy?' The ethical standard of reasonable conduct has replaced the unmoral standard of acting at one's peril.[370]

James Barr Ames, Harvard dean, legal historian,[371] advocate of fault as a morally superior rule in cases of unintentionally caused harm, says the system of civil liability was "radically transformed" in order to replace strict liability with negligence. Yet Professor Schwartz assails those modern historians who say the same thing, that the rise of negligence

---

370 James B. Ames, "Law and Morals," 99; James B. Ames, *Lectures*, 437. Whether or not the fault doctrine was "moral" at the time Ames was writing (or any other time) is a *normative* question about which Schwartz seems to feel strongly but which is clearly a separate issue from the history of negligence law. Assessing the moral dimensions of fault doctrine, however important, involves making critical value judgments (e.g., was the economy more efficient or just less equitable?) whereas the question of fault's emergence in the nineteenth century seems to me an historical issue on which there is agreement among scholars with disparate views and agendas.

See, for example, F. H. Lawson and B. S. Markesinis, *Tortious Liability:* "The moral and logical attractions of the proposition that a human being should make good the harm caused by his fault were (and still are) very great. But the converse of this principle, namely that there can be no liability where there is no fault, offered an additional attraction to an era which was more concerned in *not* making *certain* people liable than in compensating every loss....It is, no doubt, due to this rather unusual coincidence of morality and economic expediency [during the nineteenth century] that the notion of fault owes so much of its aura of soundness

and inevitability....With the growing mechanisation of the second half of the last century and the resulting multiplication of accidents, this kind of approach came more and more under scrutiny. The moral and educative basis of the fault system was also increasingly questioned. With some 35,000 deaths and 2,000,000 injuries in industrial accidents in the U.S.A. alone from about 1900 onwards, the idea of leaving all these victims uncompensated became morally intolerable and politically unwise and the same was true in the more advanced countries of Western Europe" (pp. 142–43). Whether one is for or against fault in the nineteenth century, for or against it today, cannot somehow alter the social history of the doctrine.

371 See, e.g., William P. LaPiana, *Logic and Experience: The Origin of Modern American Legal Education* (New York: Oxford Univ. Press, 1994): "Of the five Harvard law teachers, James Barr Ames was least touched by positivism. Ames was one of Langdell's earliest students, the first to follow Langdell in teaching by cases, and his successor as dean of Harvard Law School. Given Ames's intellectual lineage, it is not surprising that he was a historian of law. He never produced a comprehensive work, however. Instead, he expended much of his intellectual effort in preparing casebooks...." (p. 128–29).

"entailed the dramatic or deliberate overthrow of an ambitious prior rule of strict liability..."[372] If Professor Schwartz is right on the timing question, then Dean Ames is dead wrong—in spite of the fact that, as regards the nineteenth century foundations of American tort law, Ames was, as Dean Acheson might have put it, "present at the creation."

However much Karl Renner's conclusion that legal institutions and norms are "bricks which may be used to build a manor house in one age, a factory in another, a railway station in a third," there nevertheless remains bitter resistance to anything resembling a theory of *law as brick*, especially if it implies that decision making by business interests in capitalist societies can decisively shape particular legal outcomes or the general course of legal development over time.[373] When Bismarck rejected Theodor Lohmann's proposal to shift the burden of proof in accidental injury cases onto employers, the German Chancellor excoriated this reform as one which would be "simply ruinous for industry." Although Lohmann had been the dominant figure in a group assigned the task of drafting new social insurance legislation, "he soon discovered, as he wryly expressed it, that *Kommerzienrate* (an honorary title bestowed on businessmen) had more influence than *Geheimrate* (privy counselors in government service)."[374]

In 1967, almost a century after industrial interests trumped Lohmann's

---

372 Gary Schwartz, "Tort Law," p. 1773.
373 Eugene Kamenka, "A Marxist Theory of Law," in Csaba Varga, ed., *Marxian Legal Theory* (New York: New York University Press, 1993), p. 168. Gary Schwartz says populist legal history is "unsubtle at best, and inaccurate at worst." Schwartz, "Tort Law," p. 1773. What this suggests is that subtlety and accuracy are *distinguishable* categories for the purpose of evaluating legal theory: an individual historical account could be, for example, accurate but not subtle, and therefore although true, still unattractive. And I suspect that Schwartz is right in the sense that some scholarship is promoted within the legal academy simply because the work is fashionable or elegantly presented, quite independently of whether or not it provides an accurate or rigorous picture of reality. So one may be swimming against the current in openly endorsing a jurisprudence of "law as brick," a legal theory which so obviously appears to lack either

charm or aesthetic appeal.

Nevertheless, it is at least worth invoking, in passing, one characteristic confidence from the master builder himself, Louis Kahn: "The materials are beautiful today. Concrete is a marvelous material. It's stone that can span with guts. It's just stone and steel. Stone that can understand. I like certain things. I like brick. I like stone. I like all these materials....I got to like concrete." Louis I. Kahn, quoted in John Peter, *The Oral History of Modern Architecture: Interviews with the Greatest Architects of the Twentieth Century* 31 (New York: Harry N. Abrams, 1994), p.31; see also, Andrew Plumridge and Wim Meulenkamp, *Brickwork* (New York: Harry N. Abrams, 1993). In other words, we should at least hesitate before dismissing out of hand the aesthetic appeal of the concrete and practical. Materiality, to paraphrase Pascal, has its reasons.

374 Otto Pflanze, *Bismarck*, vol. 3, p. 153.

proposed tort reform in Germany, Georg Lukács asked the following question: "Didn't Kelsen contend in the 1920s, for example, that the formation of law was a mystery for legal science? Now it is obvious that the formation of law is not at all mysterious. There are the most complicated debates and class struggles around it. The average trader in the Federal Republic will certainly not see it as a mystery, but rather ask himself whether this particular pressure group can exert a sufficiently strong, therefore *de facto* ontological pressure on the government, for a paragraph to be formulated in its interest."[375] This may not be a solution to the mystery of law and history for which the reader hoped. Nevertheless, it is just this kind of deadpan response, and the brutal realism standing behind it, that is the hallmark of Lukács's "classical" jurisprudence.[376]

3. TWO STEPS FORWARD, ONE STEP BACK

Lincoln's policy after Sumter, Roosevelt's in the North Atlantic, at least in the eyes of most Americans at the time and most scholars in retrospect, represented a necessity—but not a precedent. By declining to use claims of inherent and abiding presidential power to justify their actions, Lincoln and Roosevelt took care not to give lesser men precedents to be invoked against lesser dangers. These two Presidents remained faithful to the spirit, if not the letter, of the Constitution: acting on the spirit to save the letter.
ARTHUR M. SCHLESINGER JR.[377]

375 Georg Lukács, quoted in Hans Heinz Holz, Leo Kofler, and Wolfgang Abendroth, *Conversations with Lukács*, Theo Pinkus, ed., (Cambridge, Mass.: MIT Press; 1975), p. 24; see also Eva Fekete and Eva Karadi, *Gyorgy Lukács: His Life in Pictures and Documents*, Peter Balaban and Kenneth McRobbie, trans. (Budapest: Corvina Kiado, 1981), pp. 230–49; Eugene Kamenka, "Lukács and Law," in Csaba Varga, ed., *Marxian Legal Theory* (New York: New York University Press, 1993), pp. 201–8; Csaba Varga, "Towards a Sociological Concept of Law: An Analysis of Lukács's Ontology," in Csaba Varga, ed., *Marxian Legal Theory*

(New York: New York University Press, 1993), pp. 361–78.

376 This is the same Lukács about whom Csaba Varga writes that "it is a little known fact that Georg Lukács, one of the most influential Marxist thinkers of recent times and the man whose personal achievement was to promote the renaissance of Marxism, obtained his first degree in law and political sciences." After describing Lukács's early friendships with Max Weber, Emil Lask, Georg Jellinek, and Hans Kelsen, "all of whom had an interest in jurisprudence and had already produced their great pioneering works in both constitutional law and in philosophy and theory of law,"

Although Roosevelt apparently did not take *enough* care to prevent the paradigmatic "lesser man," Lt. Col. Oliver North, from invoking FDR's conduct of foreign affairs as a precedent for moving secretly against the "threat" of Nicaraguan forces rolling northward through Mexico on their way to downtown Houston, Schlesinger's point, nevertheless, seems to me well taken.[378] In fact, his concluding sentence may convey greater insight than he intended.

As we have seen, Robert Heilbroner and Aaron Singer have contended that slavery was not a capitalist institution; Richard DuBoff has argued

Varga adds that the great Hungarian Marxist's "interest in law did not so much broaden as become clearer and more classical…" (Varga, "Towards a Sociological Concept of Law," pp. 361–62).

377 Arthur M. Schlesinger, Jr., "War and the Constitution: Abraham Lincoln and Franklin D. Roosevelt," in Gabor S. Boritt, ed., *Lincoln, The War President* (New York: Oxford University Press, 1992), p. 178.

378 On the Supreme Court's decision in the case of *U.S. v. Curtiss-Wright Export Corp.*, 299 U.S. 304 (1936), and its relation to the Iran-Contra scandal, see Theodore Draper, *A Very Thin Line: The Iran-Contra Affairs* (New York: Hill and Wang, 1991). Draper writes: "The issue itself was hardly one in which it was appropriate to make a sweeping judgment on the whole range of foreign affairs. The historical context is again important. A joint resolution of Congress had authorized President Franklin D. Roosevelt to prohibit arms sales to Paraguay and Bolivia, then at war. Curtiss-Wright and other companies were indicted for violating the embargo. They came up with the defense that Congress had failed to set adequate standards for the authority delegated to the President. Curiously, given the subsequent history of [Justice George] Sutherland's opinion, the policy had been set by Congress; the president was simply executing it. The case concerned the validity of a law, not the relations between the president and Congress" (p. 585).

With regard to Oliver North specifically, Draper points out: "*Curtiss-Wright* came up in Oliver North's testimony at the congressional hearings. It even provoked an exchange between North and Senator

George J. Mitchell. *North*: That was again debated in the 1930s in the *U.S. v. Curtiss-Wright Export Corporation*, and the Supreme Court held again that it was within the purview of the President of the United States to conduct secret activities and to conduct secret negotiations to further the foreign policy goals of the United States." Draper then concludes: "North was fuzzy about what *Curtiss-Wright* had actually been about; it concerned arms sales in Latin America, not secret activities or secret negotiations. But it was significant that he should have mentioned the case at all, probably because he had heard about it in reference to the president's presumed powers in foreign policy" (ibid., pp. 586–87).

See John E. Nowak and Ronald D. Rotunda, *Constitutional Law* (St. Paul, Min.: West, 5th ed., 1995): "Although [Justice] Sutherland, [in *Curtiss-Wright*] depicts presidential predominance in foreign affairs, it should not be forgotten that, in that case, the President was acting *in accord with* congressional policy. Sutherland's broad language should be read in light of the facts with which he was faced. As Justice Jackson, in his concurrence in *The Steel Seizure Case* noted, *Curtiss-Wright* was dealing with situations arising when the presidential actions are in harmony with an act of Congress, not when the President acts contrary to Congress. The Jackson interpretation places a significant limitation on the theory of an unrestrained executive plenary foreign affairs power" (p. 207). See also Peter Kornbluh and Malcolm Byrne, eds., *The Iran-Contra Scandal: The Declassified History* (New York: New Press, 1993).

that the Civil War removed a final obstacle to the spread of a capitalist mode of production across the continent; John Agnew believes that the American nation originally contained within it incompatible modes of socio-economic organization; and, finally, Benjamin Schwarz bluntly characterizes the prewar South as agricultural, aristocratic, and anticapitalist. Recall, as well, Barrington Moore's observation that "the ultimate causes of the civil war are to be found in the growth of different economic systems leading to different (but still capitalist) civilizations with incompatible stands on slavery."[379] It is clear enough that there are considerable grounds for agreement among these various positions, but Moore's description of southern plantation slavery as capitalist *but different*—a nascent form of authoritarian or antiliberal capitalist development—is most useful.[380]

On this basis, we can construct a general map of American social history which charts the Revolution as establishing a sovereign state; the Civil War as preserving the nation as a unified national market constructed on a liberal capitalist foundation; and World War II as a defense of liberal capitalism against a powerful alliance of authoritarian capitalist states.

Since the outcome of this history hinged on defeat of fascism in World War II, we may say with real conviction that the final act in this modern drama was written by the Soviet Union, a country that no longer even exists. "[T]he Red Army," Mike Davis writes, "inadvertently ensured that the American Century rather than the Thousand Year Reich would be the hegemonic system of capitalist rule in the mid-twentieth century...."[381] And while Germany and Japan have, to be sure, shared power with the United States over the last several decades of "the American

---

379 Moore, *Social Origins*, p. 141.

380 Robin Blackburn notes in *The Overthrow of Colonial Slavery* (London: Verso, 1988), "[T]he present work seeks to construct a Marxist narrative of the actual liberation struggles in the different areas of the Americas and to establish to what extent anti-slavery, either in intention or result, transcended the bourgeois democratic or capitalist dynamic" (p. 27). Although it could certainly be described as "bourgeois democratic," it was precisely the northern industrial commitment to a liberal form of capitalism which led some New England merchants, for example, to oppose the southern agrarian, albeit capitalist, dynamic—the plantation system of social and economic relations. See, for example, Richard H. Abbott, *Cotton and Capital: Boston Businessmen and Antislavery Reform, 1854–1868* (Amherst: University of Massachusetts Press, 1991).

381 Mike Davis, *Prisoners of the American Dream* (London: Verso, 1986), p. 181. See also Thomas J. McCormick, *America's Half-Century: United States Foreign Policy in the Cold War and After* (2d ed., Baltimore, Md.: Johns Hopkins University Press, 1995).

Century," they have done so only within the structure of a liberal, as opposed to authoritarian, capitalist world order.

Seen in this light, the transition from capitalism to state capitalism in the United States—during the New Deal and World War II—should be seen as part of the retrenchment of liberal capitalism, victorious in the United States during the nineteenth century only to be challenged internationally as the twentieth unfolded. Schlesinger's comparison of the seemingly disparate concerns of Abraham Lincoln and Franklin Delano Roosevelt is telling; both men tinkered with the constitutional system (Lincoln suspended *habeas corpus*, Roosevelt tried to pack the Court) in order to secure the survival of constitutionalism (understood as reflecting liberal political values and institutions).[382]

---

382 Authoritarian states may well have constitutions of their own, but the difference between them and the constitutional bases of liberal regimes is enormous; Japan and the United States provide a case in point. In *The Modernization of China and Japan* (Tokyo: John Weatherhill, 1965), George M. Beckmann notes: "The [Japanese government] had made important concessions to those groups that demanded a national parliament, but the Meiji Constitution was essentially a carefully formulated legal justification for a regime in which power was held by a small number of men with minimal responsibility to the people. Their power continued to stem from the doctrine that sovereignty rested in the person of the emperor, not by divine right but by divine descent. The government made certain that this basic principle was beyond the possibility of constitutional change by providing for uninterrupted imperial succession to the sovereignty of the state in the Imperial House Law, which was regarded as superior to ordinary legislation and could not be amended or supplanted by such" (p. 302).

Put quite simply, the Meiji Constitution was a blueprint for the police state that subsequently developed in Japan once social circumstances arrived at a point where the nation's rulers felt compelled to resort to extreme repression to prevent democratic political change. See E. Herbert Norman, "The Autocratic State," in John W. Dower, ed., *Origins of the Modern Japanese State:*

Selected Writings of E. H. Norman (New York: Pantheon, 1975), pp. 434–64. Saburo Ienaga writes in *The Pacific War*, Frank Baldwin, trans. (New York: Pantheon, 1978): "The Meiji Constitution did not guarantee basic human rights. Freedom of expression was recognized only 'within the limits of the law.' The liberties granted in the constitution could be virtually abolished by subsequent laws. Restrictions soon tumbled from the government's authoritarian cornucopia.... The Peace Preservation Law was enacted to suppress socialist ideas and the socialist movement. Later it was used against other ideas that displeased those who ran the state. The Meiji political system gagged and blindfolded the population" (pp. 14–15).

Thus we can identify Japan's own version of Imperial Germany's famous alliance of "steel and rye": a self-defensive class compromise reached by a "tame and timid bourgeoisie unable to challenge the old order" and residual, but still powerful, reactionary elements which blocked emergence of democratic institutions—what Barrington Moore describes as "feudal and capitalist features...put to work alongside one another in the effort to create a powerful modern state" (Moore, *Social Origins*, pp. 254, 275). Japanese legal and political historian Ryosuke Ishii observes that the "first codes compiled by the Meiji government were the Essence of the New Criminal Code" and, he adds, that although the first codes were based on Chinese legal principles and French jurisprudence, "after the promulgation of the Constitution the German influence became increasingly dominant" (*A History of Political Institutions in Japan* [Tokyo: University of Tokyo Press, 1980], p. 117).

As to external influences on the Meiji Constitution itself, Beckmann writes: "Upon arrival in Europe, Ito [Hirobumi] dispatched Saionji Kimmochi and several others to Paris to study the constitution of the Third Republic. The remainder of the mission proceeded to Berlin, where Ito, his assistants, and Aoki Shuzo, minister to Germany, attended a series of lectures by Rudolph Gneist, a professor jurisprudence. Gneist based his lectures on the general principle that constitutions should be firmly rooted in national history. He compared the history of Japan to that of Prussia, and he urged Ito to adopt a Prussian-style constitution. He stressed the need to protect the supreme powers of the emperor as exercised by ministers. Specifically, he emphasized that ultimate control over foreign affairs, military affairs, and legislation be entrusted to the emperor. With regard to the decisive matter of finance, Gneist recommended a clause which had been inserted in the Prussian Constitution which assured to the government the previous year's appropriations should parliament refuse or be unable to pass a budget bill....From Berlin Ito and his party journeyed to Vienna, where they attended lectures by the famous jurist Lorenz von Stein, who outlined an authoritarian system of government called 'bureaucratic constitutionalism,' in which the state and the monarch were synonymous" (*Modernization of China and Japan*, pp. 297–98).

Japan's authoritarian constitutional history was, of course, abruptly altered by the outcome of World War II and imposition of the new "MacArthur Constitution" during the American occupation of Japan. Both German and Japanese political systems were reconstructed on liberal capitalist lines after the War; see, for example, Justin Williams Sr., *Japan Political Revolution Under MacArthur: A Participant's Account* (Athens, Georgia: University of Georgia Press, 1979); Theodore Cohen, *Remaking Japan: The American Occupation as New Deal* (New York: Free Press, 1987).

There remaind, however, Japanese politicians during the Occupation period who resisted the notion that the Meiji constitutional tradition had been terminated. "Reference to foreign misunderstandings," says historian John W. Dower "and emphasis upon the positive continuities between prewar Japan and the new era of 'democracy,' were of course consistent with [Shigeru] Yoshida's unshakable conviction that Japan's interwar breakdown had been a betrayal rather than consequence of the Meiji legacy. In the Diet sessions of June 1946 he buttressed this familiar argument by referring to the 'democratic' nature of both the Charter Oath of 1868 and the constitution of 1889, arguing from this premise that the new draft constitution did not reflect 'the slightest intention to transform the political life hitherto pursued by the Japanese people.' Here again the language creaked with the ghostly voice of Ito Hirobumi, for the keynote to Ito's famous 1889 commentary on the Meiji constitution had been that 'the original national policy is by no means changed by [the new constitution] but is more strongly confirmed than ever.'" J. W. Dower, *Empire and Aftermath: Yoshida Shigeru and the Japanese Experience, 1878–1954* (Cambridge, Mass.: Harvard University Press, 1988), p. 322.

Yoshida was not alone in defending the Meiji legal heritage. See, for example, Tokyo University law professor Kenzo Takayanagi's analysis of the Meiji constitutional system, in a paper prepared in 1961 for a conference at Harvard University. Takayanagi's lengthy defense of Meiji's political credentials is replete with arguments like this one: "The statesmen who drafted the [Meiji] Constitution felt, with George Washington and eighteenth century European statesmen, that political parties were immoral." Harvard professor Arthur T. von Mehren's introduction to Takayanagi's essay is dry as dust and fails to alert readers to the way that efforts to whitewash the Meiji police state have contributed to anticonstitutionalist and neoreactionary movements in contemporary Japan. Takayanagi embraces the "dark valley" (*kurai tanima*) theory of modern Japanese history, stating that the normal development of Japanese democracy "was checked in the 1930s by the capture of political power

During the transition to state capitalism in the United States, reaction to the rising tide of fascist politics and expansionism proved critical to the shaping of American society and legal institutions. As world-system theorist Immanuel Wallerstein points out: "There were many hints—from Brest-Litovsk to Rapallo—that [the USSR.] might find it more comfortable to be diplomatically close to Germany or closer than to the US. This might have been catastrophic for the US, and one of Roosevelt's first moves in power was to establish diplomatic relations with the USSR. In 1934, the USSR joined the League of Nations and preached therein 'collective security,' a doctrine clearly aimed at Germany and its future allies, Italy and Japan. The world depression of 1929 placed both Germany and the United States in a very difficult internal situation. The political solution in Germany was Nazism....The coming to power of the Nazis facilitated the development of the New Deal as an alternative type of political solution, one that was 'centrist' rather than 'rightist'.[383]

The fact that American interests, perhaps survival, were genuinely threatened from the right meant that Roosevelt had to move his regime to the left, specifically in order to seek allies from that side of the political spectrum. As Wallerstein indicates, one of Roosevelt's earliest political decisions as president was to finally provide the Soviet Union with American diplomatic recognition.[384] Despite considerable opposition at

by army extremists and by the renewal of bureaucratic absolutism. Following the Great Depression, executive supremacy seemed to be a world-wide trend." If there was as little difference between authoritarian and liberal capitalism as Takayanagi appears to believe, one wonders why there had to be a war at all. See Kenzo Takayanagi, "A Century of Innovation: The Development of Japanese Law, 1868–1961," in *Law in Japan: The Legal Order in a Changing Society* (Cambridge: Harvard University Press, 1963), pp. 11–12.

An extremely well-informed antidote to Takayanagi's apologia for the police state can be found in Herbert P. Bix, "Rethinking 'Emperor-System Fascism': Ruptures and Continuities in Modern Japanese History," *Bullletin of Concerned Asian Scholars* (June 1982), p. 2; and in Herbert P. Bix, "Kawakami Hajime and the Organic Law of Japanese Fascism," *Japan Interpreter* 12 (winter 1978), p. 118. On "dark valley" politics and much more, see John W. Dower, "The Useful War,"

Dadealus 119 (summer 1990), p. 49.

383 Immanuel Wallerstein, "The USA in the World Today," in *The Politics of the World Economy* (Cambridge, Eng.: Cambridge University Press, 1984), p. 70.

384 "Ever since taking office, I had felt the absurdity of the inability of the United States to have any relations official or unofficial with Russia. The interchange of the following friendly letters in October [1933] paved the way for a visit from Mr. Litvinoff and the resumption of diplomatic relations with Russia the following month" (Franklin D. Roosevelt, *On Our Way* [New York: John Day, 1934], p. 128). In his response to Roosevelt's letter, Mikhail Kalinin stated that "I have always considered most abnormal and regrettable a situation wherein, during the past sixteen years, two great republics—the United States of America and the Union of Soviet Socialist Republics—have lacked the usual methods of communication and have been deprived of the benefits which such

the time and much debate since as to the reasons for Roosevelt's move, I believe that politics—specifically the sort Wallerstein outlines—were at the heart of the matter.[385]

To be sure, Wallerstein adds that once fascism was defeated "there were no longer any significant 'rightist' governments among the core states. On the world scene, the US quickly shifted therefore from being 'left of center' to being the leader of a 'free world' alliance against the world left, now dubbed 'communist totalitarianism.'"[386] While this shift to

communication could give....I shall take the liberty further to express the opinion that the abnormal situation, to which you correctly refer in your message, has an unfavorable effect not only on the interests of the two states concerned, but also on the general international situation, increasing the element of disquiet, complicating the process of consolidating world peace and encouraging forces tending to disturb the peace" (Kalinin in ibid., p. 130).

Kalinin politely points out that the United States was not resuming relations with Russia after a hiatus, as Roosevelt put it, but was initiating relations with the communist government in Moscow, relations which had not existed since Lenin and the Bolsheviks came to power. To be sure, the U.S.–Soviet alliance did not effectively discourage "forces tending to disturb the peace," if that was a reference to Hitler; neither did the brief Stalin–Ribbentrop Pact, signed six years later. Eric Hobsbawm writes: "The sheer reluctance of Western governments to enter into effective negotiations with the Red state, even in 1938–39 when the urgency of an anti-Hitler alliance was no longer denied by anyone, is only too patent. Indeed, it was the fear of being left to confront Hitler alone which eventually drove Stalin, since 1934 the unswerving champion of an alliance with the West against him, into the Stalin–Ribbentrop Pact of August, 1939...." (*The Age of Extremes* [New York: Pantheon, 1994], p. 151). But if Western governments failed to join with the "Red state" to stop Hitler in 1938–39, even Churchill did not hesitate to join ranks with the red army when the chips were down. "Stalin's brief dream," Hobsbawm concludes, "of post-war US–Soviet partnership did not actually strengthen the global alliance of

liberal capitalism and communism against fascism. Rather it demonstrated its strength and width....[T]he very nature of war confirmed the 1936 insights into the implications of the Spanish Civil War: the unity of military and civilian mobilization and social change" (ibid., p. 169). World War II thus culminated a decade-long transition in the United States from capitalist to state capitalist social organization; war and social change went hand in hand.

385   "Ultimately Roosevelt based his decision to recognize the Soviet Union primarily on political, rather than economic, considerations. Like Stalin, he feared the increasingly aggressive postures of Germany and, to a greater degree, Japan. As the tension between Japan and Russia increased during the spring of 1933, despite the President's endorsement of the Stimson Doctrine, recognition seemed to Roosevelt a subtle form of diplomatic pressure that might well give the Japanese reason to pause in their conquest of South Manchuria but would not unnecessarily antagonize them" (Joan Hoff Wilson, *Ideology and Economics: U.S. Relations with the Soviet Union, 1918-1923* [Columbia: University of Missouri Press, 1974], pp. 120–21).

Wilson's particular research context suggests that by "political, rather than economic, considerations" she means political rather than *business* considerations: the president pursued recognition for the reasons she gives here (as distinct from the claim that he was simply responding to pressure from specific business groups that would profit from increased trade between Soviets and Americans).

386   Immanuel Wallerstein, "The USA in the World", p. 71.

the right had obvious consequences for American domestic politics (for example, McCarthyism), it certainly did not roll back state capitalism or the system of productive relations which had been painstakingly assembled over previous decades.[387]

"World system" positioning alone did not shape a developing American social system during the 1930s. Coinciding with these *external* forces were a variety of domestic or *internal* forces that pushed the United States toward a centrist or, as Wallerstein describes it, "left of center" social regime. The impact of these domestic forces on the growth of state capitalism has formed an important strand in the work of some economists and historians;[388] others have analyzed domestic currents, however,

---

387 Stuart Bruchey writes: "Many business leaders were alienated in the 1930s, but the irony is that much of the reform brought about by the New Deal is now an institutionalized part of American life. So too is the relationship of government to the economy: despite regulations of economic conduct which future administrations would both introduce, modify, and even abandon; despite change in the degree to which government would intervene in the economy; despite change, too, in the industrial cast of characters subject to intervention, the basic fact remains that the reaction of both government and business to the trauma of the Great Depression has in all probability ended forever the relatively minimal contact between the two sectors that characterized American history before the 1930s" (*Enterprise*, p. 472). Whether or not that "minimal contact" was quite so modest, prior to the New Deal, or has in fact "ended forever," are important questions. But Bruchey's main point—that the innovation of the New Deal, what I have called *state* capitalism, survived the 1930s and World War II—is well taken.

388 "Never before in American history had there been an economic downturn so deep and so long lasting as the Great Depression of the 1930s. Without precedent to guide them, and in an atmosphere of crisis and collapse, the New Dealers used the powers of the federal government to experiment with a broad range of programs to deal with the problems of the Depression....The New Deal, in historical perspective, represented a decisive movement away from reliance on a traditional laissez-

faire economy toward a mixed economy, with government involvement in economic stabilization, social security, and labor-management relations. Government now participated in many areas of economic decision making that were previously the exclusive prerogative of private business" (Sidney Ratner, James H. Soltow, and Richard Sylla, *The Evolution of the American Economy* [2d ed., New York: Macmillan, 1993], pp. 486–87). Jeremy Atack and Peter Passell write: "Although the flurry of New Deal legislative activity built upon the foundation of the command economy laid down during World War I, its goal was nothing short of a complete restructuring of the American economy, a complete reform of its institutions. Whereas the law had once prohibited 'conspiracies in restraint of trade,' collective bargaining was now not only sanctioned but enforced; firms once fearful of talking to one another in the wake of the infamous 'Gary dinners' hosted between 1907 and 1911 by Judge Elbert Gary (chairman of the board of directors of U.S. Steel) at which the nation's steel producers had colluded to set prices were now encouraged to set minimum 'fair trade' prices; contracts specifying repayment in gold were nullified; caveat emptor no longer held in stock purchases. No longer would the nation's farmers be subject to the market discipline" (*A New Economic View of American History* [2d ed., New York: W. W. Norton, 1994], p. 676).

Michel Aglietta writes in *A Theory of Capitalist Regulation: The US Experience* (David Fernbach, trans., London: Verso, 1987): "The Great Depression profoundly

in conjunction with pressures arising from international politics.[389] Wallerstein and those who follow his approach, however, have provided us with an especially interesting way of looking at key developments during the New Deal and the war which provided a new foundation for legal and political relations stretching into the Vietnam era and the Reagan revolution.[390]

changed the consciousness of the working class, as well as the attitude toward industrial conflicts of a large number of social groups politically attached to the liberal bourgeoisie, especially when these conflicts occurred in branches of industry dominated by the giant corporations. On the one hand a mass movement developed and led to the formation of the Congress for Industrial Organization (CIO) in 1936. Its positions were far more radical than those of the traditional unions, and found expression in a massive unionization of workers in the key branches of steel and motor vehicles, after the spectacular strikes of autumn 1936 to winter 1937. On the other hand, the political balance of forces had greatly changed when a reformist bloc with a great majority in the industrial states and Congress carried the New Deal administration to power. One of the fundamental principles of this wide-ranging overhaul of the institutions of capitalist society was the codification of the class struggle. This involved official recognition of trade union organizations with major powers of negotiation vis-a-vis the bosses, and the means to exercise these powers without their legal existence being endangered" (pp. 134–35).

According to Richard B. DuBoff: "What had really happened between 1929 and 1933 is that the institutions of nineteenth-century free market growth broke down, beyond repair. Had the chain of circumstances been 'right,' it could have occurred in 1920–21 or possibly 1907. The tumultuous passage from the depression of the 1930s to the total economic mobilization of the 1940s was the watershed in twentieth-century U.S. capitalism. After that, nothing in the macroeconomy would ever be the same; there was no going back to the days of a pure, practically unregulated capitalist economic order" (*Accumulation and Power: An Economic*

History of the United States [Armonk, N.Y.: M. E. Sharpe, 1989], pp. 91–92).

389 For example, William Applebaum Williams, *Americans in a Changing World* (New York: Macmillan, 1978), pp. 241–337; Kees van der Pijl, *The Making of an Atlantic Ruling Class* (London: Verso, 1984), pp. 76–137; Thomas Ferguson, "Industrial Conflict and the Coming of the New Deal: The Triumph of Multinational Liberalism in America," in Steve Fraser and Gary Gerstle, eds., *The Rise and Fall of the New Deal Order, 1930-1980* (Princeton: Princeton University Press; 1989); and Gabriel Kolko, "The Political Economy of Capitalism in Crisis, 1920–1940," in *Main Currents in Modern American History* (New York: Harper and Row, 1976), p. 100.

390 Giovanni Arrighi writes in *The Long Twentieth Century* (London: Verso, 1994): "The halt in US foreign lending and investment was made permanent by the collapse of the Wall Street boom and the ensuing slump in the US economy. Faced with sudden recalls or flights of short-term funds, one country after another was forced to protect its currency, either by depreciation or exchange control....Protectionism became rampant, the pursuit of stable currencies was abandoned, and world capitalism retreated into the igloos of its nation-state economies and their associated empires....This is the 'world revolution' that Karl Polanyi traced to the 'snapping of the golden thread,' Its main landmarks were the disappearance of *haute finance* from world politics, the collapse of the League of Nations in favor of autarchist empires, the rise of Nazism in Germany, the Soviet Five Years Plans, and the launching of the US New Deal" (p. 274).

Stuart Bruchey writes: "In time, Roosevelt's policies alienated many businessmen, who came to despise 'that man in the White House.' In further time,

In his review of Morton Horwitz's second volume of legal history, Robert Gordon asks, "Was the administrative state a progressive instrument for controlling corporate power and redistributing wealth, or was it a captured and coopted instrument of corporate power?"[391] If we accept the first alternative, the New Deal might be seen as a liberal or "social democratic" adjustment in the system of law and politics—one that accomplished much but also embodied a considerably more egalitarian vision of society than what was finally achieved.[392] The first part of this

however, many of the social programs associated with the New Deal came to be regarded by the successors to the businessmen of the 1930s as built-in stabilizers in periods of falling demand. As we shall see, the New Deal marks the beginning not only of the Welfare State but also the cushioned economy" (Enterprise, p. 451). He concludes that the "New Deal, once again, did not end the Great Depression. But the president's policies did save the American economic system" (ibid., p. 472).

For our purposes here, the New Deal (and the defeat of fascism in the War) not only saved liberal capitalism but also provided the dominant model of social and economic organization in the United States for the next several decades, until what Steve Fraser and Gary Gerstle call the fall of the New Deal order (Introduction, *The Rise and Fall of the New Deal Order* [Princeton, N.J.: Princeton University Press, 1989]). "When Ronald Reagan assumed office in January 1981, an epoch in the nation's political history came to an end. The New Deal, as a dominant order of ideas, public policies, and political alliances, died, however much its ghost still hovers over a troubled polity" (ibid., p. ix).

391 Robert Gordon, "The Elusive Transformation," *Yale Journal of Law and the Humanities* (1994), p. 157.

392 "If I read correctly between the lines, [Horwitz] reads the history of [Progressive Legal Thought] as a tragic failure of a view of law and regulation that had a chance to further a social-democratic vision but was tamed and made conservative before the vision was realized" (ibid.) See Morton J. Horwitz, *The Transformation of American Law 1870-1960* (New York: Oxford University Press, 1992). Jerold Auerbach argues that it

was lawyers in the New Deal bureaucracy, including legal realists, who killed any radical potential for change: "Therein lay the source of the tension that tormented [Jerome] Frank as long as he remained in Washington. His personal commitment to Realism and to experimentalism impelled him toward policymaking; his professional preferences for process and precedent restrained him. An experimentalist as to legal means, he unquestionably accepted social ends. Standing at the cutting edge of legal thought in the Roosevelt administration, he demonstrated the compatibility of Realism with the New Deal and the strength that each derived from the other. But the conflict between professionalism and capitalism on the one hand, and social change on the other, was painful...' (*Unequal Justice: Lawyers and Social Change in Modern America* [New York: Oxford University Press, 1976], pp. 178–79).

Auerbach's case for the conflict between capitalism and social change is stronger than his case against legal professionalism; in his words, "[l]awyers' skills (drafting, negotiation, compromise) and lawyers' values (process divorced from substance, means over ends) permitted New Deal achievements yet set New Deal boundaries" (ibid, p. 227). The conflict between liberal and authoritarian capitalism which consumed the 1930s and led to war, is far more useful in explaining both achievements and boundaries of the New Deal than is the craft style of legal practice. The rise of fascism pushed the United States (including its administrative apparatus) to the left, but that threat did not and could not make New Dealers into Bolsheviks.

For exceptions that prove the rule, see John Kenneth Galbraith, *A Journey Through Economic Time* (Boston: Houghton Mifflin,

formulation, suggesting that New Deal politics checked the excesses of a business society, became the party line of postwar American liberal historiography.

However, Gordon's second perspective—which is sometimes associated with "New Left" revisionist historiography—emphasizes the extent to which the New Deal saved capitalism; in this light, the reforms of the 1930s can be seen as tools that ruling elites used to contain the Depression-inspired surge in radical sentiment favoring social reconstruction.[393] University of Massachusetts political scientist Thomas Ferguson put this well when he suggested that the Democratic Party that emerged from the Roosevelt years was no more the party of the people than the Republicans. The popular view that the Democrats were, in fact, opposed to big business, Ferguson argues, is rooted in a mistaken view of the New Deal itself which has left ordinary Americans mystified by the twists and turns of postwar politics: "[T]hey tried to puzzle out why the party did so little to help unionize the South, protect the victims of McCarthyism, promote civil rights for blacks, women, or Hispanics, or, in the late 1970s, combat America's great 'right turn' against the New Deal itself. To such people, it is always remained a mystery why the Democrats so often betrayed the ideals of the New Deal. Little did they realize that, in fact, the party was only living up to them."[394]

This view certainly suggests if not betrayal then at least an enormous disparity between what motivated New Deal reformers and the kind of

1994): "In fact, the youthful Communists and their associates were a small, if vocal, part of the New Deal community. They attracted an audience and prestige because of the exuberant assurance with which they held to and stated their views. Had such views not been present among those descending on Washington, it would have been surprising. No one of any sensitivity could look on capitalism in those years and think it a success. There was, accordingly, a choice between repair and revolt....Those seeking repair, either from choice, instinct or the desire for a measure of political acceptability, were the clearly dominant influence, and with them I was allied" (p. 84).

For a more compelling portrait of Jerome N. Frank than Auerbach's, including Frank's work for the Agricultural Adjustment Administration, see Robert Jerome Glennon, *The Iconoclast as Reformer: Jerome Frank's*

Impact on American Law (Ithaca, N.Y.: Cornell University Press, 1985). For more on the attorneys who came to Washington, see Peter H. Irons, *The New Deal Lawyers* (Princeton: Princeton Univ. Press, 1982). For more on the Legal Realists, see John Henry Schlegel, *American Legal Realism and Empirical Social Science* (Chapel Hill: University of North Carolina Press, 1995); and *American Legal Realism* William W. Fisher III, Morton J. Horwitz, and Thomas A. Reed, eds., (New York: Oxford University Press, 1993).

393 "Sometimes, however, [Horwitz] adopts the darker, instramentalist view that the progressive – New Deal initiates (and the legal theory that supported them) served large corporate interests from their inception." Gordon, "Elusive Transformation," p. 157.

394 Ferguson, "Multinational Liberalism," p. 24.

world their efforts brought about. In either case, once we acknowledge that the New Deal manifested contradictory phases[395]—or, better, that it was but one of four phases that together constitute the state capitalist period in American history—then we can appreciate why conflicting images of the New Deal continue to generate controversy.

Wallerstein's overarching critique demonstrates that the decade 1933–43 is best understood in terms of Roosevelt's "left of center" strategy to preserve and defend liberal capitalism in a time of trial; at the same time, Roosevelt was merely reflecting the world historical path staked out by liberal modernizers.[396] The first phase of the state capitalist period (1917–32) was also the last fifteen years of the previous (capitalist) period: it was what I have called a "precursor," in this instance of a nascent state capitalism. William A. Williams suggests that the legislation of Roosevelt's first three months in office "made it clear that the centralizing, rationalizing, regulative, and corporate strand of thought *that had always been strong among Progressives* had become the basis of the new liberalism."[397] Jeremy Atack and Peter Passell specifically refer to an early "foundation of the command economy laid down during World War I"[398] and many historians would now agree with Gabriel Kolko that World War I pioneered relations between public and private, the state and business, which would only become more entrenched as the century wore on.[399] This "precursor" phase of state capitalism witnessed such remark-

---

395 Douglas Dowd writes: "First, we should distinguish the three phases of the New Deal, or, more properly, of the Roosevelt Administration, for after 1938 there were no further 'New Deal' policies" (*Capitalist Development*, p. 161).

396 University of California economist Robert Pollin points out "the increasingly wide recognition that economic systems are characterized by path dependency—or the related concepts of 'complexity' and 'hysterisis'—which is to say, the specific outcomes in any given period are contingent on a range of factors, and the ways these factors happen to combine will then set the terms for the next round of indeterminate combinations. Recognizing path dependency does not deny the importance of broad historical visions and overarching theories. But it does underscore the difficulty of making such analyses hold up in considering the detailed dynamics of any given historical

period" ("Contemporary Economic Stagnation in World Historical Perspective," *New Left Review* [Sept.–Oct. 1996], p. 117).

397 Williams, *Americans in a Changing World*, p. 249 (emphasis added). See also Martin J. Sklar, *The Corporate Reconstruction of American Capitalism, 1890-1916* (Cambridge: Cambridge University Press, 1988).

398 Atack and Passell, *New Economic View*, p. 676.

399 Gabriel Kolko writes in *Century of War* (New York: New Press, 1994): "War and war organizations, as much as any factor in this century, have determined the relationship of the state to the economy both during wartime and thereafter, significantly affecting the distribution of economic power and creating crucial precedents for governments' roles in guiding and dealing with economies.... Whatever exceptions to this broad, general trend occurred did not alter the fact that during the First World War sections of the ruling-class structure articulated the forms

able superstructural developments as the emergence of Benjamin Cardozo's tort and contract jurisprudence.[400]

The second phase of state capitalism lasted from 1932 to 1947, from Roosevelt's election and recognition of the Soviet Union through the "reverse course" in New Deal liberalism, symbolically identified with 8:00 P.M., January 31, 1947.[401] This phase includes the best known, and perhaps most dramatic, shift in the legal superstructure—the Supreme Court's famous about-face on constitutionality of New Deal legislation.[402] The

and priorities for making war, thereby creating the model for business–state relations which, with some variations, has increasingly characterized most industrial nations throughout this entire century" (p. 67).

400 See, for example, Cardozo's New York Court of Appeals opinion in *MacPherson v. Buick Motor Co.*, 217 N.Y. 382, 111 N.E. 1050 (1916). For perhaps the best single essay on this transition from one way of thinking and talking about legal rules to another, see Peter Gabel, "Intention and Structure in Contractual Conditions: Outline of a Method for Critical Legal Theory," *Minnesota Law Review* 61 (1977), p. 601.

401 Historian Gabriel Kolko argues that the reverse course, or at least his version of it, actually began during World War II itself; see *The Politics of War* (New York: Pantheon, 1990). Joe Moore writes: "General MacArthur publicly issued [a written directive prohibiting a general strike by Japanese workers] the afternoon of 31 January [1947], and the leaders of the eight unions and the chairman of Kyoto were summoned once again to headquarters to be ordered by [William] Marquat to dictate a message on the spot for immediate transmission to their organizations calling off the strike. They were in effect under informal arrest until a message of cancellation was sent. All the unions complied, and chairman Ii of Kyoto made a radio broadcast at 8:00 P.M. calling off the general strike. It concluded with the words of Lenin, calling for one step backward and two steps forward..." (*Japanese Workers and the Struggle for Power* [Madison: University of Wisconsin Press, 1983], p. 239). But see Marcel Liebman's reference to Lenin's *One Step Forward, Two Steps Back*, written in 1904; *Leninism Under Lenin* (London: Cape, 1975), p. 53.

See also Bruce Cumings, "'Global Realm With No Limit, Global Realm With No Name,'" *Radical History Review* 57, (fall 1993): "No matter how much one may object, most historians of the Cold War are wedded to the idea that something terribly important and world-transforming occurred in 1947. It is true, something terribly important happened: England finally passed the baton of hegemonic maintenance to the United States. But nothing truly world-transforming occurred until 1950, when Truman and Acheson finally got the cash out of Congress to create permanent forward-basing abroad and a national security complex at home; defense spending went from $13 billion to $54 billion in six months, and for the first time in its history the U.S. had an empire abroad and a domestic complex of state and business to service it at home" (p. 51).

The reverse course can be seen as a "natural" postwar adjustment within the politics of American capitalism, as Wallerstein suggests, and certainly does not imply an abandonment of liberalism, in the sense that Barrington Moore uses that phrase to distinguish progressive from reactionary forms of capitalist modernization; see David Blackbourn, "Theme-Park Prussia," *London Review of Books* (Nov. 24, 1994): "In 1947, the Allied Control Commission pronounced the death of Prussia, symbol of militarism and knee-jerk obedience, and alleged progenitor of Nazism. It has stayed dead. The GDR was never, as some liked to believe, the continuation of Prussia by other means. Junker estates were broken up, and Prussia was distributed among the Poles and Russians as well as the Germans. Recent events are unlikely to change any of that" (p. 18).

402 See, for example, Harold J. Laski, *The*

third phase of the state capitalist period stretches from 1947 until wherever one wishes to draw the line marking what Ferguson calls the "great 'right turn' against the New Deal itself."

Historian Bartholomew Sparrow reminds us that World War II fundamentally altered the structure of American social and economic life.[403] It is to the U.S. "domestic front" that he turns his attention—specifically to how developments in the Social Security system, regulation of labor–management relations, and evolution of public finance and military procurement policies reflected modifications of the New Deal state by wartime experience.[404] This emerging "Fordist" state[405] that was compati-

American Democracy (New York: Viking, 1948), pp. 210–11; William M. Wiecek writes: "Roosevelt responded with the ill-conceived court-packing plan of 1937, which, though a tactical failure, was strategically successful in forcing a turnabout in the Court's judicial direction" ("New Deal," in The Oxford Companion to the Supreme Court of the United States [New York: Oxford University Press, 1992], p. 584). However much Roosevelt's Court-packing threat may have provided an immediate impetus for a switch in the Court's views, the underlying cause of the transition in constitutional and legal superstructure during this period was the emergence of state capitalism generally, and, specifically, an earnest national effort to find a road to recovery as well as deal with the economic and political ascendancy of Germany and Japan.

Wiecek concludes: "Beginning with West Coast Hotel v. Parrish (1937), the Court accepted state and federal regulatory legislation. It systematically dismantled the entire structure of laissez faire constitutionalism (including Lochner and Knight), and with it the dogmas of substantive due process and freedom of contract" (ibid). For some of the specific legal and political changes wrought by the war, and war production, themselves, see Thurman W. Arnold, "The Ideal of a Managed Economy," in Democracy and Free Enterprise (Norman: University of Oklahoma Press, 1942), pp. 49–62; Williams, Americans in a Changing World, pp. 297–368.

403 "Consider that the United States in 1940 was just emerging from the Great Depression,

with 14 percent unemployment, and was still very much isolationist. By mid-year 1950, however, the Marshall Plan was well under way, NATO had been established, and the U.S. government had entered the Korean War; the United States was ineluctably part of the world. On the domestic front, the economy had begun its sustained growth of the next few decades, the United States had an emerging welfare state, and suburbanization was spreading rapidly..." (Bartholomew H. Sparrow, From the Outside In: World War II and the American State [Princeton: Princeton University Press, 1996], p. x). Whether the United States was as isolationist prior to 1940 as Sparrow suggests remains an open question. His assertion, however, that war contributed to American state-building is undeniable. On the isolationsim question, see, Thomas J. McCormick, "Seeking Supremacy: The Historical Origins of American Hegemony, 1895–1945," in McCormick, America's Half-Century.

404 "The state-building of the war years did not lead to the government becoming a near-tyrannical force in American society....[T]he greater presence of the U.S. government in the economy and in individual lives was consistent with the necessary expansion of national government and extension of government-society ties during a world war. That the U.S. government became the new locus of exchange as a result of the war did not mean that the government, by itself, necessarily had greater authority. The jointness of the wartime state-building

ble with the "reverse course" and 1950s McCarthyism, yet able to provide a foundation for superstructural reform and legal innovation continuing well into the 1960s and 1970s. It was during this third phase of the state capitalist period that the Warren Court so visibly rewrote constitutional rights and private law underwent its modern transformation.[406]

implicated nominally private actors in the expansion of the government and at once constrained the scope of federal authority. The private became public, and the public included the private; both built the state" (Sparrow, *From the Outside In*, p. 311).

405 See Robert Boyer, "Fordism: The Heart of Postwar Growth—and Crisis," in Craig Charney, trans. *The Regulation School: A Critical Introduction*, (New York: Columbia University Press, 1990). In *Prisoners of the American Dream*, Mike Davis writes: "Atlantic Fordism, the economic trajectory of American hegemony, assumed the possibility of simultaneous, interdependent expansion of the major capitalist economies (although not necessarily the actual synchronization of their individual business cycles). It was, above all, the growth of the domestic US economy that provided sustained momentum in the international system as a whole, allowing the European and Japanese economies to reconstruct their productive forces on US mass-assembly principles and to achieve the 'recovery' miracles of the late 1950s....[I]t took the decade-long struggle of the new industrial CIO unions to force the way for union recognition and the codification, in the collective bargaining agreements of 1948–50, of a dynamic wage system that synchronized mass consumption with labor productivity. In this fashion, perhaps a quarter of the American population—especially white-ethnic semi-skilled workers and their families—were raised to previously middle-class or skilled-worker thresholds of home ownership and credit purchase during the 1950s. Another quarter to one-third of the population, however, including most Blacks and all agricultural laborers, remained outside the boom, constituting the 'other America' which rebelled in the 1960s. The most striking indices of the advance of the intensive regime

of accumulation were suburbanization and the growth of higher education" (pp. 190–91). See also Samuel Bowles, David Gordon, and Thomas Weisskopf, *Beond the Wasteland* (New York: Doubleday, 1983).

406 On the transformation of private law, see Eugene Kamenka and Alice Ehr-Soon Tay, "Socialism, Anarchism, and Law," in Eugene Kamenka, Robert Brown and Alice Ehr-Soon Tay, eds., *Law and Society: The Crisis in Legal Ideas* (New York: St. Martin's, 1978). Kamenka and Tay write: "Lawyers, of course, have long been aware of important changes in modern social and economic life, and in modern social and political attitudes, that affect the character and principles of many areas of private law and which have been fundamentally altering the balance between private and public law. They speak, as the late Wolfgang Friedman did, of a shift from private law, concerned with security of the individual, to public law, concerned with welfare and social utility. Even in the heart of the private law, in the law of tort or torts, and in contract, they have discerned similar developments. In torts, there is the movement from the legal-individualistic principle of fault liability to the social, actuarial cost-benefit analysis that leads to the principle of loss distribution; in contract, the concept of a bargain struck between ideally equal and freely contracting parties is increasingly infringed upon by the court's recognition of social and economic inequalities and of the one-sided restriction of the power to bargain by the existence of standard contracts. We have the emergence of whole new areas of law—industrial law, conciliation and arbitration, rent and price control, tenant and consumer protection, safeguarding of the environment—which require conceptions of the nature and function of law and of the nature and procedural characteristics of justice

The line separating the third and fourth phases of the state capitalist period simultaneously separates state and global capitalist periods. Much of the first phase of state capitalism (its precursor phase, 1917–32) emerged during the concluding decades of the capitalist period and, similarly, the final phase of state capitalism survives as a remnant within the first decades of the new global capitalist period. But where do we draw the line—and why? Economists David M. Gordon, Thomas E. Weisskopf, and Samuel Bowles suggest that postwar American society was organized around a set of stabilizing factors which helped preserve corporate hegemony, at least for a while. Regarding the course of these factors' development, they conclude: "They remained relatively solid into the 1960s, but the success of the [social structure of accumulation] in promoting economic growth proved ultimately contradictory. Workers, foreign suppliers of raw materials, and domestic citizens began to question and to resist the previously established structures of power. The growing strength of other capitalist nations, as well as the success of anti-capitalist movements in the Third World, further challenged the power of United States capital. Increased competition both domestically and internationally reduced capitalists' ability to protect their profitability from these incursions. The postwar capitalist system consequently began to erode; corporate capitalists found it increasingly difficult to control the terms of their interaction with other major actors on the economic scene."[407]

Whether the system these economists see beginning to unravel in the

that diverge sharply from the traditional attitudes, concepts and procedures of nineteenth-century common law judges and courts" (pp. 48–49).

See also Hall, *Magic Mirror*, pp. 291–99; "Private Law Present and Future," Stephen B. Presser and Jamil S. Zainaldin, eds., *Law and Jurisprudence in American History* (St. Paul, Minn.: West Publishing, 1995) pp. 821–78; Grant Gilmore, *The Death of Contract* (Columbus: Ohio State University Press, 1974).

407 David M. Gordon, Thomas E. Weisskopf, and Samuel Bowles, "Power, Accumulation, and Crisis: The Rise and Demise of the Postwar Social Structure of Accumulation," in Robert Cherry, et al., eds., *The Imperiled Economy* vol. 1 (New York: Union of Radical Political Economists, 1987). Robert Pollin observes: "There is little dispute now that the

history of Western capitalism since the end of World War II can be partitioned into two distinct periods. Its 'Golden Age', lasting roughly through the end of the 1960s, was characterized by rapid economic growth, low employment, mild business cycles and rising mass living standards, especially for the white, male sectors of the working class. The 'Leaden Age', running from the early 1970s into the present, has been distinguished by slow growth, high unemployment, more severe business cycles, and stagnating or declining living standards for the majority....As the Leaden Age advanced, the hegemony of 'big government' policies yielded to an ascendent Thatcher-Reagan agenda of unqualified support for big business and similarly unqualified opposition to any sort of downward redistribution initiatives" ("Economic Stagnation," p. 109).

1960s would have been described by Marx as a "mode of production," or by Adam Smith as a mode of subsistence, or by law professor Mitchell Franklin as a "rival system of property relations" is, of course, less important than the fact that this transition from one social structure of accumulation to another precipitated a transformation in America's legal and political superstructure. In addition to the erosion of corporate control, which these economists emphasize, there was at the same time a fundamental shift of regional power within the United States. The Civil War constituted a violent confrontation between North and South—or the regions of the nation so designated at the time—but it is one I collapsed into the more politically telling opposition between left and right, between liberal and authoritarian capitalism. Redeployed in the second half of the twentieth century, however, the North–South distinction can be translated not only in terms of a rustbelt versus sunbelt metaphor but can additionally be utilized to identify a genuine shift in the nature of who holds power in America.

Washington Post journalist David Maraniss writes in his biography of Bill Clinton that perhaps the most formative intellectual experience the President had as an undergraduate at Georgetown University was the Western Civilization course taught by Professor Carroll Quigley. Maraniss specifically refers to Quigley's "life's work, a thousand-page tome entitled *Tragedy and Hope*," which the author finally completed in 1966.[408] Describing developments in American politics in the final decade prior to his book's publication, Quigley asserted:

> [T]he economic influence of the older Wall Street financial groups has been weakening and been challenged by new wealth springing up outside the eastern cities, notably in the Southwest and Far West. These new sources of wealth have been based very largely on government action and government spending but have, none the less, adopted a petty-bourgeois outlook rather than the semiaristocratic outlook that pervades the Eastern Establishment. This new wealth, based on petroleum, natural gas, ruthless exploitation of national resources, the aviation industry, military bases in the South and West, and finally on space with all its attendant activities has centered in Texas and Southern California. Its existence, for the first time, made it possible for the petty-bourgeois outlook to make itself felt in the political nomination process instead of the unrewarding effort to influence politics by

408 David Maraniss, *First in His Class: A Biography of Bill Clinton*   (New York: Simon and Schuster, 1995), pp. 58–60.

voting for a Republican candidate nominated under Eastern Establishment influence.[409]

It is not just subsequent scholarship which has verified Quigley's initial insight into the character of this transformation in American history but, crucially, events themselves.[410] Following Joel Garreau, we might well note the regional origins of America's presidents over the past several

409 Caroll Quigley, *Tragedy and Hope: A History of the World in Our Time* (New York: Macmillan, 1966), pp. 1245–46.

410 See, for example, Richard M. Bernard, "Sunbelt South," in Charles Reagan Wilson and William Ferris, eds., *Encyclopedia of Southern Culture* 565, 565-566 (New York: Doubleday Anchor, 1989): "'Sunbelt South' and, more generally, the 'American Sunbelt' are media creations designed to give coherence and meaning to the dramatic population growth and political upheavals that have occurred in the South and Southwest since 1940. Coined by political analyst Kevin P. Phillips in his book *The Emerging Republican Majority* (1969), the concept of 'Sun Belt' (or 'Sunbelt') lay dormant and ill-defined until the mid-1970s, when a combination of census reports on migration, the growing Republican potential in the South and West, and the presidential candidacy of Georgian Jimmy Carter brought the lower tier of states to public attention. Although he did not use the term *Sunbelt*, journalist Kirkpatrick Sale, in *Power Shift: The Rise of the Southern Rim and Its Challenge to the Eastern Establishment* (1975), alerted northern intellectuals to the emergence of the nation's 'Southern Rim' as a new center of power...Most commentators attribute this increase [in population] to economic development fostered by federal and state aid to business, and to changing American lifestyles. Beginning with World War II, Washington poured enormous sums into the South and West for the construction and maintenance of military installations and the production of modern weaponry" (Vol. 2, pp. 565–66).

See also Dewey W. Grantham, *The South in Modern America* (New York: HarperCollins, 1994): "[S]pokesmen for New England cities and industries accused the South of unfair competition, violating the wage standards of the Walsh-Healy Public Contracts Act, and suppressing the development of organized labor.... Representative John F. Kennedy of Massachusetts and other congressional critics of the South's industrial promotion practices were particularly distressed by the use of public subsidies to lure industries to the South....In the debate that followed, sectional charges and countercharges were made—charges of southern 'stealing' of northern industry and of the colonial exploitation of the South by the North" (p. 275).

Earl Black and Merle Black, *The Vital South: How Presidents Are Elected* (Cambridge: Harvard University Press, 1992): "In the 1960 Democratic convention Massachusetts Senator John F. Kennedy demonstrated anew that southern votes were unnecessary to capture the party's presidential nomination. Kennedy won only 3 percent of the southern delegates, most of whom supported Texas Senator Lyndon B. Johnson, but triumphed by winning 68 percent of the votes cast by delegates outside the South....In 1963 an extraordinary chain of events made possible the Democratic party's first nomination of a southerner for president in 120 years. 'We're heading into nut country today,' President Kennedy told his wife on the morning of November 22, 1963. 'But Jackie, if somebody wants to shoot me from a window with a rifle,' he continued, 'nobody can stop it, so why worry about it?' Johnson was, of course, a backdoor president, elevated to the White House that afternoon upon the assassination of President Kennedy" (p. 107).

411 See Joel Garreau, *The Nine Nations of North America* (New York: Avon, 1981).

decades.[411] Since President Kennedy was assassinated, of our elected Presidents, two have come from Southern California, two from Texas, and one each from Georgia and Arkansas. While there are unmistakable infrastructural reasons for such shifts in the political superstructure—and presidential elections themselves are only the tip of an iceberg—such consistency in regional origins still tells us something interesting about the shift in power which most visibly reflects the close of the state capitalist period.[412]

So whether we choose Barry Goldwater's successful takeover of the Republican Party, the assassination of President Kennedy, the Vietnam War, or Ronald Reagan's dismantling of the regulatory state, it becomes necessary at some point in time between the Kennedy and Reagan presidencies to draw a line signalling the transition from one regime or social structure of accumulation to another.[413] Given the pressures on economic

412 "I describe this industrial revolution in the old hinterland as 'tax-led' because federal fiscal transfers, secured by the historically disproportionate congressional power of the South and West, were the prime movers in the creation of the Sunbelt. Thus in California, Washington, Texas and Florida, military spending sponsored the rise of aerospace and electronic industry complexes, while oil depletion allowances and agricultural credits rationalized the regional primary sectors and encouraged downstream diversification in oil technology and agricultural processing/merchandising. Immense long-term expenditures on highways, water projects and natural gas pipelines laid the basis for profligate metropolitan development in the desert West" (Davis, *Prisoners of the American Dream*, p. 194).

413 For Goldwater's takeover, see Mary C. Brennan, *Turning Right in the Sixties: The Conservative Capture of the GOP* (Chapel Hill, N.C.: University of North Carolina Press, 1995): "During the 1960s, while the majority of Americans were contemplating the fortunes and misfortunes of liberalism, conservatives methodically, and somewhat surreptitiously, became a dominant force in national politics by gaining control of the Republican Party. Disorganized and divided in 1960, defeated spectacularly in 1964, the Right at first glance appeared to be as obsolete and ineffective as liberals claimed. Yet despite its seeming

impotence, the Right evolved into a complex, organized, and effective political force that dominated the GOP by 1968 and eventually secured the election of a staunch conservative as president in 1980" (p. 1).

For JFK's assassination as the dividing line: see Carl Oglesby, *The Yankee and Cowboy War* (Kansas City, Mo: Sheed, Andrews, and McMeel, 1976): "The whole point of introducing the Cowboy/Yankee language, of course, is to bring precisely [Carroll Quigley's] old-money/new-money, Atlanticist-Frontierist tension into focus in the plane of current events. The main idea of looking at things this way is to see that a sectional rivalry, derived from the patterns of the Civil War, still operates in American politics, indeed that at the altitude of national power elites, it may be the most sensitive and inflamed division of all, more concentrated than race and more basic than two-party system attachments and ideologies. The argument of this book is that the emerging clash of Yankee and Cowboy wills beneath the visible stream of events is the dominant fact of real U.S. political life since 1960" (p. 9). Oglesby's main contention is that the assassination of President Kennedy, and the transition from North to South, Yankee to Cowboy, political regimes in the United States precipitated by the ensuing presidential succession, reveal a pattern of conspiracy that is a *normal and open* (rather than clandestine) aspect of the American

growth and the underlying shift in economic interests, it is small wonder that analogous superstructural change took an unambiguously conservative form. More than simply the "right turn" of the Rehnquist Court or corporate-sponsored pursuit of massive "tort reform,"[414] this movement precipitated a fundamental reorientation of common law thinking itself. British historian P. S. Atiyah argues: "for the past fifteen years strenuous attempts have been made to re-invigorate the area of free choice. At the same time there has been a considerable resurgence of belief in the economic virtues of the free market system, and there has also been a growing interest (especially in America) in the relationship between legal and economic principles....All this suggests that the decline of freedom of contract has been halted, and the pendulum is swinging in its favour yet again. Moreover, this renewed swing of the pendulum looks set to last for some while yet, whatever the outcome of the next few elections. All political parties now accept the virtues (within varying limits) of the free market, or free contract, and even those opposed to current trends appear now

political process.

Surprisingly, given the general Marxist hostility to "conspiracy theories," even Georg Lukács observed that "United States foreign policy, for example, has in many respects ceased to be democratically conducted, despite its ostensibly democratic character. This is quite clearly observable in Kennedy's actions in connection with Cuba. Kennedy waged a continuous struggle against the illegal intervention of the secret organizations, while today under the Johnson regime this intervention of the secret organizations and the military bureaucracy is incomparably greater" (Holz, *Conversations*, p. 103). Those for whom the phrase "deep politics" is less onerous than "conspiracy theory" should see Peter D. Scott, *Deep Politics and the Death of JFK* (Berkeley: University of California Press, 1993).

For the Vietnam War as the dividing line: in an issue of *Radical History Review* devoted to essays on imperialism, University of Chicago Asian historian Bruce Cumings argues that Vietnam was "a war propelled by Cold War liberals so addicted to containment doctrine that they redoubled their efforts precisely as they lost sight of their goals, whereas the 1990–91 Gulf War had the important goal of assuring continued

American control of that resource that had been so insistently 'present at the creation' in the 1940s—Middle Eastern oil" (pp. 47–48).

See also Richard Drinnon, *Facing West: The Metaphysics of Indian-Hating and Empire-Building* (Minneapolis: University of Minnesota Press, 1980); Gabriel Kolko, *Anatomy of a War: Vietnam, the United States, and the Modern Historical Experience* (New York: Pantheon, 1985); Lloyd C. Gardner, *Pay Any Price: Lyndon Johnson and the Wars for Vietnam* (Chicago: Ivan R. Dee, 1995); Tom Wells, *The War Within: America's Battle over Vietnam* (Berkeley: University of California Press, 1994); McCormick, *America's Half-century* pp. 147–54.

414   For the Rehnquist Court, see David G. Savage, *Turning Right: The Making of the Rehnquist Supreme Court* (New York: John Wiley, 1992); David Kairys, *With Liberty and Justice for Some: A Critique of the Conservative Supreme Court* (New York: New Press, 1993).

For "tort reform," see Michael L. Rustad, "Nationalizing Tort Law: The Republican Attack on Women, Blue Collar Workers and Consumers," *Rutgers Law Review* 48 (1996), p. 673; Mark Galanter, "Real World Torts," *Maryland Law Review* 55 (1966), p. 1093.

415   P. S. Atiyah, *An Introduction to the Law of Contract* (Oxford, Eng.: Oxford University

to have accepted many of the recent changes as fundamentally irreversible."[415]

If to a disintegrating state capitalist system of stable economic growth we add the eclipse of an Eastern Establishment by sunbelt conservatives, the rise of multinational corporations, the end of the Cold War, and parallel shifts in the legal and political superstructure, then I believe this new configuration of power deserves to be classified as a fourth distinct mode or system of economic relations,[416] as well as a fourth period in the history of American legal and social development. "The Reaganite Cold War," Hobsbawm observes, "was directed not only against the 'evil empire' abroad, but against the memory of Franklin D. Roosevelt at home: against the Welfare State as well as any other intrusive state. Its enemy was liberalism (the 'L-word' used to good effect in presidential election campaigns) as much as communism."[417]

Some readers may resist the idea that the United States could embark upon the twenty-first century, an era of *global* capitalism, under the auspices of essentially conservative rather than liberal/"responsible internationalist" political leadership.[418] Recall, however, Franz Schurmann's

---

Press, 1995), p. 27; see also, Atiyah, "Freedom of Contract and the New Right," *Essays on Contract* (Oxford, Eng.: Oxford University Press, 1988), p. 355.

416 "The foregoing data have been largely concerned with the domestic U.S. economy and the corporations that, taken together, constitute the hard core of power in the United States. But for many years now it has become analytically misleading to posit a boundary between the domestic and global functioning of our economy....[B]y far the most important development of business power since the 1960s (the years in which today's highly integrated world economy became a reality) has been the *multinational* (or transnational, or supranational) corporation" (Dowd, *Capitalist Development*, p. 115).

For the end of the Cold War, see Noam Chomsky, "From Containment to Rollback," *Z Magazine* (June 1996): "[C]hanges in the international economy in the past 25 years, accelerated by the end of the Cold War, have enabled the decision-making classes to move from containment of the threat of democracy and human rights to rollback of the despised

social contract that had been won by a long and bitter popular struggle" (p. 22). See also Noam Chomsky, "Rollback," in Greg Ruggiero and Stuart Sahulka, eds., *The New American Crisis* (New York: New Press, 1995), pp. 11–30.

417 Hobsbawm, *Age of Extremes*, p. 249. "Western constitutional capitalism, communist systems and the third world," Hobsbawm adds, were alike composed of states that, after 1945, "deliberately and actively, rejected the supremacy of the market and believed in the active management and planning of the economy by the state. Difficult though it might be to recall in the age of neoliberal economic theology, between the early 1940s and 1970s the most prestigious and formerly influential champions of complete market freedom, e.g., Friedrich von Hayek, saw themselves and their like as prophets in the wilderness vainly warning a heedless Western capitalism that it was rushing along the 'Road to Serfdom' (Hayek, 1944)" (pp. 176–77).

418 "A diverse American coalition of right and left, located in national manufacturing, small business, labor, and farming constituencies and known colloquially as 'isolationism,'

argument that it was "not accidental that the breakthrough to peaceful coexistence with Russia came under the conservative Eisenhower and that the breakthrough to China came under Nixon....While the right-wing military opposed it and ideological liberals (like organized labor) shrank back, the conservatives made the move. In both Eisenhower's approach to Russia and Nixon's approach to China and Russia, trade played a major role. Peaceful coexistence could be meaningful only if Russia and China agreed to join the world market system."[419]

Russia and China are now well on their way to being integrated into the (capitalist) world market and international trade remains as important as ever.[420] While Pat Buchanan on the right and Ralph Nader on the left challenge the globalization of American capital and its institutions,[421]

resisted the Wilson-Roosevelt-Truman march toward world power, and up until 1950 was unwilling to countenance the major defense expenditures deemed necessary to service postwar global commitments. The foreign policy output of these two tendencies is said to be, in the conventional account, responsible internationalism versus irresponsible isolationism, but Franz Schurmann is correct to term the two tendencies imperialism/internationalism and expansionism/nationalism. The isolationists just wanted isolation from Europe; they tramped through Central America and Asia in search of markets, minerals, and cheap labor" (Cumings, "Global Realm," p. 54).

419 Franz Schurmann, *The Logic of World Power* (New York: Pantheon, 1974), p. 52.

420 "The message...is that the United States is a uniquely global exporter. The Pacific region has become—very slightly—its largest market, and under current conditions will grow further, but the main point is that the United States continues to hold a massive and roughly equal export presence in all three major world economic regions. As your broker might say, no other major exporting nation is so well diversified. Neither Germany nor Japan, the world's second and third largest exporting nations, respectively, has anything like America's globally balanced export distribution, and that unique role explains the high U.S. stake in the world's multinational trading system" (Bernard K. Gordon, "Trade Blocked," *The National Interest* [fall 1996],

pp. 71–73).

421 For Buchanan, see James Bennet, "Declaring a Triumph of Ideas, Buchanan Calls for a G.O.P. Truce," *New York Times* (Aug. 12, 1996): "Mr. Buchanan had hoped to speak in prime time during the Republican convention, but aides to Mr. Dole, the presumed nominee, locked him out. They feared that Mr. Buchanan might repeat his performance from the 1992 convention in Houston, when he declared: 'There is a religious war going on in this country.' While he did not use those words in his Escondido speech, he included others certain to rattle the nerves of moderate delegates, not to mention viewers at home. He offered a fierce attack on abortion rights, on illegal immigration and on 'the New World Order' that he said threatened American sovereignty" (p. A9:2).

Buchanan specifically attacked international trade organizations and American corporations that place profits above patriotism. He and Oliver North (who introduced Buchanan to the cheering audience in Escondido, California) condemned the idea that American soldiers should be disciplined for refusing to serve abroad under the command of non-American military officers. *Z Magazine* journalist Sara Diamond reported that North "was surprised at the heckling he got when he spoke....North looked up at the Buchanans and said: 'Pat, I'm urging you to urge your followers to stay and fight.' It appeared to many in the crowd that North was a shill for

there is a broad mainstream of support for the emerging world trading system among Democrats as well as Republicans.[422] Perhaps most interesting is the way in which this new system of international trade relations threatens to become a world legal system.

One of the nagging contradictions of the fourth period has seemed to be the tenacity of residual state capitalist values, even remnants of what Horwitz calls "progressive legal thought." *Los Angeles Times* reporter David Savage has described the survival of Warren Court liberalism well into the 1970s,[423] and much more recently Justice Ruth Bader Ginsburg, a moderately liberal Jew and advocate of abortion rights, was confirmed in her seat on the Supreme Court by a nearly unanimous vote in the U.S. Senate.[424] Conservatives who had become dissatisfied with Justice Sandra O'Connor's unsteady commitment to the cause cannot have been pleased by Ginsburg's "lopsided Senate vote." In the civil law itself, damages assessed by contemporary tort juries—the modern equivalent of early-nineteenth-century ragged-trousered philanthropists—could send tobacco company stocks tumbling on the market, giving investors the jitters and making headlines on the evening news as well as *Wall Street Week*.

A solution envisioned by corporate planners is to bypass the state altogether—no state, no state capitalism to interfere with international corporate operations. In some way, this is what GATT, NAFTA, the new World

the Republican establishment. They booed at North and shouted out 'compromise,' 'hypocrisy,' and 'George Bush and the CIA'" ("Go Away, Pat, Go!" *Z Magazine* [Oct. 1996], p. 42).

For Nader, see Ralph Nader, "Introduction: Free Trade and the Decline of Democracy," in *The Case Against "Free Trade": GATT, NAFTA, and the Globalization of Corporate Power* (San Francisco: Earth Island Press, 1993), pp. 1–12.

422 See, for example, John Jackson, *The World Trading System: Law and Policy of International Economic Relations* (Cambridge, Mass.: MIT Press, 1992); Richard J. Barnet and John Cavanagh, *Global Dreams: Imperial Corporations and the New World Order* (New York: Simon and Schuster, 1994); Lester C. Thurow, *The Future of Capitalism* (New York: William Morrow, 1996).

423 Savage, *Turning Right*, pp. 11–14.

424 See James E. Simon, *The Center Holds* (New York: Simon and Schuster, 1996): "Ginsburg was the first Court nominee, for example, to provide the Senate Judiciary Committee with a comprehensive analysis of her views on *Roe v. Wade*. She had ruminated publicly about an alterative to the *Roe* analysis, suggesting that both the Court and the nation might have been better served by a more cautious ruling. Ginsburg nonetheless gave her firm endorsement to a woman's constitutional right to an abortion....Judge Ginsburg received 99 Senate votes for confirmation, 47 more than the previous nominee, Clarence Thomas. Ginsburg's lopsided Senate vote and her overwhelmingly positive public approval ratings suggested that her appointment traversed the nation's political spectrum" (p. 300).

425 Kenichi Ohmae writes in *The End of the Nation State: The Rise of Regional Economies*

Trade Organization, and what Kenichi Ohmae calls "the end of the nation state," are all about.[425] The fundamental contradiction shaping the fourth, "global capitalist" period of American legal development will likely center on how the state apparatus, however deeply ingrained with predominantly (but not exclusively) conservative political values and legal doctrines, will addresses a world system that regards the state *as such* as an unnecessary participant in the transaction of legal business on a world scale.

Rolling Stone writer William Greider, in a compelling essay on the human consequences of globalization, describes the world market as a "closet dictator." Referring to the United Nations–sponsored Codex Alimentarius Commission in Rome, he asserts: "The Codex is an obscure agency utterly unknown to ordinary citizens, but the multinational companies that help devise its standards are well aware of its significance. At a recent session of the commission, the American delegation included executives from three major chemical companies—DuPont, Monsanto and Hercules—serving alongside U.S. government officials. Among other things, the Codex standard permits DDT residues on fruit and vegetables that are thirty-three to fifty times higher than U.S. law allows."[426] Greider goes on to propose that Americans resist subordination of their imperfect domestic legal system to the emerging parallel legal system of

(New York: Free Press, 1995): "So these new claimants will turn to international bodies like the United Nations. But what is the UN if not a collection of nation states? So they will turn to multilateral agencies like the World Bank, but these too are the creatures of a nation state-defined and –funded universe. So they will turn to explicitly economic groupings like OPEC, or G-7 or ASEAN or APEC or NAFTA or the EU (European Union). But once again, all they will find behind each new acronym is a grouping of nation states. Then, if they are clever, they may interrupt their quest to ask a few simple questions. Are these nation states—notwithstanding the obvious and important role they play in world affairs— really the primary actors in today's global economy? Do they provide the best window on that economy? Do they provide the best port of access to it? In a world where economic borders are progressively disappearing, are their arbitrary, historically

accidental boundaries genuinely meaningful in economic terms? And if not, what kinds of boundaries do make sense? In other words, exactly what, at bottom, are the natural business units—the sufficient, correctly-sized and scaled aggregations of people and activities—through which to tap into that economy?" (p. 2). See also Michael Barratt Brown, "Models for Understanding Transnational Capitalism: What Comes After the Nation State?" in *Models in Political Economy* (2d ed., London: Penguin, 1995), pp. 289–304.

426 William Greider, "The Global Marketplace: A Closet Dictator," in *The Case Against Free Trade*, 195, 206. See also Noam Chomsky, "Notes on NAFTA," in Ruggiero and Sahulka, eds., *The New American Crisis*, pp. 61–65; Kristin Dawkins, "NAFTA, GATT, and the World Trade Organization," *The New American Crisis*, pp. 66–83.

427 Jeremy Brecher, "Global Village or Global Pillage?" in Ruggiero and Sahulka, eds.,

international economic institutions. If citizens do not fight back now, "offshore politics" may obviate existing legal structures—either formally through treaty agreements, or informally, through the delegation of power by national government to international trade commissions. Such gambits add up to what Jeremy Brecher calls the "loss of national economic control."[427]

Observers of this "massive transition in the whole world-system" such as Immanuel Wallerstein and Perry Anderson have urged that the only hope for effective opposition is a parallel internationalization of resistance movements.[428] Imagine if the irresistibility of international market expansion drew global traders into an endgame scenario whereby capitalism generated the system's fabled gravediggers! The globalization of capital, a decisive element in the fourth period of American social and legal history, would then amount to no more than a delaying tactic, deployed by a mode of production on the verge of extinction.

Those who suffer at the hands of the system today may not be placated by such speculation. Indeed, the human wreckage left along the way, the

The New American Crisis (New York: New Press, 1995): "The loss of national economic control has been accompanied by a growing concentration of unaccountable power in international institutions like the IMF, the World Bank, and GATT. For poor countries, foreign control has been formalized in the World Bank's 'Structural Adjustment Plans,' but IMF decisions and GATT rules affect the economic growth rates of all countries. The decisions of these institutions also have an enormous impact on the global ecology" (p. 86).

428 Immanuel Wallerstein writes in *After Liberalism* (New York: New Press, 1995): "To suggest that anyone should no longer bother about what their state does is folly, and I do not believe many people are going to be willing to turn away completely from an active concern with the actions of their state. States can make things a little better (or a little worse) for everyone. They can choose between helping ordinary people cope better and allowing upper strata to thrive still more. This is, however, *all* that states can do. These things no doubt matter a lot in the short run, but they matter not at all in the longer run. If we wish to affect in significant ways the massive transition of the whole world-system through

which we are living so that it goes in one direction rather than in another, the state is *not* a major vehicle of action. Indeed, it is a rather major obstacle" (p. 5).

Perry Anderson observes: "Much of the same paradox recurs on the ground of representative institutions proper. The attenuation of democratic forms in the major capitalist societies is increasingly evident. The executive branches of the state have gained steadily greater power at the expense of legislative assemblies. Policy choices have narrowed and popular interest in them declined. Above all, the most important changes affecting the wellbeing of citizens have been transferred sideways to international markets. In these conditions, the construction of effective supranational sovereignties is the obvious remedy to the loss by national states of so much of their substance and authority" (*A Zone of Engagement* [London: Verso, 1992], pp. 364–65). See also Samir Amin, Giovanni Arrighi, Andre Gunder Frank, and Immanuel Wallerstein, *Transforming the Revolution: Social Movements and the World-System* (New York: Monthly Review Press, 1990).

429 For the consequences of laissez-faire practices: see Walden Bello, *Dark Victory: The United*

flotsam and jetsam cast overboard by laissez faire ideology put into practice on a global scale, raises again the question of whether liberalism or
authoritarianism constitutes the typical or "really revolutionary" form of
capitalist development.[429]

States, Structural Adjustment, and Global
Poverty (London: Pluto Press, 1994); Liz Dore
and John Weeks, "The Changing Faces of
Imperialism," NACLA Report on the Americas
(Sept.–Oct. 1996): "Capitalist development in
Latin America has not improved the living
conditions of the vast majority of the
continent's population. On the contrary, only
select groups have prospered, while nearly half
live in poverty" (p. 15).

For the "really revolutionary" form of
capitalism, see Alan Ryan, "Fascism in the
Plural," London Review of Books (Sept. 21,
1995): "The collapse of the satellite
Communist regimes of Eastern Europe and
the subsequent disintegration of the USSR
were supposed to mark the triumph of the
liberal democratic ideal and the market
economy—to be 'the end of history'. What we
got instead was a revival of ultra-nationalism,
racism and ethnic strife: German reunification
celebrated by neo-Nazi skinheads; Croatian
independence marked by the rehabilitation of
Nazi collaborators. French racial discord
encouraged by Le Pen's increasingly popular
National Front; and, in Russia, the arrival of
Vladimir Zhirinovsky as something more
than a bad joke. Many people have wondered
whether 1989 would turn out to be like 1919:
what the death of old authoritarian
governments brought to life is more Fascist
than liberal" (p. 3). See also, Hans Magnus
Enzensberger, Civil Wars: From L.A. to Bosnia
(New York: New Press, 1994).